Contents

INTRODUCTION

It is hard to believe that nearly twenty years have passed since *Vegetables from Small Gardens* was first published. That was in the mid-1970s, when a new generation was discovering the delights and satisfaction of growing vegetables at home – often in much smaller gardens than their parents had enjoyed. It is always hard to pinpoint the reasons behind a trend, but it did seem then that the limited choice and poor flavour of shop vegetables, coupled with growing wariness of the chemicals used by commercial vegetable growers, were important factors in the revived interest in vegetable growing.

Ten years later, in 1986, it proved necessary to update the text. In writing the introduction for the revised edition, I commented that it might seem odd for a book on a staid subject like vegetables to need updating. But, in the ten years since it was originally written, a great deal of research had been carried out into commercial vegetable growing in this country. Much of this had a bearing on amateur gardening, throwing new scientific light on traditional practices and 'hunch'. As a result of this research we now know precisely how spacing can be varied to get the size of vegetable we require, the stage in a plant's cycle when it most pays to water and so on. Much of this work was undertaken by the National Vegetable Research Station at Wellesbourne (now part of Horticulture Research International), and the material was relayed to the gardening public in the two volumes of *Know and Grow Vegetables*, recently republished in one volume as *The Complete Know and Grow Vegetables*. This book is fascinating reading for anyone interested in vegetable growing, and I made extensive use of it in revising *Vegetables from Small Gardens* in 1986.

Another reason for updating lay in the rapid changes in vegetable varieties available to gardeners. (We should now refer to 'varieties' as 'cultivars' – the correct scientific term for varieties raised in cultivation; but 'varieties' live on in popular parlance.) Many excellent new cultivars were being introduced by plant breeders but, at the same time, many old varieties were being withdrawn, largely as a result of Common Market legislation. While this has had some benefits, for example in clarifying the situation where one variety masqueraded under a dozen different names, it has meant that some old favourites, valued by home gardeners if not by commercial growers, have been withdrawn. Fortunately organizations like the Henry Doubleday Research Association are operating a seed library, which both preserves old varieties for posterity and makes seed available to members. They certainly deserve our full support but, unless the situation changes, the best we can do is to accept these withdrawals as a fact of gardening life, and to make the most of the undeniable merits of many of the new cultivars.

A third reason for the revision was much more personal. Not long after *Vegetables from Small Gardens* was published, our family – my husband Don Pollard and our children Brendan and Kirsten, then aged seven and five – set off for a year on what we called 'The Grand Vegetable Tour'. With a caravan as our home, we travelled around Europe in a southward arc from Holland to Hungary, visiting eight countries in all. Our purpose was to study traditional and new methods of vegetable growing, and to collect the seed of old, local vegetable varieties which were, and still are, in danger of dying out. These were sent to the national Vegetable Gene Bank at Wellesbourne for conservation.

I learnt an enormous amount from that year of travel. Not only did we 'discover' many new plants, for example summer purslane, claytonia or winter purslane, iceplant, salad rocket and the many beautiful red and related chicories, but we saw at first hand some intensive methods of vegetable growing. Most important were first, the use of cut-and-come-again techniques for salad seedlings and second, to increase the productivity of mature crops, and closely spaced cultivation in narrow beds – both methods making optimum use of available ground.

When we returned we experimented with these new plants and methods in the small organic market garden we then established, finding much of what we had learnt particularly relevant to small gardens. So some of these ideas were incorporated in the revised edition.

As mentioned above, ever since returning from the 'Grand Vegetable Tour' we have gardened 'organically'. We no longer use any artificial fertilizers, chemical weedkillers or pesticides, other than the few approved by the organic standards authorities in this country. These break down into non-toxic compounds, doing minimum damage to other life forms.

Organic gardening undoubtedly involves a little more labour than chemically aided gardening. Building up the soil fertility with manure and compost, keeping beds and paths mulched to control weeds and hand picking pests all require physical effort – but the crops ultimately benefit. A body of natural predators builds up within the garden to help keep down pests and the joys of eating fresh produce untainted by chemicals far outweigh the inconvenience of the odd caterpillar-carved hole. Moreover, compared with conventionally grown vegetables, organically grown vegetables keep fresh longer after picking – and most people find they are better flavoured (although this is hard to prove). So this new edition is devoted entirely to organic methods of gardening.

As it happens, the last ten to fifteen years have seen widespread acceptance of the organic philosophy among gardeners. This has been accompanied by limited research into organic methods, focused mainly on pest and disease control and variety trials, studying which are most suited to organic production. Admittedly some of the research has been prompted by the fact that pests have built up resistance to the chemicals previously used to control them, so commercial growers have been forced to resort to more benign methods, such as 'biological control', where a pest's natural enemy is introduced to control it. Although successful use of biological control agents requires some skill, they are a boon to organic gardeners. And there are exciting developments in the pipeline. Only last week I tried out the new biological control for slugs, based on naturally occurring nematode parasites. It seems to be working well.

For various reasons interest in eating and cooking vegetables, if not necessarily in growing them, is higher now than it has been for many years. The number of vegetarians has increased dramatically, with many other people cutting down on the amount of meat in their diet and eating more fruit and vegetables to compensate. Compared with the 1970s, a far greater range of vegetables can be found in supermarkets and markets; exotic vegetables, imported from all corners of the globe, are becoming commonplace. Slowly, too, the supermarket chains are demonstrating an interest in quality and flavour: tomatoes no longer have to be perfectly red and round to sell! (It still remains true, however, that you will have a far greater choice if you decide to grow your own.)

Since 'The Grand Vegetable Tour' my own excursions into foreign fields have focused on oriental vegetables, lured by the tempting names of unknown plants, mainly in Japanese seed catalogues. The quest for information eventually took me to China, Japan, Taiwan, the USA and Canada – and it is probably true to say that the whole character of our own garden has changed as a result of these excursions. We now grow a wide range of oriental vegetables, concentrating on the many types of greens. As it happens, in our climate these are at their best from late summer to early spring, so follow on naturally from our standard summer vegetables and offer variety during the leaner vegetable months. Almost all these oriental greens can be grown as cut-and-come-again crops, both as seedlings and when mature, making them some of the most productive vegetables for temperate climates. The full story is told in my book *Oriental Vegetables*, but oriental vegetables tend to play a much larger part in this new edition of *Vegetables for Small Gardens* than they did before, and they are strongly recommended to anyone who only has limited space for vegetable growing. (Herbs have been squeezed out to make space for the oriental newcomers, but their cultivation is covered in the companion volume, *Salads for Small Gardens*.)

Several of the oriental vegetables are beautiful to look at, which brings me to another aspect of vegetable growing in small gardens – how to compromise between utility and beauty. While many owners of small gardens are content to devote the whole space to vegetable growing, others long for the colour and beauty associated with flowers. The answer, I feel, lies in the 'potager' approach – shorthand for a decorative vegetable garden. On a grand scale this implies laying out the kitchen garden in a (usually symmetrical) pattern of designed beds, with trellises, arches and espalier fruit forming the background and linking the beds. The vegetables grown are selected, to some extent, for their decorative qualities, and are often planted in groups, rather than rows, to enhance the effect. Flowers, herbs and fruit can be grown among, beside or around the groups to create a beautiful, colourful vegetable garden.

I feel this approach can be adopted on a much smaller, cottage-garden scale, so that even a tiny vegetable plot can be as colourful as any conventional garden devoted to flowers and shrubs. It is also feasible to incorporate vegetables into an ordinary flower garden: use arches and trellises for climbing beans and cucumbers; edge beds with the pretty 'Salad Bowl' types of vegetables; sneak a few plants of the purple-leaved 'Bull's Blood' beet or ornamental kale into a flower border; put some asparagus into the herbaceous border. This book is not about potagers but, where plants have decorative qualities which lend themselves to 'potager' treatment, they will be pointed out.

But now for the problems of small gardens. There is, of course, no such thing as the typical small garden, and I'm ducking the question of defining what I mean by a small garden. Take it to mean any garden that feels small to you, or that is too small to fulfil your needs.

The classical books on vegetable growing talked about the ideal 'open site' for a vegetable garden. But the modern gardener is far more likely to be struggling with a garden overshadowed by his neighbour's house or a tower block, with the wind funnelling across his plot through the gap between his house and the next.

Again, gardening books in the past tended to assume that your garden had reasonably fertile, well-drained soil, and advocated three and four year rotations to help maintain fertility. But it is not unusual for the modern gardener to find himself faced with a waterlogged patch of raw-looking clay, or little more than the pile of rubble the builders left behind. And you can't practise much rotation on a pocket handkerchief.

It's no good pretending that vegetables will grow anywhere. The old standby crops of the kitchen garden – Brussels sprouts, cauliflowers, leeks and cabbages, for example, need good conditions and there is no getting away from it. The same holds true for the newer oriental greens. A lot of work has to be done to bring poor sites into a sufficiently fertile state to grow vegetables, but it can be done with even the most unpromising sites. Be resigned to the fact that it may take a year or two.

In the meantime small areas can be made fertile enough to grow less fussy or fast-growing crops such as radishes, turnips and salad seedlings; or a start can be made with tomatoes in pots, or lettuces and herbs in a window box, tub, or growing-bag.

With small gardens there are always competing demands. You need somewhere for the children to play, to hang out the washing and to put out a picnic table in summer. Most people want some flowers, and possibly fruit trees or soft fruit. And what about a shed? A place to keep the tools and deck chairs and hang the onions is essential.

Every family wants something different from its vegetable plot. It is obviously difficult to keep an average family continually supplied with vegetables from a very small plot but it is quite feasible, in, say, a plot that is 10 metres (roughly 10 yards) square, to have something worthwhile from the garden all year round. If you are prepared to put the whole garden down to small patches of cut-and-come-again seedlings, perhaps you could keep the family in greens and salads all year round.

The decision about what to grow is a very personal one. Some people prefer to concentrate on vegetables that are difficult or expensive to buy: kohl rabi or celeriac for example, and sweet peppers. Others concentrate on those which lose most, in terms of quality and flavour, in the journey from field to shop to consumer; these include such as salads, peas, young carrots and sweet corn. The flavour of freshly picked peas and sweet corn, or young carrots just pulled from the ground, is a world apart from anything you can buy. For other people it is a question of maximum bulk and, to this end, I have tried to calculate a 'value for space' rating for each vegetable. (See the Planning Information Table on pp.128-9.)

The vegetable lover with a small garden is inevitably trying to get the proverbial quart out of a pint pot. The intensive cultivation methods which make this possible – catch cropping, intercropping and cut-and-come-again techniques – depend largely on soil fertility (see Chapter 1). But the modern gardener has a lot of outside help. Plant breeders have produced more compact, faster maturing, higher yielding cultivars – often with good disease resistance as well. These can often be planted more closely than old-fashioned varieties and are much more productive. Then there are the new materials, from the fleeces which offer protection from the cold, to the fine nets which exclude flying pests, and the polytunnels which can double any garden's capacity.

The newcomer to vegetable growing is sometimes at a loss as to how to start. He may be bombarded with conflicting advice. This is hardly surprising: gardening is a very inexact science, and there are few wrong or right answers. What works one year may well fail the next; what is suitable for a mild coastal area would be most inappropriate in a hilly inland area. Each soil has its own characteristics. The real gardener is inevitably an experimenter, constantly trying out different ideas until he discovers what is best for him, his conditions and his requirements.

Then there is the weather to consider. One of the first lessons we have to learn is the role played by our climate. A gardener is not quite his own boss! The 'master plan' is pre-ordained by the seasons. A farmer once advised me to 'co-operate with the weather', and it was very sound advice. Even if your book tells you to sow parsnips in late winter, there is no point in trying to sow them on sticky wet soil. Better to wait until it has dried out. If there is a sunny spell in late summer when the onions are ready for harvesting, do not procrastinate for a moment. The weather might turn nasty on you, your onions will start to sprout or rot and your crop will be wasted.

It probably takes a newcomer to gardening three or four years to get the 'feel' of how the annual pattern of gardening operations fits into the overall pattern of the seasons. When the ground first becomes workable in spring, the shallots and onion sets can be planted; when the cold spring wind has dried out the surface, the seedbed can be raked to a tilth for the early sowings. When the danger of frosts is over the tender crops, such as tomatoes and cucumbers, can be planted out. When frost threatens again in the autumn, some crops will need harvesting, others protection. These are the indicators to which an experienced gardener reacts instinctively. Everything else fits neatly in between.

For anyone new to gardening, or new to an area, it is worth investigating what established gardeners in the locality are doing. What they grow, how and when, provides many a clue to success. It is always best to start with what does well naturally – the 'difficult' vegetables can be tackled later.

I would also advise anyone growing vegetables to keep records. It is always useful to know which cultivars proved successful in previous seasons, how many rows you found you needed and where there were gaps in the household supply which could be remedied. Records of sowing dates, quantities of seeds or plants needed, cultural details and pests encountered prove immensely valuable. You may be inundated with advice from experts, but your personal garden diary will be the only source of information about the unique conditions which constitute your garden.

And, finally, a word of encouragement for complete beginners. I often come across people who, although they had never before grown anything, in their first season had results anyone would be proud of. They simply 'followed the instructions on the packet'. That could be beginners' luck, green fingers, or plain common sense. Get a feel for the sort of conditions plants like and, from then on, gardening is very largely common sense.

Newcomers to gardening who want to reinforce beginners' luck will find the advice in gardening magazines, on the radio, on television and in seed catalogues (almost always free), most valuable. They should also consider joining a local gardening club or society, where they will pick up hints from more experienced gardeners, and from the lectures and demonstrations. Many gardening societies are able to obtain seeds and gardening supplies at discounts – a useful service for their members.

I hope this revised edition will prove useful to a new generation of gardeners. I am always interested in readers' experiences in different parts of the country, and in their comments on how this book could be improved.

CHAPTER ONE

Soil Fertility

I have based this book on two assumptions. First, that most people reading it have only a small garden, or small part of a garden, to devote to vegetable growing. Second, that they want the maximum returns from that area, however small. In other words, they want to cultivate the vegetable plot as intensively as possible.

This means that every inch of space should be in use. Vegetables should be planted as close together as is reasonable and as soon as one crop is finished, another should be sown or planted in its place – at least during the growing season. Space between rows can be intercropped, cloches and crop cover films can be used to extend the growing season, and even concrete corners and paths can be made productive with the use of boxes or compost-filled polythene bags. With careful planning, it is astonishing how much can be produced from a tiny but intensively worked garden.

However, to get the best results, the garden needs to be reasonably sheltered, well watered and, above all, fertile. Shelter and water are fairly easily provided. Fertility can pose more of a problem. Some soils are naturally fertile but, in most cases, steps have to be taken to increase, and then maintain, soil fertility. Once the soil is fertile, crops grow fast and vigorously, stand a better chance of overcoming pests and disease, and yield heavily. To borrow a commercial term, turnover is greatly increased.

Soil fertility, then, is the key to getting the most out of a small vegetable garden. So I make no apology for devoting a whole chapter to the subject. It is the foundation stone for growing good vegetables.

What is soil fertility? To answer that question we must take a look at what soil is, how it functions and what it does for the plant.

THE NATURE OF SOIL

Although soil looks solid, in an average garden slightly less than half of the soil consists of solid matter. This is mainly made up of mineral particles of sand, silt and clay which have been formed over the centuries by the breakdown of rocks. About 5 per cent of the soil, an extremely important 5 per cent, is organic matter. This is a mixture of the remains of plants and animals, decomposing vegetation and humus, and the tiny creatures living in the soil known as micro-organisms, many of which play a vital role in breaking down all this material. The rest of what we call the soil, about half of it, consists of air and water, which fill the spaces or pores between the crumbs of soil.

What does soil do for plants? It supplies an anchorage, and a medium through which the roots can breathe. It supplies water, which is essential for all living things, and this again is absorbed through the roots. And it also supplies most of the nutrients, or foods, required by plants.

Sources of nutrients

A plant gets its nutrients from two sources. Through its leaves it takes in carbon dioxide from the air which, together with water absorbed through the roots, is converted in the presence of light into sugars and starches in the 'factories' of the leaves during the process known as photosynthesis. The rest of the nutrients which are necessary for healthy plant growth are obtained from the soil and absorbed into the plant's system in dilute solution through the roots. Of these nutrients, the plant requires nitrogen, phosphorus and potassium (usually called potash) in large quantities, calcium, sulphur and magnesium in more moderate quantities and, in really minute quantities, the so-called 'trace elements', such as iron, manganese, zinc, boron and a number of others.

Some of these nutrients are found in the mineral particles of the soil, particularly in clays. But they occur mainly, in highly complex forms, in the organic matter in the soil. Nitrogen comes mainly from decaying organic matter (plant remains) in the soil, but also from atmospheric nitrogen in the soil, which is 'fixed' and converted into forms plants can use by bacteria which live in soil organic matter. Nitrogen, the most important nutrient for plants, is easily washed or leached out of the soil, especially during the rainy winter months and, on the whole, plant growth deteriorates most seriously when there is a shortage of nitrogen.

The most important process at work in the soil is the breaking down of organic matter by minute micro-organisms, mainly types of bacteria, to release nutrients in simple forms which can be taken up by plants or – as the jargon has it – making them 'available'. This can only take place provided conditions are 'right' for the micro-organisms, that is provided they have enough oxygen and moisture, the soil is not too acid or too alkaline for them, and, of course, provided they have an adequate supply of organic matter to work on.

Fertility can be summed up as creating the best conditions for soil micro-organisms to go about their work of breaking down organic matter into humus. (Humus is organic matter in a very advanced state of decay, and it is from humus that plant nutrients are released.) Good soil structure is an important factor in creating these conditions.

TYPES OF SOIL

It is useful to understand what types of soil there are, how a soil develops its structure, what can be done to improve it and hence its fertility.

The mineral element in soils is made up of particles of varying size, which are classified, according to their size, as sands, silts and clays. The particles of sand are the largest – the individual grains are visible to the naked eye; then next come silt particles, which are infinitely smaller and which cannot be distinguished by the naked eye; the smallest of all are clay particles.

Most soils in Britain are loams, a mixture of one or more types. But because sands and clays, to take the extreme types, have very different characteristics, the proportion of these predominating in any particular soil largely determines the characteristics of the soil, such as its structure and how rich it is in nutrients.

Sandy soils have large particles, which are most reluctant to stick together naturally to form crumbs. (See Soil Structure opposite.) The spaces between the particles are also large, so water drains away easily and the soil contains plenty of air. Sandy soils warm up quickly in spring, but dry out in summer. They are usually poor in nutrients, because nutrients are washed out of the soil in the drainage water. Sandy loams, however, are richer in nutrients than pure sands and hold water better.

A clay soil, on the contrary, consists of microscopic particles which have a great tendency, because of their chemical nature, to stick together. A pure clay is extremely sticky, there are few spaces for air, and water cannot drain through it easily. When it does dry it is apt to dry into hard, impenetrable lumps. A clay soil, however, is very rich in nutrients and, when organic matter is worked into it, can develop an excellent crumb structure.

Silts have some characteristics in common with clay, in that they retain moisture well but can dry into hard clods. They are often very fertile and, like clay, respond well to the incorporation of organic matter.

Sandy soils are generally considered 'light', clay soils 'heavy', and silts intermediate. Other distinct types of soil are peats and chalk soils. The Fenland peats are rich fertile soils, but the high, boggy moorland peats are usually too acid to grow vegetables. Chalk soils can cause problems by becoming very sticky when wet and drying into steely lumps, leading to a shortage of water for plants. The remedy lies in frequent additions of organic matter, which decompose rapidly on chalk soils. Most vegetables can be grown very successfully on the deeper chalky soils, though it is a little more difficult on thin chalk soils.

The ideal soil, the loam that gardeners dream about, is a balanced mixture of sand, silt and clay. The sandy elements make for good drainage and aeration, the clay elements for richness, retention of water in summer and the cohesiveness which is essential for the formation of crumbs. Even soils such as these are dependent on fresh organic matter being added continually so that they can develop a good crumb structure.

Assessing your soil type

It is useful to be able to tell what type of soil you have – although this is not easy for an inexperienced gardener. But you can get some indication by what is called 'finger analysis'. Hold some soil in the palm of your hand, and then rub a little between your fingers. If the predominant feeling is of grittiness, it is basically a sandy soil. If it feels silky, it is a silty soil; if it feels sticky and can almost be 'polished' under pressure from the fingers, it is a clay soil. If it doesn't really feel either gritty, silky or sticky it is a loam.

After cultivating a soil for a few years, you acquire a 'feel' for the type of soil you have and how to cater for its particular characteristics. Even within a small area, soil can be very variable.

SOIL STRUCTURE

In all except very sandy or silty soils, the mineral and organic particles in the soil join together to form small lumps, or crumbs, of varying sizes. The crumbs can easily be seen if you crush a small clod of garden soil in your hand. You can break it down so far, but after that only the resistant crumbs are left, and to break them down into dust-size fragments is a much harder business.

In a good soil the crumbs, which vary in size, are very stable. Around them and between them a network of spaces or pores is built up, and it is this combination of crumbs and spaces which makes up the soil structure. The channels made by the spaces between the crumbs form the aeration and drainage system of the soil. When rain falls on the soil, the surplus water drains off through the channels, preventing it from becoming water-logged. Water remains in the smallest pores, forming a moisture reservoir for the roots and soil organisms. The large spaces are filled with air, supplying the oxygen which is necessary for the plant roots and the various living organisms in the soil. A soil with a good structure is one in which the crumbs remain stable even when wet, allowing effective drainage and aeration that will encourage plants to thrive.

Tilth

The soil structure has a direct bearing on what gardeners call 'tilth'. This is the physical condition of the surface of the soil where the seeds are sown. Soil with a good structure can be broken down, often simply by raking in the spring, to a 'mellow' tilth where the individual soil crumbs are roughly the size of breadcrumbs. This is ideal for sowing seeds. It is very difficult to get a good tilth either on soils which dry out so much that the surface virtually becomes dust, or on those which are so sticky when wet that they dry into solid, almost unbreakable clods. In both these cases the fault of the soil originates in poor structure.

Soil structure test

If you have a loamy soil, as most people have, you can do a simple test to see if your soil has a good, stable, crumb structure. It is worth comparing samples from different parts of the garden, ideally taking them from different depths, anything down to 45cm (18in) deep. For each sample take half a trowel of soil, dry it overnight on a saucer, then sieve it through a household sieve to remove all the very light material. Then take a tea-spoon of the soil, put it in a glass, cover it with water and shake. Poor soil disintegrates rapidly making the water cloudy, but the crumbs of a well-structured soil will remain intact however long you shake the glass. Soils of intermediate quality come between these extremes. You'll find the best samples come from ground that has been mulched, or from soil beneath a compost heap, or from worm casts. Aim to bring your poorer soils up to the quality of these. There are various methods of improving the quality of your garden soil and these are clearly explained overleaf.

The part humus plays in soil structure

Apart from the size of the soil particles, several other factors have an important influence on the development of a good soil structure, and here we get back to humus. Besides being a storehouse of plant nutrients, certain elements in humus have the ability to 'coat' particles of sand and silt together to make crumbs. Conversely, in heavy clay soils, humus helps in the process of breaking down the large clods into smaller clods which, in turn, break down into crumbs.

Another important feature of humus, especially in sandy soils, is that it has a great capacity for holding water. Apart from making sandy and chalk soils more resistant to drought conditions, this also prevents the nutrients from being washed out so rapidly.

The part earthworms play in soil structure

Earthworms, especially the burrowing and casting species, play a most important part in creating a good soil structure. Their burrows, some of which are permanent with 'cemented' sides, open up the soil and create aeration and drainage channels. They work and plough through enormous quantities of earth, literally eating their way through the soil. They take in soil and organic matter, mix it intimately together and treat it with gums and lime as it passes through their stomach. This is the first vital stage in the breakdown of organic matter. With several types of worm the result is the familiar coil-like casts which are deposited both on the surface and within the soil, and bestow enormous benefits.

The casts are remarkably rich, containing more micro-organisms, more inorganic minerals and more organic matter than the soil from which they were derived; moreover the nutrients are converted into forms plants can use immediately. Of equal importance, the casts are remarkably stable even when wet, and perform a key role in the formation of stable crumbs in the soil.

Worms feed on fresh organic matter. Their preference is for animal manure; semi-rotted compost is second choice. The fastest way of increasing the worm population is to add organic matter to the surface of the soil. The traditional method of improving soil structure was the use of grass leys, grassing down for several years. (Soil structure in old pasture land is excellent.) It is now thought that this is effective primarily because the decaying grass roots provide a constant source of food for worms; subsequently the grass roots reinforce the casts so making stable 'aggregates' of soil crumbs.

Finally, when worms die their protein-rich bodies decay and nitrogen is returned to the soil. This could amount to the equivalent of 454kg (100lb) of nitrogen fertilizer per 4,000sq m (100lb per acre) per annum!

HOW TO IMPROVE SOILS

In practice, the structure of almost any soil can be improved by adding organic matter, which will eventually be converted into humus. Organic matter is anything with animal or vegetable origins – manure, compost, straw or seaweed, for example (see Chapter 2).

With heavy soils, cultivation itself, letting in air so that earthworms, bacteria and other micro-organisms can get to work, results in an improvement of soil structure. It is also remarkable how the action of frost, alternately freezing and thawing the soil, will break down the clods of a clay soil to produce a crumb structure. This is why clay soils should be 'dug over rough' in autumn, say by the end of November, exposing the clods to the frost. My own garden is laid out in narrow beds about 1m (1yd) wide, and in autumn I like to spade the sides of the bed into the middle to form a single ridge before covering them with manure. The ridges ensure good drainage and maximum exposure of the soil to the frost.

Sharp sand, coarse grit, or weathered ashes can be worked into the surface of a heavy soil to improve drainage and help it to warm up in spring. As for fresh organic matter, which, as mentioned earlier, is food for worms, this should be added to the surface leaving the worms to work it in. If it is dug in there will initially be a loss of nitrogen as the bacteria break it down. Well-rotted manure or compost, however, should be dug in.

The structure of light sandy soils is easily destroyed, so they are often left uncultivated until the spring, though they can be mulched in autumn with, say, straw, bracken or compost, or even left weedy, to protect the surface from the elements. In spring dig in well-rotted manure or compost as a source of nutrients – feeding earthworms is far less important in well-drained, well-aerated soils.

Soil conditioners

Various artificial soil conditioners appear on the market from time to time, claiming to help the formation of crumbs or tilth on sandy or clay soils. They are generally raked into the surface. The extravagant claims made for some of these products should be taken with a pinch of salt, and personally I would not want to use any that were not organic in origin. However, if properly used they can certainly help in the formation of tilth under bad conditions, for example where most of the topsoil has been removed in building operations. If cost is a limiting factor, confine their use to special areas such as a seedbed. It seems that some of the seaweed-based products are among the most effective. Calcified seaweed, for example, can be considered a natural soil conditioner.

SOIL ACIDITY AND LIMING

The acidity of a soil is another factor which influences soil fertility. Acidity is measured on a scale known as the pH scale, which ranges from 0 to 14. A neutral soil has a pH value of 7.0, an acid soil a pH below 7.0, and an alkaline soil one above 7.0. The change from one pH level to the next indicates a soil that is ten times as acid (or alkaline) as the one below it.

Broadly speaking, the acidity of a soil reflects the amount of calcium, that is chalk or lime, in it. In our humid climate, rainwater is continually washing calcium out of the soil, so there is a tendency for soil to become more acid all the time. This process is most marked in parts of the country with a very high rainfall, in cities and industrialized areas where acids in the atmosphere wash the calcium out even faster, and on light sandy soils. Heavy soils such as clays are less likely to become seriously acid, and may have enough reserves of calcium to last for many years.

The ideal pH for a soil is 6.5, which is slightly acid. In fact most British soils tend to be slightly acid.

Why does pH matter?

Firstly, because plants only grow well within a certain pH range, varying from plant to plant. Most vegetables do best on a slightly acid soil. This is mainly because the pH value has an effect on the availability of the soil nutrients which plants need. At pH 5.0 most nutrients are 'available'. However, phosphate, one of the key nutrients, becomes 'locked up' if the soil becomes too acid and the pH falls below 5.0. Calcium, potassium and magnesium may be washed out of the soil altogether under very acid conditions. At a low pH other nutrients may be present in such large quantities that they become phytotoxic, that is poisonous to the plant.

When the pH rises above 7.5, that is if the soil becomes too alkaline, most of the trace elements, which are essential for healthy plant growth, become locked up and unavailable to plants. In other words, if the pH is seriously wrong, plants will be starved, or poisoned.

Secondly, micro-organisms such as bacteria, which break down the organic matter into humus, become progressively less active as the soil becomes more acid. When the pH falls to 4.5, they cease to function altogether. This means that, not only are no more nutrients released into the soil, but that the soil structure starts to deteriorate through lack of humus.

Most earthworms cannot tolerate very acid conditions and will move out of very acid soils, which should be limed as the first step towards encouraging their return.

Finally, certain plant diseases are worse in notably acid or alkaline conditions. Clubroot in cabbage is most serious in acid soils, potato scab in alkaline soils.

Putting the pH right

The most common pH problem in this country is over-acidity, which is corrected by liming. However, over-liming can be very harmful, so only lime your soil if it is really necessary. If plants seem to be doing well and there is a large worm population (particularly if your soil is on the heavy side) assume everything is all right.

Indications that a soil is too acid and needs liming are a 'sour look', typified by moss growing on the surface, certain weeds such as sorrel and docks, and vegetation on the surface which is not rotting.

A chemical test is the only certain way of finding out what the pH is and if lime is needed. Soil testing kits are available for the amateur, or tests can be carried out by advisory services. The kits give an accurate indication of the acidity of the soil, but they cannot tell you precisely how much lime you require, as this varies with the type of soil. Lighter dressings of lime will be required for a sandy soil, heavier for a silt and the heaviest of all for a clay. Consult an expert, otherwise, if in doubt, err on the light side. Sandy soils in particular are easily over-limed.

As a general rule, if you have a soil which tends to become too acid (see Soil Acidity and Liming p.15), apply lime dressings every third or fourth year at the most. Lime needs a while to take effect, but further dressings can be made later if necessary. Liming is best done in the autumn and, although lime is traditionally spread on the surface of the soil, with medium and heavy soils it is far better to work it thoroughly into the top spit of soil when digging.

Never apply lime at the same time as fertilizers, farmyard manure or composts, as undesirable chemical reactions occur. Allow about a month to elapse between applications of any of these materials and liming. Slow acting forms of lime, such as ground limestone or dolomite, are the most suitable for organic gardeners.

Recommended dressings of ground limestone for a moderately acid soil (pH 6) are as follows: sandy soil 270g/m^2 (½lb/sq yd); loamy soil 550gm^2 (1lb/sq yd); clay or humus-rich soil 800g/m^2 (1½lb/sq yd). The lime content of the soil can also be increased by using mushroom compost, which has chalk in it. Ground limestone and mushroom compost can also be worked into a compost heap in small quantities, as an indirect means of adding lime to the soil

Correcting soils which are too alkaline, for example soils with a great deal of chalk in them, is more difficult. Working in organic matter will always help. Foliar sprays, such as liquid seaweed, often prove the quickest method of correcting deficiencies which arise on alkaline soils.

TOPSOIL AND SUBSOIL
Soil fertility is usually concerned with the dark layer of soil we cultivate known as the topsoil. This varies in depth from only a few centimetres to several metres thick, and it generally lies over a lighter coloured, poorer layer of subsoil. The main difference between the two layers is that the topsoil contains organic matter, which has given it a relatively good structure, while the subsoil has no organic matter and is solid, lifeless, of poor structure and often badly drained as a result. Roots cannot penetrate it easily and so plants will tend not to do well.

From a gardener's point of view, the deeper the topsoil the better. The easiest way of increasing the topsoil is by the gradual addition of more organic matter to the surface, and indeed by the mere process of cultivation. On the whole, subsoil is best left alone and should never be brought to the surface. Over the years cultivation of the topsoil will gradually lead to an improvement in the subsoil through the infiltration of roots, worms and so on from the topsoil.

Thin topsoil

There are two exceptions to the general rule of not disturbing the subsoil. Where the topsoil is very thin, say only a finger length deep, it is worth double digging the soil, which means penetrating the subsoil, working a layer of organic matter into it, and then replacing the topsoil (see Chapter 3 for double digging). This will improve the fertility of the subsoil, and it will gradually assume the character of topsoil.

Hard pan

The other case in which interference is justified is where an extremely hard layer, known as a hard pan, is found in the subsoil. This can be caused by a layer of mineral salts, possibly 30cm (12in) or so down; or it may be the result of extreme compaction due to heavy machinery having worked on the soil – a situation which could arise on new housing estates. A hard pan can be so impenetrable that it prevents all natural drainage, thus making the topsoil waterlogged.

You may suspect the presence of a hard pan when you dig the soil. At a certain depth the fork or spade seems to encounter far greater resistance. The only answer is to break up the hard pan by physical means. A spade will usually do the job; or plunge the tines of a fork in at an angle and move them about. Failing that, use a pickaxe.

DRAINAGE

This brings us to the question of drainage, which has an important bearing on soil fertility. A waterlogged soil is one in which surplus water cannot drain away. As a result all the spaces between the soil crumbs are filled with water and air is driven out. The roots are unable to breathe and bacteria cease to function, which in turn means that the level of nutrients in the soil falls and its structure deteriorates. A waterlogged soil can never be fertile. A badly drained soil is also a cold soil, and plants never do well in such soils. The best way to raise a soil's temperature is by drainage.

Often it is obvious that a soil needs drainage. If water lies on the surface for several days after a heavy rain, or if water is encountered when you dig a foot or so deep (this is what is meant by a high water table) drainage is necessary. Less obvious indications of a badly drained soil are poor vegetation, plants with a mass of small shallow roots rather than deep roots, lack of worms, and soil that is grey, bluish, black or mottled rather than brown.

Bad drainage occurs either because of the nature of the topsoil itself (as in the case with a heavy clay soil with little organic matter in it) or because the topsoil lies over a non-porous layer of subsoil or rock which does not allow water to drain away – clay or granite for example. Where the underlying layer is porous, such as gravel or sand, there will be no problem. As already mentioned, hard pan or general soil compaction can also cause poor drainage.

If the poor drainage seems to stem from the nature of the topsoil, digging in plenty of organic matter, which encourages worm activity, will go a

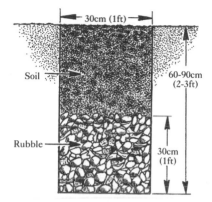

Simple trench drain filled with rubble. Clay or plastic pipes can be laid at the bottom of the trench to remedy more serious drainage problems

long way towards putting the matter right. This has certainly been the case with my present garden. During the winter we moved in, half the kitchen garden was semi-permanently under water and the rest waterlogged, making it quite unworkable until early the following summer – and hard work then. By digging in vast quantities of spent mushroom compost over the next few years we now have a reasonably well-drained and fertile soil in the kitchen garden.

Where the drainage problem is caused by the nature of the subsoil, the addition of some form of artificial drainage will be necessary. In a small garden, drainage can often be improved sufficiently by making a few 'trench drains'. This is done by taking out a trench about 30cm (1ft) wide and 60 or 90cm (2 or 3ft) deep, and filling the bottom 30cm (1ft) with a layer of large clinkers, stones, broken bricks, and similar material before replacing the soil (see diagram above). A trench like this could be made across the lower end of a slope, or at both ends of a level site. It could also be incorporated into a path; a meandering path through a small garden could easily conceal a most effective drain as well as provide an additional, decorative feature. I've been told that in the past reasonably effective drains were made simply by filling trenches with brushwood.

In a persistently wet garden, the only solution may be to lay a proper system of drains, draining into a ditch, artificial soakaway or sump. Clay or plastic pipes can be laid in the drains. Both are satisfactory, but for the amateur modern plastic pipes, 4–5cm (1½–2in) diameter, are easier to handle and lay. It is common practice to lay the pipes at the bottom of the trench and cover them with 30cm (1ft) or so of drainage material such as clinker or rubble.

Laying drains is a skilled job, so, if it is necessary, it would be well worth seeking expert advice on the sort of drains to use, their depth, spacing and gradient, and the most suitable layout for your particular plot.

Growing in raised beds (see p.39) often provides a satisfactory solution to a poor drainage problem.

IMPROVING FERTILITY: A SUMMARY

A fertile soil is well drained, probably slightly acid or neutral, has a good crumbly structure and is rich in nutrients which are available to the plants.

If things are growing well in your garden, assume it is fertile. A vigorous crop of weeds in a neglected garden can be taken as a sign of fertility, even if it does mean a lot of work before you produce an equally vigorous crop of vegetables. But if either cultivated plants or weeds seem poor and sickly, something more radical is wrong. In this case, the steps to take in restoring fertility are:

1 Improve drainage if it is faulty. This often brings dramatic results.

2 Check acidity. Faulty pH is often at the root of failure, especially in city gardens. It can be corrected by liming.

3 Work in bulky organic matter such as manure, compost, seaweed, sludge or whatever is available. This will improve the soil structure and provide nutrients, and of course encourage earthworm activity. It may also be necessary in the early stages to increase the supply of nutrients with regular organic feeds, for example of liquid seaweed or comfrey liquid.

Maintaining fertility

Once soil has been brought into a fertile state, it pays to keep it that way. Vegetables remove considerable quantities of nutrients from the soil, and these must be replenished by frequent applications of organic matter.

Conserving the soil structure is also most important. It can easily be destroyed by cultivating when the soil is too wet or too dry, by heavy rain on the bare surface, or by walking on the bare surface more than is necessary. The practice of keeping the surface continually mulched, that is covered with a layer of compost or other form of organic matter, goes a long way towards improving and conserving the soil structure. In fact, over the years I have become such a mulching addict that the sight of bare soil in the kitchen garden makes me feel distinctly uneasy. The fertility of the soil depends chiefly on the rate at which organic matter is added to it.

One of the great advantages of laying out a vegetable garden in narrow beds is that they can be worked from the paths, so avoiding the necessity of ever treading on the soil.

SPECIAL PROBLEMS

The neglected garden

Neglected gardens create special problems. They can be weedy, may have a low level of fertility, and the soil is often intractable and difficult to work.

A suggested line of approach is as follows:

1   Cut down and clear away all surface vegetation.

2   Dig over the ground, removing the roots of all perennial weeds by hand. Ideally complete this by the autumn. If the weed problem is very severe it may be necessary to mulch with heavy carpeting or black polythene for several months before proceeding any further. (See Chapter 5 for more on perennial weeds and weed-suppressing mulches.)

3   If the soil is compacted try to at least fork over the soil surface to help get air and rain into it. Then spread a thick layer of bulky manure, compost, straw, sewage sludge, spent mushroom compost, seaweed, or any other kind of organic matter over the ground. It can easily be 15cm (6in) deep. If it is reasonably well rotted it can be dug in; if it is very fresh, or digging proves extremely hard, leave it in place over the winter, allowing worms to work it into the soil.

4   In spring, dig in the residue and rake down the surface of the soil.

5   Before attempting to sow or plant anything allow the first flush of weed seeds to germinate: there is bound to be a huge reserve of weed seed in the soil. Hoe off the weeds before sowing or planting. Don't try to sow too early. If the garden proves very weedy, don't sow directly into the ground during the first season, but raise the first plants in pots, planting them out when they are a reasonable size (see Chapter 4). Alternatively plant through weed suppressing black plastic films.

6   Concentrate the first year on vegetables which are naturally vigorous and cover the ground well, such as potatoes and Jerusalem artichokes (both excellent crops for breaking in neglected soil), broad beans, Swiss chard, New Zealand spinach, turnips and Chinese artichokes. These all keep weeds down well once established. Another option is to make frequent sowings of 'cut-and-come-again' seedling crops which will grow in shallow soils. Suggestions are garden cress, salad rape, salad mustard and salad rocket. Feed regularly with organic liquid feeds to stimulate growth.

7   Mulch as much as you can to prevent weeds from germinating and to control the perennial weeds. After two years or so of cultivation, weeds become less of a problem.

Do not expect marvellous crops the first year. However, by growing something and working the soil, you will see it start to improve. If crops do not seem to be doing better in the second year, it may be worth having a professional soil analysis to check on the pH and to see if there are any serious nutrient deficiencies. This can, of course, always be done at the outset.

Digging up lawns and rough areas

Tackle this job in the autumn. It is best to double dig the area which is being converted into a vegetable plot (see Chapter 3 for double digging). Slice off the top 5cm (2in) of turf, and bury it grass-side down in the first trench. Chop it up before covering with soil from the next trench.

If the soil in the lawn is acid, it will probably be necessary to lime after the autumn digging.

The rubble the builders left behind

Owners of new houses are often faced with the prospect of converting a pile of rubble or raw clay into a vegetable garden. The topsoil has been removed, and the soil that remains looks impossible. Don't despair. It can be converted into a garden.

A common practice is to import topsoil but this is very expensive and, if the soil has been stacked in a heap more than 1m (1yd) high, it will be devoid of worms. The cheaper and most effective method is to import large quantities of organic matter.

I suggest you tackle the problem as follows:

1   Remove the largest stones, bricks and similar rubbish. Don't worry about removing every stone over the whole area: their main drawback is making it difficult to grow root crops like carrots and parsnips, and it may be easier to prepare a special area for them, or grow them initially inside deep boxes.

2   Fork over the soil as much as possible.

3   In the autumn cover the soil with a thick layer of organic matter as suggested for the neglected garden. Make no attempt to dig it but leave it undisturbed during the winter.

4   Proceed as for the neglected garden.

Pockets of fertility

In the early days of a raw garden, concentrate your resources. Use any spare compost or manure in one area, dig it in, and plant or sow there initially. Fertile 'pockets' can be created by making small trenches up to 15cm (6in) deep, filling them with commercial potting compost, topped with a couple of centimetres or an inch or so of soil. Lettuce, spring onions, radishes, early carrots, dwarf beans, seedling salads and so on could be sown in these pockets.

Green manuring

Green manuring is a time honoured method of maintaining and improving the fertility of a soil, by growing a crop which is dug into the soil to enrich it, rather than being removed for consumption. For the benefits and use of green manures see Chapter 2.

CHAPTER TWO

Manures, Fertilizers, Compost, and Green Manures

The term 'manure' usually refers to a bulky product derived from animals, and 'fertilizer' to a concentrated powder, granules or liquid, in most cases man-made or 'artificial'. But there is no hard and fast rule, and in practice the terms are very loosely interchanged. Both manures and fertilizers can be either organic or inorganic in origin.

Essentially manures improve the soil, as described in the previous chapter. They are also a source of plant foods or nutrients, which are released slowly when they are broken down by soil micro-organisms; in addition they are a source of food for earthworms. Artificial fertilizers have a minimal effect on the soil, supply no food for earthworms, but are a quick source of plant foods.

THE ORGANIC VERSUS INORGANIC CONTROVERSY

Modern gardeners tend to be divided into two camps – those who are happy to use chemical products such as artificial fertilizers, weedkillers, and chemical sprays for pest and disease control, and the 'organic' school, who avoid the use of chemicals.

In relation to manures and fertilizers, organic gardeners use only those which are derived from animal or vegetable material, ruling out manufactured 'artificial' fertilizers and most of those that have been extracted from rocks (unless they are subsequently broken down in the soil by natural processes). The basic philosophy of organic gardening is 'feed the soil, not the plant'. Bulky organic manures primarily feed the soil; artificial fertilizers are directed at feeding the plant.

There are other practical reasons for not using artificial fertilizers:

~They are, in the main, water soluble and very fast acting. Plants respond quickly, but the resultant sappy soft growth is more susceptible to pest and disease attack, and more vulnerable to bad weather.

~Artificial fertilizers have only a short term effect. However the nutrients in organic fertilizers, released by the action of soil bacteria, become available slowly but over a much longer period. Plant growth is therefore steadier and sturdier.

~Artificial fertilizers only supply a limited range of the key elements such as nitrogen, phosphorus and potash. Most organic fertilizers also supply minor elements, trace elements and other growth promoting substances.

~The dosage of artificial fertilizers is critical; it is easy to apply too much, so damaging the plant or, through chemical reactions, leading to deficiencies in other key nutrients. This is most unlikely with the gentler action of organic fertilizers.

~Artificial fertilizers can easily pollute the environment. The high level of nitrates in the water supply in farming areas is an example of this. There is far less risk of pollution with the use of organic manures and fertilizers.

AIM OF THE MANURING PROGRAMME

In organic gardens the main aim of the manuring programme is to be constantly improving the soil fertility, by the addition of as much bulky organic manure as possible. (Where bulky manures are in short supply, homemade compost and green manuring can be used to make up the shortfall.) Once a garden is brought to a high level of fertility, and maintained at that level, little supplementary feeding is required. But reaching this level may take a few years, and organic fertilizers can play a useful role in bridging the gap.

Generally speaking, nitrogen, which is essential for all plant growth but needed in greatest quantities by leafy, bulky plants, is the nutrient most likely to be in short supply. Nitrogen is washed out of the soil in winter, and the natural supplies are not replenished until soil temperatures are warm enough in spring for the soil organisms to start breaking down organic matter. This is when conventional gardeners apply a nitrogenous fertilizer to stimulate plant growth. Organic gardeners either have to be patient, or they can use slower working concentrated organic fertilizers, such as forms of seaweed.

Most gardens have considerable reserves of the two other main elements, phosphorus and potash, and in gardens where all plant wastes are returned to the soil as compost, overall losses are low. The average garden's requirements for phosphorus and potash would be met with annual applications of manure of about 5.5kg/sq m (10lb/sq yd), or at least 2kg/sq m (5lb/sq yd) of good compost.

Potash deficiency is most likely in chalk and light sandy soils; phosphorus deficiency in heavy soils and peat soils. Amateur soil testing kits give some indication of major nutrient deficiencies but, where growth is consistently poor, and a soil problem is suspected, it is advisable to have a professional soil analysis carried out. Under organic systems serious deficiencies of phosphorus or potash can be corrected in the long term by the use of rock phosphate and rock potash. They will also be gradually corrected by the addition of organic matter.

TRACE ELEMENTS

Most soils contain sufficient quantities of the trace elements required by plants but occasionally deficiencies occur, usually in fairly extreme soil types. Typical deficiency symptoms are stunted growth and pale, often yellowing leaves. Boron, manganese and copper deficiencies are the most likely to show up in vegetables. Once diagnosed (professional help may be needed for this), they can be corrected by applying specific foliar feeds: borax, for example, is used to correct boron deficiency. Seaweed foliar feeds also appear to help correct trace element deficiencies. Indeed some crops respond surprisingly well to treatment with fertilizers containing trace elements, such as seaweed extracts, even though no deficiencies are particularly apparent.

In the long term the best remedy for trace element deficiencies is adding organic matter and correcting the soil pH (see the previous chapter). One of the many benefits of organic systems is that soil deficiencies are, in fact, far less likely to arise.

BULKY ORGANIC MANURES

It is no longer easy to find supplies of the traditional bulky animal manures such as horse, cow, and pig manure. If you have a supply, make the most of it. It should be mixed with as much straw as possible, as this is as valuable as the manure element. If wood shavings or sawdust have been used as litter, stack the manure in a heap for up to a year to break it down. Otherwise nitrogen will be 'robbed' from the soil in the early stages of decomposition. Poultry manure, other bird manures and rabbit manure are very concentrated, and are therefore best added to the compost heap in small quantities as an activator.

Some modern alternative bulky manures are treated sewage sludge, slaughter house waste and municipal waste. Just make sure they are guaranteed free of heavy metals.

In many areas spent mushroom compost is available, and is an excellent manure, especially on heavy clay soils. Rotate it around the garden, to avoid the build up of lime in any one area.

If you are close to the sea, seaweed is a valuable manure. It contains roughly the same amount of organic matter and nitrogen as farmyard manure, as well as numerous trace elements, and can be used fresh, dried or composted.

Straw, if you can obtain it, is an excellent source of organic matter. It is best to compost it (see p.31).

Tracking down organic matter calls for a fair amount of initiative. But it is not impossible, even in cities. I have friends in London who get free horse manure from police stables, sacks of rotting leaves and vegetable waste from markets and greengrocers, and packing straw for composting from shops. Those great piles of leaves, swept up in city parks and streets and so often burnt, rot down beautifully (see Composting leaves p.31). The boom in pony riding must mean there is a lot of very useful muck somewhere for the asking!

As a general rule, well-rotted bulky manures are best dug into the soil, though they can be used for mulching during the growing season (see Chapter 3). Fresh manures and half-rotted compost, on the other hand, are best spread on the surface of the soil in autumn, several centimetres thick for the worms to work in. It is inadvisable to apply fresh animal manure onto growing vegetables; much better to let it age for a period of time first in a covered heap. Don't worry too much about the do's and don'ts: the main step towards achieving a vegetable garden you can be proud of is to be working something organic into your soil, somehow!

Peat

In the past peat was fairly widely used to improve soil structure, particularly in clay and chalk soils, though it has very little nutrient value. With current anxiety about destruction of peat bogs and depletion of the natural reserves of peat, its use is not recommended.

CONCENTRATED ORGANIC FERTILIZERS

In highly fertile soils it is unnecessary to use organic fertilizers, but they can help to raise fertility in the following situations:

~Where substantial soil deficiencies need to be corrected.

~To raise nutrient levels in the interim period before a poor soil has been brought up to a reasonable level of fertility; nitrogen is most likely to be in short supply.

~To obtain higher yields, notably of 'hungry' crops such as potatoes and brassicas. Tomatoes, to take another example, will respond well to extra potash once they are flowering and fruiting.

APPLYING FERTILIZERS

Fertilizers are available in dry forms – generally powders or granules – or as concentrated liquid solutions. The dried forms are spread on the surface and raked into the soil. It is advisable to water them in afterwards.

Liquid forms are diluted and are usually watered on the ground around the plants using a watering can. The soil should be moist before applying fertilizer, so water beforehand if necessary.

Diluted liquid fertilizers can also be sprayed on the plants as a foliar feed, using standard spraying equipment or a can with a fine rose. Do it in the evening or in dull weather, spraying so that the leaves are covered. Foliar feeding is sometimes used in dry weather to avoid watering.

In conventional gardening fertilizers are applied as a *base dressing* or a *top dressing*. A *base dressing* is worked into the soil two to three weeks before sowing or planting in the spring, to meet the plant's requirements for nitrogen and, to a lesser extent phosphorus, in the early stages of growth. *Top dressings* are applied during growth as a booster. For example crops which have over-wintered in the soil, such as spring cabbage and over-wintered onions, can benefit from a nitrogen-rich top dressing in spring. Top dressings can also be applied as a foliar feed.

With the slower acting organic fertilizers the feeding system is more flexible. Slow acting general purpose fertilizers like seaweed meal can be applied to the soil several months before sowing or planting. During growth, comfrey, seaweed and other general purpose organic fertilizers can be used as a top dressing.

Foliar feeding, especially of seaweed extracts and comfrey, is also used quite frequently. They seem to act as a tonic, with leaves often developing a deep, healthy looking green very soon afterwards. No one is quite sure why this is so. However, foliar feeding should not be the *sole* method used; plants can only take in limited amounts through their leaves.

The following are some concentrated organic fertilizers which can be purchased. It has to be said that on the whole they are a fairly expensive way to buy nutrients, and are relatively slow acting. Their composition can vary considerably.

Dried blood A fast acting source of nitrogen. Use as a top dressing to boost growth in spring or early summer.

Hoof and horn Primarily a source of nitrogen, which is released within a couple of weeks of application. Useful as a top dressing on over-wintered greens, and leafy crops in early summer.

Blood, fish and bonemeal A source of nitrogen and phosphorus. Use as a base dressing two to three weeks before sowing or planting, or as a top dressing during growth.

Bonemeal and boneflour A source of phosphorus, used mainly for perennial plants, but can be useful where vegetables are grown on light land. Only use steamed or sterilized bonemeal, as anthrax can be contracted from raw bonemeal.

Seaweed meal Supplies potash, some nitrogen and phosphorus, as well as trace elements. Use as a base dressing several months before sowing or planting, or as a top dressing. It should be dug in as, otherwise, it may 'gel' on the surface.

Liquid comfrey concentrate A general purpose liquid feed containing high levels of potash. Use as a top dressing to encourage plant growth. (This can also be homemade. See below.)

In addition various proprietary concentrated organic composts, quite frequently made from chicken manure or from worm-worked wastes, appear on the market. Their precise value varies from product to product.

Domestic organic fertilizers

Soot Contains nitrogen, and is a good general stimulant. Don't use it fresh as the sulphur released can damage plants. Store it somewhere dry for about three months, then apply it as a top dressing on young plants. It also improves the texture of clay soil and, because of its dark colour, helps to warm soils through absorption of heat. It is said to deter pests such as pea weevil, celery fly, carrot fly and slugs.

Ash From wood fires and bonfires contains potash. Slow burning hardwoods are particularly rich in potash. Either work fresh ash into the compost heap or store it in a dry place. If exposed to rain the potash is rapidly washed out. Apply it to growing crops in spring.

Liquid manure or *'Black Jack'* A valuable and cheap liquid manure, can be made by suspending a sack of well-rotted animal manure in a barrel of water (see diagram p.28). Grass cuttings and soot can be included in this mixture. Leave about ten days before using, and stir before use. Dilute it to the colour of weak tea before watering plants with it.

Comfrey liquid manure The deep-rooting perennial plant comfrey can be used to make a useful liquid fertilizer, rich in potassium (and therefore excellent for feeding tomatoes).

Sack with rotted
animal manure,
soot and grass
cuttings

'Black Jack' tub; simple method of making liquid manure by hanging a sack of manure, which can be mixed with soot and grass cuttings, in a barrel of water

The best comfrey for this purpose is the highly productive 'Bocking 14' cultivar of Russian comfrey. It is worth making space for half a dozen plants in even a small garden: fortunately they tolerate light shade. Start with purchased plants, or by taking root offsets or root cuttings from healthy established plants. Plant them at least 60cm (2ft) apart. (For Further Reading see p.248.)

There are several ways of making comfrey manure. The simplest method of making concentrated comfrey is in a large barrel, rain butt, or rubbish bin, supported on bricks to raise it a short distance off the ground. Either insert a tap near the bottom, or drill a 1cm (½in) hole in the bottom, standing a jar beneath the hole to collect the juice. Stuff the barrel with fresh or wilted leaves, weighted down with a heavy board to compress them. Cover the barrel with a lid. The concentrate will start to drip through within about ten days. Keep it in a jar in a cool dark place. Dilute it from 10 to 20 times with water for use. Avoid getting it on your skin, and be warned: it can be very smelly!

Nettle manure Popularly known as 'nettle tea', this is also a useful, home-made general fertilizer, made and used in the same way as comfrey manure. An alternative recipe, given to me by 'forest gardener' Robert Hart, is to half fill buckets with compacted nettles and cover them with water. Use the resulting liquid without dilution 'when it starts to smell!'

Compost

Bulky manures cost money and, as mentioned earlier, are not always easy to obtain. Homemade compost costs nothing, and is an invaluable source of humus. Anyone growing vegetables, in however small a garden, should make space for a compost heap. You can never have too much compost: it's extraordinary how a huge heap settles into an insignificant pile!

A compost heap is essentially a pile of vegetable and animal waste, which generates heat and decomposes naturally with the aid of bacteria. When fully decomposed the resulting compost is blackish brown in colour, moist, crumbly, and uniform in texture, with no half decayed stalks or vegetation that is still recognizable as such. However, even partially decomposed compost benefits the soil wonderfully: it is just slightly more awkward to handle.

There are many theories about the best way to make compost, with even the experts often failing to agree – at least over details. The main point is that to bring about decomposition relatively quickly the bacteria need moisture, air, warmth, and a source of nitrogen, which is normally leafy vegetation. The key to making good compost is ensuring that these conditions are met satisfactorily.

A simple heap

This can be made by piling up wastes as they accumulate or, better still, collecting together enough material to build it up a layer at a time. When it is about 90cm-1.2m (3-4ft) high, cover it with 2.5cm (1in) of soil, then cover it completely with an old carpet, hessian or heavy duty plastic, and leave it to rot. This could take about a year. The drawback with this anaerobic (that is, airless) method is that high temperatures are not generated, so weed seeds and disease spores may not be destroyed, and tough material may not all be broken down.

Aerobic compost heap (see diagram p.30)

In this case air circulates through the compost heap and, provided it is large enough and well insulated, high temperatures are generated, weed and disease spores are therefore killed, and the rotting process is therefore faster and more complete.

The bin In a small garden, compost is best made in a semi-permanent bin at least 90cm-1.2m (3-4ft) high and the same width – the larger the better. It should stand on a soil base. A long narrow bin might prove feasible in some gardens, tucked alongside a fence or hedge.

It must be a robust construction. Three sides should be made of material with good insulation properties such as timber, bricks, breeze blocks or even hay or straw bales. The front should be designed so that it can be erected in stages, making it easy both to put in raw materials and, later, to remove the rotted compost. Slipping plants or poles between upright posts or pipes at the corners is one way of doing this. Where space allows you to build two bins side by side, one compost heap can be decomposing while the other is being built up. Provided they are reasonably strong, some of the patented bins on the market can be useful in small gardens. A simple bin can be made from strong wire mesh, lined with carpet or cardboard as a form of insulation.

Foundations When you start to build the heap, fork the soil underneath. This improves drainage and helps worms to move in later on. Start the

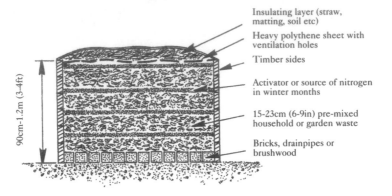

Aerobic Compost Heap

heap with a 7·5cm (3in) layer of tree prunings or brushwood, or build it on a layer of drain pipes or rows of bricks, or lay rigid mesh wire on bricks or wood blocks to support the heap – all to improve aeration.

What to use Almost any material of vegetable or animal origin can be used – for example, kitchen waste such as vegetable peelings, egg shells, orange peel, tea leaves, teapot dregs and vacuum cleaner waste; garden waste such as weeds (nettles are excellent), vegetable remains, old potting soil, lawn mowings, autumn leaves (even pine needles), thin prunings, bonfire ash and straw; green bracken gathered between late spring and early autumn; animal manure such as pigeon droppings and so on.

Do not use Diseased vegetables (burn or bury them); perennial weeds such as docks, couch grass, bindweed or ground elder, unless they have been laid out first to die off in the sun; evergreens such as holly or ivy; woody material; scrap pieces of meat which would attract rats; any materials such as plastic, tin, glass, or man-made fibres that will not rot.

Building the heap Ideally wastes should be pre-mixed before putting them on the compost heap. The easiest way is to collect them in airtight plastic bags or rubbish sacks. Keep one purely for household wastes and one for weeds and, when there is enough material, make them into one layer 15-23cm (6-9in) thick. Avoid a thick layer of any one material, especially grass cuttings, which can become compacted, prevent air circulation and stop the biological activity in the heap.

If the compost heap is short of fresh green material (which is most likely to occur in the winter months), each layer can be sprinkled with a source of nitrogen or an activator to stimulate bacterial activity. Use a proprietary organic compost activator, animal or poultry manure, seaweed meal, or blood, fish and bonemeal.

Moisture The compost heap needs to be damp, but not soaking wet. Water if necessary. In areas of very high rainfall it may be necessary to protect it with a cover to prevent it from becoming waterlogged.

Completion When the heap reaches the top of the bin, cover it with a sheet of heavy polythene punctured with holes for ventilation. Make the holes about 2·5cm (1in) in diameter and 30cm (12in) apart. Then cover the whole heap with permeable insulating material, such as a thick layer of straw, matting, 5cm (2in) of soil or an old carpet.

Turning The heat generated in the heap will not reach the outer 15cm (6in), so theoretically the heap should be turned 'sides to middle' after about three weeks to give the outer edges a chance to rot. Where this is difficult, slice off the outer 7·5-15cm (3-6in) before the compost is used, and put it aside to start the next heap.

In summer a heap made this way will be ready in three or four months; in winter it will probably take at least six to eight months.

The compost can either be dug into the soil or spread on the surface, using up to a barrow load per square metre (yard).

Composting straw

If you are able to get a supply of straw, it is advisable to compost it. Either incorporate it gradually into your normal compost heap, or build it up into a heap on its own. Make it in layers about 15cm (6in) thick, water each layer until thoroughly moist, and sprinkle each layer with a source of nitrogen (see p.29). Turn in dry material on the outside and bury it in the heap. It can be made up to 1·8m (6ft) high, and should be ready in a few months.

Composting leaves

Autumn leaves are best composted on their own, as they eventually decay into wonderful leaf mould. This can be used in sowing and potting compost, or when half rotted, as drainage material in pots or for mulching. Pack the leaves into a wire-netting enclosure 60-90cm (2-3ft) high. They may take up to two years to rot down completely. Leaves can also be gathered in black plastic sacks and left to rot.

I have recently learnt that leaves from trees grown on very alkaline and chalky soils make poor leaf mould. The best way to utilize them is to dig them into trenches.

Worm compost

A useful system for making compost in small households has been developed by American biologist Mary Appelhof, author of *Worms Eat My Garbage* (see Further Reading p.248). It consists of feeding domestic and garden waste to the small, red, manure, brandling or fishing worms, *Eisenia foetida*. These eventually convert it into a material called 'vermicompost', a pleasant peat-like substance, which can be used either as ordinary compost or in making potting compost.

Use a box roughly 45 x 60 x 25cm deep (18 x 24 x 10in), filled with about 1.6kg (3½lb) of shredded newspaper which serves as 'bedding'. This is moistened with about 4.5 litre (1gal) of water, then a handful of fishing worms are put in. The box is covered to keep it moist. The worms are fed regularly with wastes. The squeamish need have no fear of the worms escaping. Once the food supply is exhausted, the worms die, but before that stage is reached some can be transferred to another box with fresh bedding to keep the system going.

Worm casts
Worm casts, usually reared on a seaweed diet, are occasionally offered for sale. They can also, of course, be collected from the garden, most easily from lawns. They are a very rich source of nutrients, and benefit the soil and plant growth. Sprinkle them along the drill before sowing, or use them to top dress young plants.

GREEN MANURES
Green manures are grown to dig in to the soil to improve its fertility. I used to think green manuring was impractical in small gardens, but I am now convinced it is worth doing, even on a very small scale. Depending on the plant used, green manures can:
~ Increase the organic matter in the soil.
~ Increase the nitrogen in the soil.
~ Protect the soil surface over the winter so nutrients are not washed out.
~ Help to smother weeds.
~ Increase the drought resistance of the soil.
~ Produce extra material for the compost heap or for mulching.
Green manures cannot provide all the nutrients and organic matter a garden needs, but can be a very useful supplementary source of both.

In small gardens the two most practical options for green manuring are as a quick catch crop during the growing season, or an over-wintered crop sown in late summer or autumn and dug in the following spring. It can be worth sowing very small areas, even, say, a couple of square metres (yards). Remember also that green manuring can be done in greenhouses and polytunnels, rather than leaving ground bare.

There are many green manures to choose from, and it is worth experimenting in your own garden, sowing a few rows of different ones side by side to see which grows best in your soil and climatic conditions. I have found the following very useful.

Spring or summer 'catch crop'
Sow where ground is vacant for four to eight weeks. Suitable plants are:

Mustard (*Sinapsis alba*) and rape (*Brassica napa* var. *napa*) Both are very fast growing. Sow from early spring to early autumn. Dig in from three to eight weeks later, before they flower, as a quick source of nitrogen. Don't grow on soil infected with clubroot.

Phacelia tanacetifolia A pretty, fast growing, feathery-leaved plant. Sow as above, digging in four to eight weeks later before it flowers, as a source of nitrogen and some organic matter from the root systems. Leave a few to flower: the lovely blue flowers attract beneficial insects.

Buckwheat (*Fagopyrum esculentum*) A fast growing plant. Sow from spring to late summer. It will tolerate poor soil. Dig in within six to eight weeks before it flowers, mainly as a source of organic matter. Again, a few left to flower will attract beneficial hoverflies.

Hardy over-wintering green manures

Sow these after the ground has been cleared in late summer or autumn.

Field beans (*Vicia faba*) Sow from early to late autumn, spacing seeds 13cm (5in) apart. Dig in the following spring before they flower. They are a source of organic matter and nitrogen, both from the leaves when they rot and from the nitrogen fixing nodules on the roots. Closely related to broad beans, the young leaves and tops can be eaten raw in salads or cooked. The plants are unsuitable for light soils.

Winter tares (*Vicia sativa*) Sow from mid-summer to early autumn. Dig in the following spring. For benefits see field beans (above). The plants do best on heavy soil.

Grazing rye (*Secale cereale*) Sow from late summer to early autumn, protecting it well from birds at least in the most vulnerable early stages. Dig in the fibrous root system in spring as a source of organic matter.

With the exception of the beans, all these green manures can be sown in rows, wide drills or thinly broadcast. Provided they have grown well, the first leafy growth can be cut and then used for mulching or worked into the compost heap.

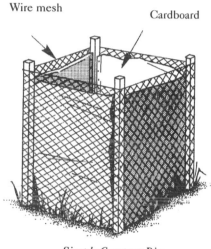

Wire mesh   Cardboard

Simple Compost Bin

The secondary growth can be dug in a couple of weeks later. The stems, roots and leaves take a while to break down after being dug in, so it is normally easier to plant the following vegetable crop, rather than sow *in situ*.

MANURING GUIDELINES

~ Whenever a piece of ground needs digging, organic matter is worked in.
~ Whenever a crop is planted, it is mulched with an organic mulch.
~ During the growing season, seaweed liquid feeds and foliar feeds are used on any plants that look as if they would benefit.
~ Every winter some vacant beds will be ridged and covered with a heavy organic mulch.
~ A couple of beds will be sown with an over-wintering green manure.

CHAPTER THREE

Tools and Techniques

BASIC TOOLS AND EQUIPMENT
Even for a small garden, money has to be spent on basic tools and equipment. Always buy the best you can afford. Cheap tools are false economy. They make the job harder, and have a depressingly short life span. The best quality tools are made of stainless steel with ash handles, and often carry a ten-year guarantee.

When buying tools, try them out for size (particularly the handles) and weight, as it is most important that they should feel comfortable.

It is worth taking care of good tools so they give long service. Soil should always be scraped off before the tools are put away and, ideally, they should be wiped with an oily rag. Spades and hoes need occasional sharpening with a sharpening stone. Needless to say, this does not always happen – even in the best gardening circles.

The following tools are almost essential: a spade, a digging fork, a rake, a Dutch hoe or a draw hoe, a hand fork and trowel, an onion hoe, a garden line and a watering can. A dibber is always useful. If you intend to raise plants from seed indoors, a set of miniature tools (often sold as a houseplant set or 'rockery tools') and a small dibber, are worth having.

The *spade* is the traditional digging tool and the best for thorough digging on heavy soil, for breaking up clods, and for work which involves moving soil. However, in a small garden with reasonably well-worked soil, you could manage using only a fork. Various sizes of spade are sold, the smallest, the border or ladies' spade, being the most suitable for women.

The *fork* is also used for digging. It is preferable to a spade on a very stony soil. It is also used for breaking up soil which has already been turned with a spade, and generally 'working' the soil. For ordinary garden use the round-pronged fork is the most popular, though some people prefer the flat-pronged fork, also used for lifting potatoes and other root vegetables.

Rakes are mainly used for levelling soil, removing stones, and preparing the tilth on a seedbed. For general purposes an eight- or ten-tooth metal-headed rake is adequate. I am very attached to a handmade, rosehead nail-tooth rake (a wooden head fitted with iron teeth) which is perfectly balanced and easy to use. These are worth getting if you come across them. A springbok rake comes in handy for raking up leaves and rubbish.

The *Dutch hoe*, in which the blade is pushed lightly through the soil, is for removing weeds and loosening the soil when it is not too heavy. It can also be used for drawing a drill. When hoeing with a Dutch hoe walk backwards as you work, so that no footmarks are left on the soil. In small gardens, of course, it is often possible to hoe most of the garden while standing on the path. Always hoe with gentle movements, or hoeing can soon become surprisingly tiring.

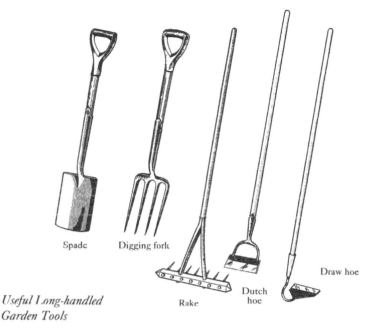

Spade   Digging fork

Draw hoe

Useful Long-handled
Garden Tools

Rake

Dutch
hoe

The *draw hoe* is pulled towards you, rather than pushed. It can be used for hoeing on heavier soils, and for such jobs as earthing up and drawing a shallow flat-bottomed drill for peas.

The *onion hoe* is a small, swan-necked draw hoe on a 15cm (6in) handle. It is invaluable for weeding, specially in confined spaces, for thinning, drawings drills and even earthing up. If restricted to one hoe in a small garden, this would be my choice (see below). New to this country is the short handled 'Ibis' hoe, an oriental hoe with a subtly curved triangular blade, tapering to a point. It is ideal for weeding and drawing a drill.

Triangular, serrated-edge, oscillating and double-edged hoes are very useful. It is really a question of finding what suits you best personally.

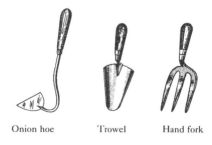

Onion hoe   Trowel   Hand fork

Some Essential Small Hand Tools

The *cultivator* is a tool with three to five claw-like prongs, which can be very useful for breaking up ground and for weeding between plants.

A *hand trowel* is the best planting tool, and a small *hand fork* is useful for weeding near plants and loosening the soil in small areas. I mainly use the *dibber* for planting leeks. It enables you to make a straight 20cm (8in) hole into which they can be dropped. It is also handy for planting large seeds.

Garden lines can be bought, or made by attaching twine to a pair of skewers or tent pegs. If your garden beds are a constant width, make your line the same width: that will save hours of ravelling and unravelling.

It is useful to have a 7 or 9 litre (1½ or 2gal) *watering can* with a fine and a coarse rose. A can with a very narrow spout is handy for watering seedlings. Most gardeners will find that they need a wheelbarrow, or at least a trug basket for collecting weeds, a small sprayer, ½ litre (1pt) capacity is probably sufficient, and a hose, preferably with a fitting for adjusting the spray.

DIGGING

Digging is necessary for several reasons: to get air into the soil; to expose as much soil as possible to the elements; to break soil down so that roots can penetrate, and as a means of working manure and other organic matter into the soil. Unless soil has been dug properly at regular intervals, it is difficult to get it into a suitable condition for sowing or planting.

The 'degrees' of digging, according to how much effort is involved, could be described as first forking, second plain or single digging, and third double digging, also known as bastard trenching (real trenching is a complex business, and not necessary or practicable in small gardens).

The easiest operation, *forking*, is generally done between clearing one crop and sowing or planting the next. After clearing early peas, for example, fork over the ground before sowing the next crop of, say, lettuces, beetroot or carrots. In spring, after the soil has been broken down by the frost, it can often be forked over easily. If you are fortunate enough to have a really good loamy soil, forking may be sufficient to keep it in good condition permanently, but most soils benefit from being dug annually, with double digging until they are in good condition.

Single or *plain digging* Work the top spit of soil only – 23-25cm (9-10in). To allow room for manoeuvring, the traditional way of digging is to start by taking out a small trench, the depth of the spade and 30-38cm (12-15in) wide, across the width of the area you are digging. Remove this soil to the end of the plot, where your digging will finish (see Stage 1). Then dig the strip beside your trench, turning the soil into the first trench – and so on. If you are adding manure lay this in the bottom of the trench before turning in the soil from the adjacent strip. Then fork it over to ensure the soil and manure are mixed together (see Stage 2). Fill the last trench with the soil you removed from the first (see Stage 3).

Double digging. Here a wider trench is made, about 60cm (2ft) wide, and the top spit is turned into the preceding trench in the same way. The bottom spit is then forked over to the depth of the fork, and manure or organic matter is worked into the broken up soil as thoroughly as possible. The top spit of soil from the next trench is then used to fill it in.

Although double digging is harder work, it is worth doing, especially if you are starting off with poor soil or bad conditions. It helps to improve the drainage of heavy soil and increases the moisture reserves deeper in the soil, so encouraging roots to go deeper in search of moisture. We now know that Brussels sprout roots can penetrate 60-90cm (2-3ft) deep. By using the deeper moisture reserves, moisture near the surface is conserved: this is

Single Digging

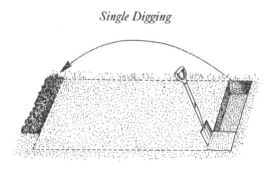

Stage 1 Dig the width of the plot, removing the soil at the far end

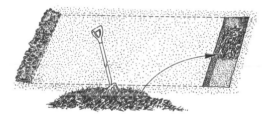

Stage 2 Lay manure in the bottom of the trench

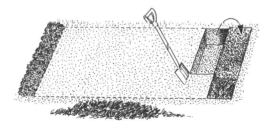

Stage 3 Cover the manure with soil from the adjacent strip, then fork it over so soil and manure are thoroughly mixed

important because it is from the upper layers that the surface roots extract nutrients, and they can only do so when the soil is moist. Where you have a thin sandy soil, or a shallow soil over gravel or chalk, double digging helps to deepen the topsoil.

The manure or organic matter which is being dug in can either be spread evenly over the surface first, or kept 'at the ready' in small heaps.

There are several points to make about digging:

1 Always put the spade in as vertically as possible. You get through the ground faster and penetrate deeper.

2 As far as possible, dig out and remove the roots of perennial weeds such as dock, ground elder, bindweed, dandelions, couch grass and thistles. Remove all seeding weeds. Young annual weeds can be dug in. (See also Weeds, Chapter 5.)

3 With heavy soil, digging is easier if you use the spade to make preparatory 'slits' in the soil at right angles to the trench. The soil can then be removed cleanly.

4 Do not attempt to break up the soil finely. Just turn it over and leave it rough as frost action helps to break up the clods. Frost 'tilth' is very beneficial for soil structure. When you see it on the soil surface, leave it undisturbed for a week to get the maximum benefit.

5 Never dig when it is very wet, very dry or very frosty. However, if you keep your soil covered with a light mulch, say of bracken or straw, the surface is protected and will remain 'diggable' in adverse conditions. The mulch itself can be dug in. On heavy soils, aim to complete the digging by early winter, to allow plenty of time for frost to break down the clods. On light sandy soils digging is best left until mid- or late winter.

6 Where possible, allow at least six weeks for the soil to 'settle' before sowing or planting.

7 Digging is hard work. Always go at it gently, taking smaller 'slices' of soil if the going is tough.

One of the problems with very small gardens is finding the space to double dig: there rarely seems to be a large enough vacant patch of soil. So often forking has to suffice, and opportunities to dig more thoroughly and incorporate organic matter deeper into the soil have to be snatched as they arise. For this reason it is worth trying to plan your garden so that crops which will mature at roughly the same time are adjacent – which is not always as simple as it sounds!

Narrow beds

The typical modern kitchen garden is still a rectangular plot with the vegetables grown in widely spaced rows. But more people are returning to the market gardener's traditional method of growing closely spaced vegetables in narrow beds. Beds can vary from 1·5m (5ft) to 1m (3ft). I've personally settled for a 1·2m (4ft) compromise. Work out something that suits you and the dimensions of your garden. The beds don't have to be straight: they can be curved if this helps to make the most of the space available.

Paths between beds can be about 30cm (1ft) wide, with an occasional wider path to allow for wide barrow loads.

Narrow beds have several advantages:

1   There is no need to tread on the soil, so the soil structure is preserved. All cultivation and harvesting can be be done from the path.

2   All manure is concentrated precisely where the plants will grow.

3   No energy is wasted digging ground that will merely be trodden.

4   They lend themselves to intensive planting and equidistant spacing (see Chapter 7). The foliage of most plants then makes a canopy over the soil which prevents weed seeds from germinating. This effect can be reinforced by mulching between the plants.

5   Being accessible, they are particularly easy to ridge up in winter. (See How to Improve Soils p.14.)

6   They are similarly easy to cover with low polytunnels, supporting either insect proof netting or polythene films.

7   It is easier to work out a flexible rotation system with several narrow beds rather than a few larger plots.

Raised beds

These are beds that are anything up to about 30cm (12in) above ground level. To make them manageable, they are generally wider at the base than the top, a 1.2m (4ft) base and 90cm (3ft) top being fairly standard. Raised beds have good drainage and warm up quickly in spring. However, the sides are exposed to sun and wind and dry out rapidly – a factor to consider in areas of low rainfall.

The top of the bed can be flat or rounded. (Flat topped beds are often edged with boards in order to keep them in place.) In small gardens, rounded beds have the advantage of increasing the potential surface area for cultivation. Moreover, in northern latitudes, if the beds are orientated in an east west direction, the south facing side and top benefit from increased exposure to sunlight and radiation. Research in California showed that the benefits of a 5° slope were equivalent to moving 50km (30 miles) to the south!

The fertility of raised beds is normally maintained by keeping the surface heavily mulched, which helps to prevent the sides being eroded. Digging, which tends to distort the shape, is kept to a minimum. The beds can be re-made every few years, double digging the ground at the time if it seems necessary to build up fertility.

Making a raised bed

~ Initially cultivate the whole area to a depth of 15-20cm (6-8in). If the soil is poor it can be double dug.

~ Mark out the position of the beds, allowing about 38cm (15in) for paths.

~ Spade 15-20cm (6-8in) of soil from the path onto the bed area to raise it.

~ Rake the bed to level it, then shape it into a curved shape if required. Firm the sides with the back of a spade.

Built up raised beds

Here a bed is made within a frame, normally of concrete, wood or brick, so that it is about 60cm (2ft) high. This means it can be cultivated without bending down: an asset for disabled, elderly and wheelchair gardeners. The bottom 30cm (12in) would be filled with a layer of rubble to ensure good drainage, topped with about 30cm (12in) of good soil. This type of raised bed is sometimes used to overcome exceptionally bad soil conditions , or to make a garden on concrete foundations.

Intensive deep beds

These are beds that are made outstandingly fertile, both by very deep digging, and by working in large quantities of organic matter.

'NO-DIGGING'

The 'no-digging' technique is worth a mention. This is a system where digging is abolished in favour of continually mulching the soil, with cultivation more or less restricted to light forking and hoeing. A small area of mulch is scraped away when seeds are sown or planting is carried out. I have no first-hand experience of a total 'no-digging' system, which is usually combined with narrow beds. It is probably most suited to light soils, and certainly the soil must be well drained and brought into a high state of fertility before it can be worked successfully. The more fertile your soil becomes, the closer you are to that nirvana where no digging is necessary.

SEED AND SOWING
Seed quality

Most garden vegetables are raised from seed and, for the majority, minimum standards of purity and germination are laid down, so the seed you buy is normally of good quality. All seed deteriorates with age, however, losing its viability, that is its ability to germinate. This process varies with the species. Deterioration is most rapid under damp or hot conditions. For this reason, seed should always be kept as cool and dry as possible, *never* in a hot kitchen or damp shed.

The best way to keep seed is in an airtight tin or jar, in which there is a handful of cooked rice grains, or a bag or dish of silica gel, to absorb moisture. If possible use cobalt-treated silica gel, which is blue when dry and pink when moist. When it becomes moist, redry it in a low oven and then return it promptly to the tin.

Vegetable seed today is often packed in hermetically sealed foil packs. In these seed remains viable much longer than in paper packets, but once the foil packs are open, normal deterioration sets in.

Types of seed

Besides ordinary 'naked' seed, seed firms now offer seed in different forms and with various treatments.

Pelleted seed Individual seeds are made into tiny balls and are given a protective coating that breaks down in the soil. They are very easy to handle and can be spaced out accurately so little, if any, thinning is necessary. There can be germination problems, however. Sow shallowly, in watered drills (see Sowing in adverse conditions p.46) if conditions are dry, and water if necessary until the seed germinates. It will not do so if it dries out.

Seed tapes and sheets Seeds are embedded into soluble tapes, or tissue-like sheets, well spaced out so that subsequent thinning is minimized. The tapes or sheets are 'sown' by laying them on the soil, or on a seed box, and covering with soil in the normal way. Although they come and go on the market, those I have used have been successful.

Chitted or pre-germinated seed The seed has just started to germinate – a tiny root can be seen – and is despatched by a seed firm in a small sachet ready for pricking out (see p.60). It is a useful short cut for amateurs with seed, such as cucumbers, which require a high temperature in order to germinate, but can be grown in slightly cooler conditions once they have germinated. You can also chit your own, if you want to give a head start to seeds that are unlikely to germinate if sown outside in cold soils such as French beans and sweet corn. Use the technique for testing seed viability (see p.60). Sow the seeds as soon after they have germinated as possible, handling them extremely carefully when you do so as the tiny root tips are easily damaged.

Primed seed The seed is brought to the point of germination, then dried and packeted. Once sown, it germinates exceptionally fast. This is very useful with seed that may germinate slowly when sown *in situ*, such as carrots, parsley and onions. To be on the safe side, primed seed should generally be sown within a few months of purchase.

Dressed and treated seed Seed is quite frequently treated or dusted with chemicals, either to combat soil-borne diseases which prevent germination (especially in cold wet soils), or to overcome certain seed-borne diseases, such as celery leaf spot. Strictly speaking organic gardeners should not use these seeds. Untreated seed is available from companies supplying organic gardeners, and other seed companies can often supply untreated seed on request. Treated and dressed seed tends to lose its viability fairly fast, so should not be kept for a second season. Always wash your hands after handling it.

F_1 Hybrids F_1 hybrid seed is made by crossing two parent lines that have been inbred for several generations. The resulting hybrid plants have exceptional vigour, quality, and uniformity. The seed is expensive, as the cross has to be re-made every time seed is required. On the whole it is well worth the price. Never save F_1 seed, as it will not breed true.

Saving your own seed

Amateur gardeners are generally advised against saving their own seed because of the risk of cross pollination and the difficulty in ripening seed in our climate and maintaining its quality. However, I sometimes save seed from vegetables that seed in early summer, such as broad beans, cress, and Mediterranean or salad rocket. Always save seed from the very best, healthiest plants and, as far as possible, let it ripen naturally on the plant. If the weather turns wet, pull up the plants and hang them under cover. When the pods are brittle the seed can be shaken out and stored in jars or paper envelopes.

Sowing methods

The majority of vegetables are raised from seed. Depending on the circumstances, they can be sown:

~*In situ*, that is in the ground where they will grow to maturity.

~In a seedbed, usually in closely spaced rows, from which they will later be transplanted into their permanent position.

~'Indoors', that is in a greenhouse or anywhere under cover, sown in some kind of seedtray (see Chapter 4).

The first method is generally used for root vegetables such as beetroot, carrots, parsnips, radishes and turnips, none of which transplant easily, and also for peas and beans.

A seedbed is favoured for brassicas (members of the cabbage family such as cauliflower, Brussels sprouts, kale) mainly to save space. These vegetables are planted out at least 60cm (2ft) apart, so the space they eventually occupy can meanwhile be used for other groups.

Vegetables are raised under glass or indoors, either because they are tender and cannot be planted outside until late spring or after the danger of frost is over, or else to extend the growing season and so obtain better or earlier crops.

There are no hard and fast rules about which method to adopt for any particular vegetable. It will vary according to the part of the country, the cultivar (some cultivars are bred to withstand colder temperatures) and what you are trying to achieve. Take lettuce: it can be sown under glass to provide an early outdoor planting; it can be sown in a seedbed early in spring for the early summer crop, and later sowings can be made *in situ*, when conditions are drier and transplanting more risky. These plants would be thinned out to the required distance.

In the next few pages, sowing methods are described in some detail for the benefit of new gardeners. They may sound a little complicated at first but, in fact, soon become as instinctive as driving a car.

The site for a seedbed

1   If possible make the seedbed in an open position. It is tempting to tuck it into an odd corner near a hedge, for example, but unless the seedlings are transplanted very young, they will become drawn and spindly if they have to strain towards the light, and will suffer from lack of moisture.

2   Make sure the site chosen is free of perennial weeds, as it will be difficult to weed without disturbing the seedlings.

3   Don't use last year's potato plot as tiny sprouting potatoes be a menace among small seedlings.

4   There is a lot of capital locked up in a seedbed so, if it is plagued by cats and dogs, children, and so on, it is worth wiring it off. Single strands of strong black cotton over individual seed rows will usually deter birds.

Preparing the soil

The same principles apply to sowing in a seedbed or sowing *in situ*. The ground needs to be firm but not consolidated, with the surface free from stones and large lumps of soil, and raked to a fine tilth.

The art lies in knowing the precise point at which to start making the seedbed, that is when the soil is not too wet and not too dry. As a rough guide, if the soil sticks to your shoes as you walk on it, let it dry out for a few more days before tackling it. On the other hand, don't wait until it is completely dry and dusty. Choosing the right moment is largely a question of experience. It is particularly important on clay soils, which are apt to turn from a wet and sticky state into hard intractable clods almost overnight.

If the soil is kept mulched after the spring digging, it will be much easier to make a good seedbed when the time comes. Just rake the mulch aside before starting to work.

Assuming the soil is dug over in the winter or spring, the following are the steps in preparing a seedbed:

1   Fork the soil lightly to a depth of 5-7·5cm (2-3in) or hoe it, to allow it to dry out.

2   When it is dry enough to crumble to a tilth (possibly the same day, or maybe a few days later), break down any clods with the back of the rake, rake it level, and rake off stones and any remaining lumps of soil. Small lumps can sometimes be crumbled in your hands.

3   Rake the soil gently backwards and forwards until you have the sort of tilth you want. The finer the seeds being sown, the finer the tilth should be. Large seeds like peas and beans are best sown in a fairly coarse tilth, which helps to reduce weed germination.

In the past, treading over the soil before raking was recommended, but now that is felt to be advisable only on very light soils.

Sowing in standard drills

The commonest method of sowing is in drills, perhaps best described as slits in the soil, anything from 1·5cm (½-2in) deep. Once the ground has been prepared for sowing the various stages are as follows:

1   Try to choose a day when the soil is moist, and there is not much wind.

2   Mark out your row with the line. Put sticks in at either end. In the seedbed rows can be very close, say 10-13cm (4-5in) apart for lettuces or leeks, about 20-23cm (8-9in) for brassicas.

3   Make a straight, shallow, smooth drill along the line, for most seeds no more than 1-2cm (½-¾in) deep, with the blade of the trowel or the corner of a draw hoe, or even a pointed stick.

4   Sow seeds very thinly. I find it easiest to put some seed into the palm of my left hand, taking a few from there with the thumb and forefinger of

my right hand. Before covering, press them gently in the ground with your hand or the back of the rake. In the seedbed it is often best to sow the seeds evenly spaced, about 2·5cm (1in) apart. It is laborious but much better than shaking a packet at random along a row (see top diagram below).

If sowing *in situ*, 'station sowing' is advisable, that is sowing a small group of three or four seeds together at intervals (see bottom diagram below). This makes eventual thinning much easier. For plants that will finally be, say, 20cm (8in) apart, station sow 10cm (4in) apart.

Careful spacing and 'station sowing' both save a great deal of time in thinning, make weeding easier, and prevent seedlings from becoming too 'leggy' and entangled with each other, as happens when sown too thickly. A fast growing crop such as radishes can be 'station sown' between a slow growing crop such as parsnips. The radishes are cleared before the space is required by the parsnips.

5   As far as depth is concerned, most small seeds need to be just covered with soil; larger seeds by about 1cm (½in) of soil. Exceptions are peas and beans which are sown 3-5cm (1¼-2in) deep. As a general rule sow slightly deeper on lighter soils than heavy ones.

6   Cover the drill by pushing the soil back gently with the fingers, the rake, your boot or the edge of the hoe. Put in a label to remind you where you sowed them.

7   Once the seedlings are through and well established, put a 2·5cm (1in) thick layer of dried grass cuttings or well-rotted compost between the rows as a mulch. This keeps down weeds and helps retain moisture in the soil. If the ground is not already moist, water before mulching.

8   Watch out for attacks from the usual garden pests such as slugs, flea beetle and birds when your plants are in the seedling stages. (See Pests, Diseases and Weeds p.63.)

Methods of Seed Spacing

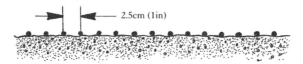

2.5cm (1in)

Evenly spaced seeds to minimize thinning

'Station sowing'

Sowing in Wide, Parallel Drills
This is an excellent way of sowing cut-and-come-again seedlings

Sowing in wide drills

A 'wide drill' is a flat bottomed drill, generally, but not necessarily, the width of a hoe blade. It is a convenient way of sowing seeds that require little or no thinning, such as radishes or peas, or that will be harvested as 'cut-and-come-again' crops, for example seedling salads (see p.104). In this case several drills can be made side by side, the seedlings eventually spilling over the edges to make dense patches. A wide drill can be considered a half way house between a standard drill and broadcasting; it is easier to weed than a broadcast area.

1   Prepare the seedbed in the normal way.
2   Use the blade of an onion hoe or draw hoe to make a flat drill of the depth required. Where fairly dense patches of salad seedlings are being sown, make adjacent drills as close as they can be without spilling soil from one into the next.
3   Sow seed evenly across the drill and press it in.
4   Cover with the soil from the edge of the drill.

Broadcasting

Here seeds are scattered over the surface of the soil and then raked in. Again, the method is used where little or no thinning is required, traditionally for early carrots, turnips when grown for turnip tops, and also for mustard, cress, salad rocket and other cut-and-come-again seedling crops (see pp.104-5). It is unwise to broadcast in weedy soil, as subsequent weeding is difficult.

1   Prepare the seedbed normally. If the soil is suspected of being very weedy, prepare it first, allow the first flush of weeds to germinate, and hoe them off before sowing.
2   Scatter seed evenly over the surface.

3   Rake the soil first in one direction, than at right angles to the first direction, to cover the seed.

Sowing singly
Very large seeds like beans and peas can be sown in holes made with a dibber. Just make sure they are not suspended in a pocket of air. Always sow a few spares alongside the rows: they will be useful for filling in gaps if there are casualties.

The less hardy seeds like cucumbers, marrows and sweet corn can be sown under jam jars to give them extra protection. Sow them in pairs, removing the weakest after germination.

Sowing in adverse conditions
It is not always possible to sow in ideal conditions.
Wet conditions If the ground is very wet, drying out can be accelerated by putting cloches or clear polythene film over the area you want to sow several days beforehand.

If you must sow while the soil is still sticky, put a wooden board alongside the row, and stand on it while working. This takes your weight and prevents the soil from becoming consolidated.

A little sharp sand or potting compost sprinkled along the drill will provide more hospitable conditions for the seed.
Dry conditions If it is necessary to sow when the soil is very dry, for example in one of the dry spells which occur in late spring, or for mid-summer and late summer sowings, either give the seedbed a very thorough watering the night before, so that it is moist to the depth of a few centimetres, or make the drills, and water the *bottom of the drills only*, until almost muddy. Use a small houseplant can, or an ordinary can in which a cork with a V-shaped notch cut in it has been inserted into the spout. Sow the seeds in the moist soil and cover with the *dry* soil from beside the drill. This acts like a mulch and prevents moisture from evaporating, so keeping the seeds moist until they germinate. In dry conditions drills can be lined with moist sand or potting compost to help germination.

A final word on outdoor sowing. Almost all vegetable seeds germinate very much faster in warm rather than cold soils. Lingering in the soil before germination is often, literally, fatal. So never be in too much of a hurry to start early in the year unless you can provide protective covering, such as cloches. The precise time of sowing will depend on where you are and your type of soil. This is one case where the early bird does not catch the worm: he is more likely to catch a cold.

THINNING GUIDELINES
1   Seedlings must never be allowed to overcrowd each other either in their permanent rows or in the seedbed. If they are to develop properly, they must be thinned and surplus seedlings removed. Unless the thinnings are to be transplanted (as is possible with, for example, onions, leeks

and lettuces) the best way to thin without disturbing the remaining seedlings is to nip them off at ground level.

2   The ultimate distance to which you thin varies according to the vegetable. Recommendations are given in Chapter 9.

3   Start thinning as soon as you can safely handle the seedlings, removing intermediate seedlings so that the remaining seedlings stand just clear of their neighbours.

4   Thin in successive stages to offset any losses from pests or diseases.

5   Choose a time when the soil is moist. If it is dry, then water a couple of hours beforehand.

6   Make sure remaining seedlings are not unduly disturbed and firm the soil around them if necessary. Remove all thinnings as their smell can attract the plant's pests.

PLANTING GUIDELINES

1   As a general rule, the earlier seedlings can be transplanted to their permanent position the better. For example, lettuces can be transplanted when they have four leaves, brassicas when they are about 10cm (4in) high. Beetroot, parsnips and carrots can only be transplanted when they are very small, before the tap root develops.

2   If possible transplant in cool, dull weather, never in the heat of the day.

3   If the soil is dry, water both the seedbed and the soil into which the plants are being moved, either overnight or several hours beforehand.

4   Handle plants by the leaves rather than the roots, to avoid damaging the delicate root hairs.

5   Use a trowel, dibber, or smaller tool to make a hole large enough for the roots without cramping them. Hold the plant in the hole as you replace the soil. If planting brassicas in dry weather, 'puddle' or water the hole first.

6   Finally firm the soil around the stem with your fingers and water gently, with a rose on the can. Firm planting is essential. Give a leaf a tug when you have finished; if the plant is wobbly, replant it!

7   I like to mulch after planting, to keep moisture in and weeds out.

8   Transplanting is inevitably a shock to a plant; it can be softened by raising plants in pots or any kind of module. (See Sowing Indoors p.52.)

HEELING-IN

If plants are bought but cannot be planted immediately, they are sometimes 'heeled-in' temporarily. Make a shallow V-shaped trench or hole, lay the plants in it close together, cover the roots and part of the stem with the soil, and water them. This technique can also be used for mature crops which have to be lifted because the ground is needed – leeks, celeriac or parsnips, for example. Heeled-in plants will keep in reasonable condition for several weeks (see diagram p.184).

STORAGE

Root crops such as carrots, beetroot and swedes, which are susceptible to heavy frost but will tolerate light frost, can be lifted and stored in autumn. The simplest method is to store them in boxes or barrels in a cool but frost proof shed or cellar. Lay them in single layers, each layer separated with sand, sieved ashes or a similar material to prevent them losing moisture. Discard any diseased or damaged specimens. If there is no suitable space under cover, roots can be stored in a heap or 'clamp' in the garden in a well drained spot. Start with a thick layer of straw, pile the vegetables on it and, when the heap is completed, cover it with another 15-20cm (6-8in) layer of straw. In very cold areas cover this with several inches of soil, taken from around the base of the clamp to create a small drainage ditch.

MULCHING
Mulching is the practice of keeping the soil covered, either with an organic material (such as compost), or an inorganic material (such as polythene film). It generally increases soil fertility and productivity, so is a very valuable technique in small gardens. Remember that it is also beneficial under cover, for example in greenhouses and polytunnels. Here are some of the potential benefits of mulching:
~ It preserves soil moisture by preventing evaporation. This is most valuable in areas of low rainfall. It also keeps the soil surface in good condition.
~ It keeps down most weeds.
~ It improves the soil structure, by encouraging earthworm activity (this is equally true with organic and inorganic mulches); by preventing compaction when the soil is walked on; and with light soils, by protecting them from winter weathering and the adverse effect of heavy rain.
~ It has an insulating effect, making the soil cooler in summer and warmer in winter.
~ It keeps sprawling plants like bush tomatoes and trailing cucumbers clean, so making them less prone to disease.
~ Organic mulches add organic matter and some nutrients to the soil. They can eventually be dug in.

Organic mulches
The choice of mulching material is very wide in range: virtually any of the bulky manures mentioned in Chapter 2 can be used, provided they are well enough rotted to spread easily on the ground and around plants. They should be loose enough in texture for both air and water to penetrate. For this reason avoid *fresh* lawn mowings, which can become very compacted if put on in a thick layer. Allow them to dry out for several days before spreading them on the ground. (And don't use them if they have been sprayed with a hormone weedkiller.) Garden compost, straw, hay, spent mushroom compost, wilted green manure tops, wilted comfrey, spent hops, seaweed, leaf mould, peat substitutes such as coir and cocoa shell, and also various manufactured biodegradable mulches are all possibilities. Seaweed is apt to attract flies in summer, but they can be deterred with a thin covering of lawn mowings. Woody materials such as sawdust and

shredded and pulverized bark are best avoided on vegetable beds, as nitrogen will be robbed from the soil in the process of their breakdown. They are excellent, however, on paths.

The thickness of the mulch depends on the material and, to some extent on the reason for mulching. This is one of the things one learns with experience. On the whole the thicker the better, provided plants are not in danger of being physically swamped. To be of most benefit, I would suggest a minimum 2.5cm (1in) layer of garden compost, 5cm (2in) of mushroom compost or lawn mowings and up to 15cm (6in) of straw, which 'settles' to much less.

Incidentally, I have been very impressed with the effect of straw mulching in our polytunnel. In summer we mulch the paths thickly with straw, then dig them in to make winter beds. The soil, which would otherwise have been baked solid, is in a beautiful condition when it comes round to planting time.

Inorganic mulches

These suppress weeds and help retain moisture, but supply no nutrients to the soil. Most of the inorganic mulches used in gardens today are made from some kind of polythene film, with new, potentially useful products, continually being launched. The following types are current examples of mulching films.

Impermeable black film Keeps down weeds; plant through it.
Impermeable clear film Warms up soil.
Opaque white film Reflects heat and light up on to plants; useful for fruiting vegetables like tomatoes and peppers.
Double sided black and white film Laid with the black weed-suppressing side on the soil and the white, light-reflecting side uppermost.
Chequered films Deter insects such as aphids.
Perforated black films Keep down weeds, while allowing some water to penetrate through to the soil. Used for long term mulching, and very good on strawberries, for example.
Permeable woven polypropylene films The heavier types are designed for long term, weed-suppressing mulches on paths. Because they drain well weeds don't get established on the surface. They can also be used for mulching sturdy plants. Newer softer and lighter films suppress weeds in the short term, and are good mulches for less robust plants like salads.

Many other materials can be used for mulching. Carpets are excellent for keeping down weeds on paths, though they eventually disintegrate, or need weeding themselves! Thickly piled newspaper and cardboard are good for mulching plants.

In some arid areas plants are traditionally mulched with stones; in Spain stone mulching is used in polytunnels, the stones conserving moisture during the day and radiating heat at night. Stone mulches probably need to be at least 7.5cm (3in) deep in order to be properly effective.

Mulching techniques

~ Mulching tends to maintain the *status quo* in the soil. So always mulch beds when the soil is warm and moist, and then it will remain that way. Mulching cold, very wet and very dry soils will be counter productive. Mulching immediately after planting often works well.

~ The easiest way to mulch growing plants with films is to lay the film on the prepared ground, cut slits or triangles in it at the required spacing and then to plant through the holes. Except where perforated films are used, water carefully by the plant when it is necessary.

~ Dig in organic mulches at the end of the season.

There is scope for mulching all year round. Here are some suggestions:

In autumn, mulch over-wintering crops (such as celeriac, leeks, parsnip and winter radish) to keep the soil warm, preserve soil structure and make lifting easier in frosty weather.

In early spring, mulch after digging: it keeps the soil in a beautiful condition before making the seedbed.

In late spring and summer, mulch between rows in the seedbed after seedlings have germinated, and between growing crops such as peas, beans, onions and carrots, to keep down weeds and preserve moisture.

In summer mulch tomatoes, cucumbers and similar crops to keep their fruit clean and of good quality.

WATERING

In spite of our apparently wet climate, most vegetables benefit substantially from an increased supply of water, particularly in the drier eastern regions of the country.

The golden rule of watering is to water gently and thoroughly. For young seedlings and small plants, use a can with a fine rose, a hose with a nozzle which can be adjusted to a fine spray, or a houseplant can with a narrow spout. Useful watering aids are perforated polythene tubing and porous seephose. They can be attached to a tap or hose and laid on the ground between plants. The water seeps out through the holes or porous wall, watering steadily and gently. Some forms of seephose can be buried in the ground, so minimising the loss from evaporation.

A good occasional watering is far more beneficial than light intermittent waterings, which are worthless. Never just sprinkle the surface for ten minutes or so. Go for a 'good heavy watering' of about 22 litre/sq in (4 gal/sq yd), which will soak the surface to a good depth. This takes much more water than most people realize. It is salutary to poke your finger into the soil after what seems like a heavy shower; it is often remarkably dry. To minimize evaporation losses water towards evening (allowing time for the plants to dry before nightfall). Rainwater is said to be preferable to tap water, so it is good practice to collect your own water in tubs from roofs. Wherever practicable, mulch immediately after watering.

Vegetables must have water throughout their growth – key periods being germination and transplanting. But apart from this, different types of vegetables have 'critical periods' during their growth, when lack of water is most damaging. If water is scarce, confine watering to one really heavy watering during the critical period.

For leafy vegetables such as brassicas, spinach and lettuce, among the thirstiest of crops, the critical period is 10 to 20 days before they are ready for harvesting. In hot weather they would benefit from weekly watering at the rate of 11 to 16 litre/sq m (2 to 3 gal/sq yd). Where this is difficult, give a single 'good heavy watering', as above, during the critical period.

Fruiting vegetables, such as peas, beans, tomatoes and courgettes, need water most in the flowering to fruiting period. In the absence of rainfall, give a weekly 'good heavy watering' once flowering starts. Before flowering water the plants just enough to prevent them from drying out. Overwatering can result in too much leaf development, rather than the pods or the fruits forming.

With root crops the key is a steady moisture supply throughout growth. Overwatering in the early phases results in the development of leaves at the expense of roots; over-watering in the later phases, especially after a dry spell, can lead to roots cracking. Moderate watering in dry conditions is all that is required.

A final point about watering: the closer plants are spaced, the more competitive they are and the more water they require. Take this into account if you are 'packing them in' and doing a lot of intercropping in a small garden. Make sure they have enough water to reach their full potential.

WINDBREAKS

As anyone with an exposed garden is only too aware, plants hate being buffeted by wind. It has been proved that, by sheltering vegetables from even light winds, yields can be increased by as much as 20 or 30 per cent.

The best windbreaks are about 50 per cent solid, allowing the air to filter through, for example a well-grown hedge, a lath fence, or wattle hurdles. A completely solid windbreak, such as a wall, can create a destructive area of turbulence on the lee side.

Where wind is a problem, it is worth erecting or growing some sort of barrier. Windbreak netting, for example, can be battened firmly to strong posts. Even a wire netting enclosure around a vegetable patch has a sheltering effect. Nylon netting or hessian sacks 30cm (12in) or so high can be strung between rows of vegetables to provide a shelter. Such shelter is considered effective for a distance of roughly six times its height: so 60cm (2ft) high barriers would need to be about 3.6m (12ft) apart.

In small gardens draughts caused by gaps between buildings are very damaging and should be remedied. Erect a windbreak extending some way beyond the gap on each side to make sure the gap is fully protected. Gusts of winds have nasty sneaky habits!

CHAPTER FOUR

Sowing Indoors

While most of our vegetables can be sown directly in the soil outdoors, there are several cases where it pays to start them in a more protected situation 'indoors'. Examples include:

~ Tender, generally semi-tropical vegetables like tomatoes, peppers and cucumbers that would not otherwise mature in a short summer.

~ Vegetables where seed is exceptionally small, or tricky to germinate, or particularly vulnerable in the seedling stage, or very expensive.

~ Crops that can be sown early to get an out of season crop.

~ To get high quality plants.

The alternative to raising these vegetables yourself is to buy them in from a garden centre or nursery at the planting out stage. Provided you have sufficient space, there's a lot to be said for raising your own. It's intrinsically satisfying, it saves money, and you have an enormous choice of varieties from seed catalogues compared to the limited range offered for sale. Moreover there is always a risk of importing pests like vine weevil and diseases such as clubroot on bought-in plants. Once established these can be a nightmare to eliminate. With modern equipment raising plants from seed is not difficult.

Sowing 'indoors' or 'under cover' generally implies sowing in a heated or unheated greenhouse, or in your own house, perhaps in a porch or on a windowsill, or in frames or under cloches outside. The common denominator is protection from the elements.

For a small garden, elaborate and costly facilities such as a heated greenhouse are unnecessary. A reasonably early start, with adequate results, can be obtained by using small domestic propagators, or warm cupboards or shelves above radiators; slightly later sowings can be made in cold greenhouses or cloches or frames outside.

But a word of warning. With modern sowing composts, getting seeds to germinate is no problem. The skill, especially for the tender plants, lies in providing good growing conditions *after* germination, in the intervening weeks before planting out. If the temperature at this stage, particularly at night, is too low the seedlings may die off; if the light is inadequate they will become weak, spindly and pale. So make sure you have somewhere warm and light to keep plants in the interim period. Otherwise there may be a lot of casualties.

The great temptation with sowing indoors is to start too early. But the tender vegetables cannot be planted out in the open until all risk of frost is over, which in much of the country is not until the late spring or early summer. If plants are ready too soon they simply hang about deteriorating.

The aim should always be to maintain steady growth, which leads to sturdy healthy plants. Recommendations on sowing times will be given under the individual vegetables.

There are several stages involved in raising plants indoors, though some can be bypassed.

Sowing
Seeds are sown in special compost, either in standard containers such as a seedtray, or singly in some kind of 'module' (see p.54).

Pricking out
Young seedlings are moved into a larger container so they have room to develop. Pricking out is unnecessary when sown in a module.

Potting on
Young plants are moved into an individual pot. This is done where they will be grown to maturity in large pots or containers, or to obtain exceptionally high quality plants for planting out.

Hardening-off
Plants need to be acclimatized gradually to lower temperatures and rougher, windier conditions before planting them outside, otherwise they suffer a setback on planting. It is unnecessary where they will be grown finally in greenhouses or frames, or under cloches.

Planting
They are finally planted, either in the ground outdoors or in a greenhouse or equivalent or, in some cases, into a large container.

PLANT RAISING EQUIPMENT
To raise plants indoors, you need a container, sowing or potting compost, and, in most cases, a propagator or some means of creating warm, damp air.

Containers
All sorts of things can be used for sowing. For seed that will be pricked out soon after germination, fairly small containers are sufficient, as space is at a premium in most propagators. Unless the container is porous, it should have drainage holes in the base, or there is a risk of the compost becoming sour and the seedlings waterlogged. Typical sowing containers are:

~ Shallow plastic or clay seedpans or seedtrays, which need be no more than 5-7·5cm (2-3in) deep.

~ Clay, plastic, fibre, polythene or sturdy paper pots: 7·5cm (3in) diameter is generally large enough.

Cheap containers are easily improvised from plastic punnets, cartons, beakers, yogurt pots and so on, simply by poking drainage holes in the base. Use a heated poker or knitting needle to make the holes. Plastic sandwich boxes with fitted lids make excellent 'seedtrays'.

Various types of seed-raising kits, with seed pre-sown in compost, are on the market. The container lid is used as a watering tray after germination. They can be very handy, especially where facilities for mixing up compost are limited.

Modules

A 'module' is any sowing container where one seed (or occasionally several seeds) is sown and grown to potting or planting stage. Module raised plants are often known as 'plugs'. They have several advantages:

~ As the seedling has absolutely no competition from other seedlings it develops into an exceptionally good, healthy plant with a strong, compact root system.

~ When planted out, there is virtually no root disturbance. Vegetables that normally dislike being transplanted, such as Chinese cabbage, can be planted out very successfully from modules.

~ There is some flexibility over planting because of the protection the module gives the root system. Planting can succeed in, for example, fairly wet soil conditions that would be quite unsuitable for planting a 'bare root' type transplant. Plants can 'hang about' in modules without too much of a setback, and spare plants can be kept in the wings for planting in gaps, or in vacant ground as the space becomes available.

~ A variety of plants can be raised in a small space. A 40-cell tray, for example, could easily be used for raising ten plants each of four different vegetables. In a small garden

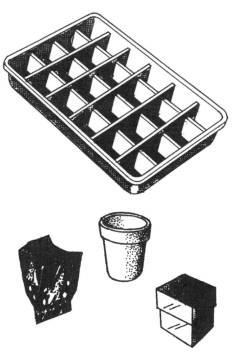

Some Examples of Modules
Above: seedtray with interlocking dividers
Below: various small pots

it is better to raise a few, first class plants than lots of poorer quality plants.

The main drawback to modules is that they take up considerable space in a propagator. So sometimes plants are sown in small seedtrays or containers, then pricked out into a module.

Typical modules are moulded plastic and polystyrene trays, consisting of a number of cells. Any small pot or container can be considered a module if used to raise a single, individual plant (see diagram opposite).

Modules can also be improvized. Convert a standard seedtray into a module by dividing it into cells with interlocking plastic or cardboard dividers (see diagram on previous page). Or use fibre egg cartons, sowing in the egg compartments. When it comes to planting, split the cartons apart and plant out the sections; the roots will grow through them. (You can sow seed in the lid, and prick out into the lower section.) Half egg shells can also be used as modules, best stood in plastic egg boxes to keep them upright. Again, the plant's roots will eventually penetrate the shell, so it can be planted out intact. However, if the shell is not already cracked when it comes to planting, squeeze it gently to crack it and help the process along.

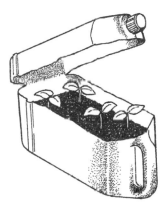

Improvized Container
Drainage holes must be made in the base of the plastic bottles

All the above containers and modules are filled with some kind of compost for sowing. However, there are systems in which compost and container are integrated – for example soil blocks (see p.57) and compressed netted blocks, such as the well known 'Jiffy 7's'. These are flat discs of compressed peat-based compost held in a fine net. When watered they swell into small pots in which a seed can be sown and grown to planting out stage. The plant roots grow through the net, so the whole thing is planted as one. It is to be hoped that this system will be adapted in future to some of the peat substitutes coming on the market.

Sowing and potting compost

Compost is the general term for a mixture into which seeds are sown, pricked out, or potted on. It should not be confused with 'compost heap' compost, which is too rich for plant raising. Ordinary garden soil is unsuitable, as it is not porous enough, and is liable to be full of weed seed.

Traditional sowing and potting composts were made by mixing sterilized sieved garden loam, peat and sand with chemical fertilizers. Apart from being laborious, this requires a great deal of time and space and is difficult to do well. Most gardeners today, especially where space is limited, use commercially available composts.

Theoretically seed is sown in a very fine, almost inert sowing compost, then pricked out and potted on into a coarser, richer potting compost. In practice multi-purpose composts are now widely used for all stages and prove very satisfactory. Organic fertilizers can be used to supply extra feed where necessary in the later stages of growth.

Types of compost
The committed organic gardener has a restricted choice of plant raising composts. The well-established 'John Innes' range of soil-based composts include peat and chemicals; most other composts are peat based. However, various composts which are developed from peat substitutes, such as coir and forestry waste products, are being developed. I have had good results with composts based on recycled municipal waste, into which worm casts have been incorporated. The best advice is to watch the organic gardening press for suitable products you can try out for raising plants.

Module composts
Although standard potting compost can be used in modules, commercial growers use specially formulated composts which give better results. The reason for this is largely because this type of compost doesn't become too compacted in the modules. Suitable organic composts are being developed: use them where you can.

Homemade organic sowing compost
Mix one part of coarse builder's or silver sand with two parts of leaf mould. The leaf mould is easier to handle if it is sieved through a 6mm (¼in) sieve. The mixture can be watered with liquid seaweed to enrich it. This compost would be suitable for germinating seeds and growing them to the pricking out stage.

Comfrey potting compost
This recipe, developed by organic gardener Terry Marshall, has proved very successful. The main ingredients are leaf mould and Russian comfrey (see pp.28 and 31), preferably using the cultivar 'Bocking 14'.
~ Cut the leaves of well-established comfrey plants in early autumn.
~ Take a strong plastic sack and line the bottom with a layer roughly 7·5cm (3in) deep of well-rotted leaf mould, ideally 12-18 months old.
~ Cover with a similar thickness of comfrey leaves, pressed down lightly.
~ Alternate comfrey and leaf mould layers until the sack is full.
~ Tie the sack at the neck, make a few ventilation holes with a garden fork and leave in a sheltered place until spring, when it will be ready for use. This can be used as a multi-purpose compost.

Composts based on worm compost

If you make your own worm compost (see pp.31-2), try the following HDRA recommendations:

For a sowing compost, mix one part sieved leaf mould with one part worm compost.

For a general purpose compost, mix 1 part worm compost with 3 parts well-rotted leaf mould (or peat alternative) and 1 part sharp sand. To every 4·5 litre (10gal) of mixture add 90g (3oz) calcified seaweed.

Soil blocks

So called 'soil blocks' are made by compressing loose soil or potting compost into a cube with a blocking tool, which also makes a small indentation in the upper block face into which the seed is sown. Block sizes can range from tiny 'miniblocks' about 1cm (½in) square, to blocks 5cm (2in) or more in diameter. (Different blocking tools are needed for each size.) The miniblocks are most economical with space at the germination stage; if necessary they can be transferred into a larger block for the later stages of growth. Blocks can be stood side by side in a standard seedtray.

It is easiest to make blocks with proprietary blocking composts which contain an adhesive additive but, with skill, blocks can be made from ordinary soil or potting compost. It is a question of getting the moisture content correct. Some organic blocking composts are now being introduced.

CREATING A WARM ATMOSPHERE

Most vegetable seeds will germinate satisfactorily at soil temperatures of 13-16°C (55-61°F). The ideal source of heat is from below – or 'bottom heat' as it is called – which is easily supplied by the standard plug-in electric propagator. These small propagators are economic to run.

The heat source is either a low wattage light bulb or electric cables, which are housed beneath a tray on top of which the sowing container is placed. The atmosphere is kept moist by a plastic dome fitted over the seedtray, or a sheet of clear polythene over the top. An ordinary, free-standing, table hot plate can be used as a propagator base.

Without a propagator germination, certainly early in the year, will be slower and more erratic. However, some reasonable results can be obtained by putting the sown container anywhere warm,

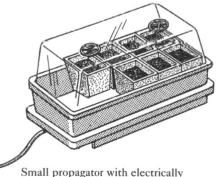

Small propagator with electrically heated base plate

for example in an airing cupboard, over a radiator or near a stove. Try to avoid direct sunlight, a very dry atmosphere, or draughts.

SOWING IN CONTAINERS

Composts vary in texture and ability to absorb moisture but, on the whole, it is easiest to start with fairly moist, rather than dry, compost. Water it beforehand with a rose on the can, turning it with your hands so that there are no dry pockets. (If you find it easier, fill the container with dry compost, then stand it in a tray of water so that it can soak up water before sowing.)

~ Fill the container with moist compost. Press it down with a small board or flat surface to make it reasonably firm and level, leaving a 1cm (½in) space below the rim of the container. Where pots are used for sowing, a layer of broken crocks or foam rubber can be put at the bottom to economize on compost.

~ Sprinkle the seeds evenly over the surface, or else space them carefully 6mm-2.5cm (¼-1in) apart, depending on the seed.

~ Cover the seeds by sieving a little dry compost or sharp sand over them. Sand seems to reduce the risk of seedlings being attacked by fungal diseases. As a general rule, seeds need to be covered to about twice their depth. Very small seeds can be left uncovered. Firm the soil again after sowing.

~ If necessary, water the surface lightly, or stand the container in water until the top surface is moist. This latter method is preferable with small seeds, which are easily swamped by overhead watering.

~ To prevent the compost from drying out, cover the container with a sheet of glass or polythene, or a fitted plastic

Stages in Seed Sowing

Fill the container with loose compost

Make the surface smooth and level by pressing with a small board

Sprinkle or space seeds evenly over the surface

Cover seeds with sieved compost or sharp sand

dome, or slip it into a plastic bag. Remove the covering once the seedlings have germinated.
~ Put it into the propagator or somewhere warm.

SOWING IN MODULES

With most of the purpose-made module composts, it seems easiest to fill the modules loosely with dry compost, then to water them gently from above, and/or stand them in a tray of water for a period, until they are thoroughly moist.

The aim of sowing in modules is to have only one germinated seedling in each cell or block. To ensure that you achieve this, either sow just one seed per cell, or sow several seeds and then nip out all but the strongest seedling in every cell once they have germinated. (For the exception of multi-sowing, see below.)

Pushing seeds off a piece of paper so they can be sown single in soil blocks or any other type of module

Picking up individual seeds on the tip of a piece of glass so they can be sown singly in soil blocks or any other type of module

Large seeds are easily sown individually. Small seeds can be trickier to sow on their own. Either push them carefully off a piece of paper, or put them on a saucer and pick them up individually, spillikin style, using the moistened tip of a piece of broken glass, or a plant label. The former works best: a single seed adheres to the glass, but drops off neatly when the glass touches the compost (see diagram above). Cover the seed gently with compost from the edge of the module or block.

Multi-sowing is a practice where several seeds are sown together in a cell, the seedlings left unthinned, and eventually planted out 'as one' at a wider spacing than normal. It is appropriate for the few vegetables which are not adversely affected by competition from close neighbours – onions, round beetroot and round carrot being some of the examples. The technique saves on space and time.

TESTING SEED VIABILITY

Successful use of modules depends on reliable germination. If, for any reason, the seed viability is in doubt, do a germination test before sowing: put a piece of foam rubber or sponge in a dish, cover it with a double layer of paper towels, lay the seeds on top and put the dish in a propagator or somewhere warm to germinate. In most cases, if the seeds have not germinated within a couple of weeks, it is better to get fresh seed.

TREATMENT AFTER SOWING

~ Examine your seeds daily – things can happen very fast. Every morning, remove the cover – glass, polythene, or bag – wiping off any condensation before replacing it.

~ As soon as seedlings have germinated, remove them from the dark (if they were in a cupboard), or they will become weak and drawn; remove any close-fitting lids or covers that would cramp growth.

~ Keep them in airy, well-lit conditions, but keep very small seedlings away from direct sun for a few days: bright sun can massacre them. If you cannot move them from a windowsill, prop up some newspaper or netting to shade them lightly.

~ Once seedlings are sturdy and established give them as much light as possible. If on a windowsill, give them a half turn daily, so they do not get drawn in one direction.

~ Water gently to prevent them drying out, but don't overwater. Fragile seedlings are best watered by standing the container in a tray of water so it can soak it up from below. If peat-based or similar composts are used, particularly for soil blocks, take great care to prevent them drying out. Re-wetting dried-out compost can be very difficult.

~ Prick out seedlings as soon as possible.

PRICKING OUT

Seedlings can be pricked out as soon as they are large enough to handle. In most cases this is once they have developed two true leaves, as opposed to the first tiny 'seed leaves'. The purpose of pricking out is to give them plenty of space to develop, in a reasonably fertile compost. If they were initially sown well spaced out in multi-purpose compost, there is no need to prick out. They can be pricked out into seedtrays, preferably 5-7.5cm (2-3in) deep, or into any kind of module or small pot. Only prick out healthy looking seedlings: duds rarely recover. Most seedlings can be kept at lower temperatures once pricked out. Special requirements are mentioned in Chapter 9.

~ Fill the new containers with moist potting compost, which has been gently firmed and levelled.

~ Water the seedlings beforehand; allow the compost to drain.

~ Uproot each seedling carefully, using a miniature dibber or any small

Pricking out seedlings so they are well spaced out in a larger container. Always handle them by their leaves to avoid damaging the delicate root hairs

bladed tool, even something like a large nail. Hold the seedling by the leaves, never by the root as this could damage the delicate root hairs.

~ Make a small hole in the compost, large enough to take the root.

~ Hold the seedling slightly above the compost, ease it into the hole, then press soil firmly but gently around it, so the seed leaves are just above soil level and there are no air pockets beneath it.

~ Water if necessary, using a fine rose.

~ Shade seedlings from direct sun for a day or two, especially if they show any signs of wilting.

POTTING ON

Seedlings can often remain in this container until they are planted out. However, when they are going to be grown in large pots, as may be the case with tomatoes and peppers, or when they are outgrowing their containers before it is time to plant them out, it may be necessary to move them into a larger pot to give them room to develop. There is also a risk of disease setting in if they become overcrowded.

It is always best to move plants into larger containers in stages, rather than into a very much larger container in one move. Tomatoes that will eventually be grown in, say, 20cm (8in) pots, should be potted first into pots of at least 7·5cm (3in) diameter as an intermediate stage.

~ Water plants well in advance and allow to drain.

~ Put a good layer of compost in the container, on top of drainage material such as old crocks if a soil compost is used. Tap the pot base on a flat surface a couple of times to settle the compost.

~ Hold the plant in the centre with the lowest leaves just above soil level.

~ Fill the pot with compost, leaving 1cm (½in) space at the rim.

~ Firm around the plant with the finger tips, tapping the pot on a surface from time to time to consolidate and level the compost.

~ Water lightly; water more heavily later when the plant is established.

~ Shelter the plant from direct sun for a couple of days.

Plants often grow very rapidly in pots and need plenty of ventilation. Never allow them to get overcrowded. If necessary move them a little further apart every day or so, so the leaves of adjacent plants are not touching.

Sometimes plants start to outgrow their pots before conditions outdoors are suitable for planting, and it may not be practical to pot them into larger pots. As a holding operation, stand them in trays lined with potting compost and, in the case of fibre or paper pots that will disintegrate, pack compost around them. Water the compost with a seaweed-based fertilizer. Roots will continue to develop and feed.

HARDENING-OFF

Plants raised indoors tend to be 'soft' and need to be toughened up over a two to three week period before planting out. The standard method is to gradually expose them to colder conditions, first by increasing the ventilation, then by putting the plants in a cold frame outdoors for longer periods each day. Initially either cover them at night, or bring them back indoors. Eventually they will only need protecting on exceptionally cold nights.

'Brushing' is an alternative method of hardening-off, which saves moving the plants outdoors. Using a piece of paper or cardboard, or a special brush, literally brush the seedlings in each direction. It can be done for up to a minute a day, over the normal hardening-off period.

CHAPTER FIVE

Pests, Diseases and Weeds

Pests, diseases, unfavourable conditions and weeds take their toll of vegetables in terms of quality and quantity. Commercial vegetable growers spend a great deal of money on insecticides, fungicides and weedkillers so that they get the biggest possible yields and completely unblemished produce for marketing.

On a small scale this is unnecessary. It does not matter if there are a few holes in a cabbage leaf or the odd maggoty pea. However, it is most annoying to lose all the carrots to carrot fly, or to find most of the brassicas have succumbed to clubroot. But there are practical, non-chemical solutions to most of these problems, which can be used successfully in small gardens.

The main pests and diseases to which particular vegetables are prone will be covered in Chapter 9. But here, let us take an overall look at the various types of trouble.

Pests

To start with, there is the damage to vegetables caused by insects and closely related species. Vegetables are mainly attacked by the caterpillars of various moths and butterflies, by the adults and grubs of some beetles, by weevils and by the maggots of tiny flies such as the onion fly and the carrot fly.

Pests which live in the soil (see p.64) include millipedes, cutworms, wireworms, chafer bugs and leatherjackets. These last three are the larval forms of the click beetle, May and June bugs, and the crane fly, *alias* daddy-long-legs, respectively. Besides these there are eelworms or nematodes, microscopic soil pests which can be particularly damaging to potatoes.

Working mostly above ground, night-feeding slugs skeletonize leaves by the morning. Their cousins the snails, though less damaging, are by no means innocent inhabitants of the garden. All these creatures feed on plants by biting the leaves, stems or roots.

Another group of insects, most notable among them the aphids, greenfly and blackfly, and the related whitefly, pierce leaves and other parts of the plant and suck the sap. Aphids not only cause physical damage but often transmit virus diseases in the process. Instead of the typical holes left by biting insects, leaves attacked by sucking insects are distorted, often twisted, curled or blistered.

Fortunately there are effective ways and means of dealing with most of these pests.

In many gardens it is the larger pests which are the real problem: mice taking peas and broad bean seeds, moles tunnelling unmercifully through rows of seedlings and uprooting plants, and cats and dogs scratching

SOIL PESTS

LARVA ADULT	APPEARANCE: LARVAE	APPEARANCE: ADULT & TYPICAL DAMAGE
LEATHERJACKET CRANEFLY	Legless No distinct head Fat, soft Earthy colour Up to 4cm (1½in) long	Cranefly body 2cm (¾in) long Lavae eat root, lower leaves, stem of many vegetables Attack above and below soil Most destructive early spring to mid-summer
CUTWORM TURNIP MOTH	Caterpillars 3 prs legs and sucker feet Distinct head Fat Soil coloured Up to 5cm (2in) long	Adults are turnip moths, body 2cm (¾in) long; heart and dart moths and others Cutworms damage lettuce, beet, carrots, etc Cut off stems at soil level Mostly night feeders
CHAFER GRUB COCKCHAFER BEETLE	3 prs good legs Large brown head Tail end of body swollen Lies with bent body Whitish, inactive Up to 4cm (1½in) long	Adults known as May bugs, body 4.5cm (1¾in) and June bugs, body 2cm (¾in) Larvae eat all kinds of root
WIREWORM CLICK BEETLE	3 prs good legs Shiny, hard Tough, wire-like Golden yellow About 2.5cm (1in) long	Click beetle body 2.5cm (1in long) Adults fling themselves into air with a click when lying on their backs Wireworms attack potatoes, brassica roots, beans, tomato stems, lettuce
    MILLIPEDES	2 prs legs on most segments, slow moving Flat type: flat, light brown, 1.5-2cm (½-¾in) long Thin snake type: smooth round bodies up to 2cm (¾in) long Usually black and shiny Curl up when disturbed	Eat roots, seed and seedlings of peas, beans, carrots, potatoes
   SLUGS	Soft bodied, slimy Various colours Horns on head Up to 2.5-5cm (1-2in) long	Eat almost anything – seedlings, lettuce etc Feed all year round Attack above and below soil

around as they go about their business. Last, but by no means least, are birds. The ravages of pigeons, jays and pheasants on young peas, winter greens, or on a seedbed of brassicas is heart-breaking. Sparrows are very serious pests in some areas. They usually attack seedlings, in particular those of lettuce, beetroot and spinach. With most of these pests, the answer lies not so much in destroying them as in deterrents, and in physically protecting the crops. Birds, it should be added, also do much good in the garden by devouring insect pests.

DISEASES

The diseases which affect vegetables can be divided into two groups. The first includes those caused by fungi, bacteria and viruses. The fungi produce mycelia, threads which are visible to the naked eye, while the bacteria and viruses are microscopic; you only see the resulting damage.

Clubroot: a serious disease on brassicas, producing distorted galls and swellings

Fungi and bacteria cause greyish moulds and mildews on leaves; clubroot gall in brassicas; the various rots which can ruin stored onions, and damping off diseases, which cause seedlings to droop and die shortly after they come through the soil.

Virus diseases are very strange, often fatal, and still something of an unknown quantity. One example of this disease is cucumber mosaic. The leaves become mottled, develop a yellowish mosaic pattern, and the whole plant becomes stunted and dies. If you suspect a plant of having a virus disease (obviously stunted growth and mottling are fairly common symptoms), it is wisest to pull it up and burn it to prevent the spread of infection.

All these diseases are infectious, and can spread very rapidly in conditions which suit them. They are much harder to control, either with chemicals or by other means, than pests. Indeed, in many cases, once the disease has become obvious it is too late to do anything about it. Prevention is better – and easier – than cure.

The second group of diseases, usually dubbed 'physiological', are not infectious in the same sense. They are caused by poor conditions: for example temperatures that are too high or too low for the vegetable; lack of water or faulty watering; poor nutrition; a mineral deficiency or even an excess of a chemical salt in the soil due to excessive use of artificial fertilizers. Again, these troubles can be prevented. In well-grown plants they should not arise.

GENERAL PREVENTATIVE MEASURES

If this catalogue of plant ills seems unduly long, take comfort from the fact that many pests and diseases can be avoided, or their effects considerably minimized, by growing plants well. Vegetables growing in a fertile, well-drained soil with plenty of organic matter, a balanced supply of nutrients and adequate moisture are much more likely to withstand attacks by pests and diseases.

It is the seeds which are slow to germinate because the soil conditions are poor, the lingering seedlings unable to develop a good root system and the plants which never 'get away' which are most vulnerable to attack by pests and diseases.

In very acid soils that bane of the cabbage family, clubroot, is often prevalent. Liming is the first step towards prevention of future attacks. In light, hungry soils potato scab, a disease which gives potatoes an unwholesome look, is often a problem. It can be remedied by digging in organic matter such as decayed leaves or grass mowings – anything up to a barrow load per 4sq m (4sq yd), or digging in a green manure before planting.

So the first and most important step in preventing disease is to improve the soil's fertility.

Garden hygiene

The next series of preventative measures come under the general heading of garden hygiene. At some stage in their life cycle many of the common garden pests and diseases depend on rubbish, bricks, any debris that is lying about, or weeds, to provide them with protection. Remove these sources of protection and you are hitting the pests where it hurts. There are many examples.

The fungi which cause downy mildews over-winter in plant debris; aphids, which attack cabbages and many other plants, hide in cabbages, broccoli and Brussels sprouts in winter and, in late spring, produce a winged generation which immediately flies off to infect the nearest victim. That wretched pest of young seedlings, the flea beetle, shelters in convenient rubbish or patches of weeds throughout the winter; slugs are permanently on the look-out for sheltered spots, such as rubbish, bits of wood or rotten cabbage leaves under which to lay their eggs or shelter from bad weather.

One of the virus diseases which attacks lettuce survives the winter in weed seeds, particularly chickweed. Weeds also harbour pests such as cabbage root fly, carrot fly, the blackfly which attacks broad beans and the fungus which causes clubroot. I often find clusters of leatherjacket grubs in the fibrous root systems of grassy weeds.

For these reasons rubbish should always be removed from the garden. Dead wood and diseased material of any kind should be burnt; everything else that will rot can go on the compost heap. Odd bits of slate, wood, bricks and so on should be tidied away. Never leave the roots of vegetables in the ground when they are finished. Chop them up and put them on the compost heap if they are healthy; burn them if they are diseased. If possible, try to clear those old brassicas out of the ground by late spring, to prevent the spring hatch of aphids. Keep weeds down and clear out hidey-holes for pests: old dry leaves under hedges and debris in the bottom of ditches are favourite haunts.

Cultural practices
By adopting certain cultural practices diseases and pests can often be avoided, or at least minimized.

Sowing
Many seedling diseases result from seeds being sown too thickly or in cold conditions. Always sow thinly and wait until the soil has had a chance to warm up; if possible put cloches over the soil a couple of days before sowing in early spring. A firm seedbed with a good tilth is the best guarantee of quick germination, which in turn is the first step towards avoiding the pests and diseases which attack seeds and seedlings.

It is sometimes advisable to prepare a 'stale seedbed' about ten days before sowing. This deters the bean seed fly, which is attracted by the smell of freshly disturbed soil. The flies lay eggs in the soil, and these hatch into maggots which attack onions, leeks, peas and beans.

Rotation
Many of the pests and diseases which live mainly in the soil only attack plants of a particular family. They can be starved out if they are deprived of their favourite hosts, to use the technical term. So it is always advisable to move crops around as much as possible from year to year. For example, if a piece of ground has been used for root crops such as beetroot, carrots and parsnips, you should grow onions, peas, beans, spinach or cabbages there the next time, and so on. Rotation is almost impossible in a very small garden; but whenever there is a chance to use a particular piece of ground for a different type of crop, take it. Long term rotation, anything up to seven years, is the only practical means of overcoming some eelworm pests. (For more on rotation, and rotation groups see pp.118 and 122.)

Overcrowding
Never overcrowd plants. There must be room for air to circulate around them; fungus diseases in particular spread rapidly in stagnant conditions. Where plants are too close they will compete for water and nutrients. There is no need to be as extravagant with space as our forefathers, but better results will often be obtained from a few plants given sufficient space rather than too many crowded together – this is another case of finding a happy medium.

Handling vegetables for storing
Always handle vegetables that are being stored very carefully. This

applies particularly to onions and garlic. The rots which destroy stored bulbs are most liable to infect those which have been cut or even bruised in handling.

Timing and deterrent tactics

Some pests and diseases can be avoided by varying the sowing time. For example, autumn and early spring sowings of broad beans escape the worst of the blackfly aphids; turnips sown in early summer largely escape flea beetle attacks; early and late carrots may avoid carrot fly.

If onions are grown from sets rather than seed, damage by the onion fly is avoided. In my experience, planting French marigolds between tomato and pepper plants, when they are grown under cover, lessens whitefly attacks, perhaps on account of the strong scent of the foliage.

In a garden where both potatoes and outdoor tomatoes are being grown, plant the tomatoes as far as possible from the potatoes to cut down the risk of infection from potato blight.

Resistant varieties

Scientists have had considerable success in breeding cultivars of vegetables which are immune to, or at least display considerable tolerance towards certain pests and diseases. Unfortunately there is no guarantee that the resistance is permanent: pests and diseases are quite capable of developing new strains to overcome the resistance. Varieties with resistance, however, are invaluable to organic gardeners. Useful introductions include the swede 'Marian', which is highly tolerant of mildew and clubroot; lettuce 'Minetto', which has good resistance to downy mildew and mosaic virus; lettuces 'Avoncrisp' and 'Avondefiance' with resistance to lettuce root aphid, and the parsnip 'Avonresister', with resistance to canker. Carrots with resistance to carrot fly are in the pipeline. Watch out for developments in the organic gardening press.

CHEMICAL CONTROL OF PESTS AND DISEASES

Organic gardeners only use chemical sprays as a last resort and then only those allowed under the organic standards 'rules'. These few are permitted on the grounds that they do minimum damage to the soil and the environment, and less damage to bees, pollinating insects and other beneficial predators and parasites than other chemicals. More importantly, they are generally made, or extracted, from plants and break down rapidly into non-toxic compounds. This means that they avoid the worst risks stemming from the more powerful mainstream garden chemicals – notably the likelihood of killing a broad spectrum of insects (many of them beneficial) as well as birds and other creatures in the food chain. There are risks to humans from some types, ranging from harmful residues on food to children swallowing chemicals, with inevitably serious consequences.

Even so, the fact remains that they *are* chemicals, they do damage life other than the specific pest or disease being targeted and, with frequent use, the pests and diseases develop a natural resistance to them rendering the chemicals useless. So their use should always be minimized.

For organic gardeners – besides the general hygiene measures and cultural practices already mentioned – the answer lies in using biological control and various traps, barriers, nets and preventative devices to deter or control the most common vegetable pests (see pp.72–8). After a few years of organic gardening, the population of natural predators builds up in a garden, to a considerable extent keeping pests and diseases under control. But there are occasions when the bad guys get the upper hand, when the alternative methods are insufficient, and spraying may be needed.

If you do use chemicals, it is important to keep to the rules:

~ Always follow the manufacturers' instructions meticulously.

~ Always spray in the evening or in dull weather when pollinating insects are not flying.

~ Never spray water, ditches, ponds, rain tubs and so on, or allow spray to drift onto water.

~ Never spray when it is windy, or allow spray to drift onto neighbouring gardens.

~ Try to make up no more spray than is needed, as the surplus will have to be disposed of.

~ Never transfer chemicals to other containers such as beer or soft drink bottles that people might drink from.

~ Store chemicals in tightly shut containers or tins, in a cool dry place well out of the reach of pets and children.

~ Wash hands and equipment very thoroughly after use.

Applying Pesticides

The term pesticide covers all chemicals used for controlling pests and diseases. It includes insecticides for controlling insects and fungicides for preventing fungus disease attacks.

All the insecticides approved for organic use act as 'contact' poisons, killing pests on the surface at the time or shortly after application. They break down rapidly after use so there is no residual effect, but fairly frequent spraying may be necessary. Follow the manufacturer's instructions.

In vegetable gardens the most widely used 'permissible' fungicide is 'Bordeaux Mixture', which is sprayed on potatoes and tomatoes against blight, and celery against leaf spot. To be really effective, plants have to be sprayed thoroughly in advance of an attack. It is, however, a mixture of chemical compounds and is not used by committed organic gardeners.

Pesticides can be applied as dusts, sprays, aerosols, paste or pellets. In the case of insect pests, it does not always follow that the same range of pests will be controlled by all forms of the pesticide – so study labels carefully to make certain.

On a small scale, there are puffer packs of dusts and aerosols, in both of which the chemical is in a form ready for use. These are very handy. Sprays have to be made up from the concentrated powder or solution and applied through some form of sprayer. As spray goes a long way, a 0.5 litre (1pt) capacity hand sprayer, preferably with an adjustable nozzle, is quite adequate for average use in a small garden.

Some pesticides, but not all, are compatible with others, and can be mixed together or applied with foliar feeds. Always check first before using a particular mixture.

The safer insecticides

The following are the safer insecticides in current use. Consult organic organizations and catalogues for information on new developments. All these products should be stored in dark, cool conditions. Remember, they are not as powerful as other chemicals and results may be disappointing.

Safer Insecticides

Product	Comments	Effective against
Derris	Main active ingredient is rotenone Available as powder and liquid Can harm some beneficial insects Harmful to fish so keep away from ponds Can mix with pyrethrum to make more effective insecticide	Aphids (greenfly, blackfly, cabbage mealy aphid) Small caterpillars Flea beetles and pollen beetles Turnip fly, weevils, red spider mite
Pyrethrum	Available as dust and spray Harmful to some beneficial insects and fish Can mix with derris to make more effective insecticides	Same pests as derris, but particularly against flying insects like aphids – blackfly, greenfly, cabbage mealy aphid; whitefly, red spider mite
Insecticidal soap	Available as dilute or concentrated liquid May damage small beneficial insects Best used as spot treatment on infestations	Aphids – blackfly, greenfly, cabbage mealy aphid; whitefly, red spider mite
Bacillus thuringiensis biological spray	Powder diluted to use as spray Harmless to all beneficial insects	Moth and butterfly caterpillars only (no effect on sawfly caterpillars)

Homemade rhubarb spray

The recipe for this mixture was devised by organic pioneer Lawrence Hills to kill aphids, and many people have found it effective. I believe that, strictly speaking, using such mixtures is illegal under current EU legislation. However, I will include it here for gardeners outside the EU and in the hope that the relevant restrictions will eventually be removed!

Chop up 1.4kg (3lb) rhubarb leaves.
Boil for ½ hour in 3.5 litre (6pt) water.
Strain off liquid and cool.
Dissolve 28g (1oz) soapflakes in 1.2 litre (2pt) water, mix with rhubarb liquid and spray.

Note: Some rhubarb cultivars are considered more effective than others. 'Glaskin's Perpetual' is not recommended

Biological Control

Biological control is the use of a pest's natural enemy to control it. It is acceptable to organic gardeners because it avoids the use of chemicals and there are no harmful effects on beneficial insects, other forms of wild life or human beings. As far as can be seen, there is no damage to the environment, as a biological control is *specific* to the pest and, once the pest is eradicated, the control itself dies out. It has to be reintroduced when there is another infestation.

With the increased interest in avoiding the use of chemicals, a lot of research is being undertaken on biological control. New forms are regularly being introduced: watch out for them in the gardening press. Currently, biological control is most widely used in greenhouses, where the conditions are much easier to control. However a few are available for use outdoors (see below).

Applying biological control can be tricky. Generally speaking, the most critical factors are choosing the right moment to introduce the predator or parasite (which must have a sufficient food supply of the pest) and maintaining the necessary temperature for it to remain active. Whatever biological control is used, follow the instructions carefully. The controls can be obtained by mail order from specialist suppliers and are increasingly being offered in seed company mail order catalogues.

Effective biological controls are currently available for the following vegetable pests:

Outdoors
Caterpillars – the bacteria *Bacillus thuringiensis* (see The safer insecticides opposite).
Red spider mite – predatory mites (effective only in mid-summer, or in very hot weather).
Lugs and small snails – parasitic nematodes. (Introduced in 1994.)

71

In greenhouses
Aphids – predatory midges or parasitic wasps.
Whitefly – parasitic wasps.
Red spider mite – predatory mites.

Alternative measures for controlling pests and soil pests

Slugs and snails Other than using biological control, which is fairly expensive, the best way of reducing the slug and snail population is to hunt them with a torch at night, when they are feeding. Collect them in yogurt pots, beer cans or buckets – depending on the scale of your problem. If you can't bear to squash them, make it an instantaneous death by pouring boiling water over them. During the day slugs can be found hiding in cool damp places such as under pieces of wood, plastic film, carpeting and so on.

My own view is that catching slugs by hand is a much more effective means of control than using sunken slug traps, which are usually baited with beer. They only catch limited numbers of slugs but, in addition, catch the beneficial carabid beetles – and the larger carabids feed on slugs. Incidentally, carabid beetles are killed by slug pellets – which is a good reason not to use them.

Slugs and snails can certainly be deterred by dry sharp materials such as grit, sand, coarse ashes and broken egg shells, which can be placed around vulnerable plants. Surrounding a vegetable patch with a fairly wide gravel path may also help to keep out slugs.

Individual young plants can be protected with barriers made from plastic pots or bottles with the bottom removed. (See Cabbage root fly p.74.)
In general, cultivating the soil exposes slugs to their natural enemies, birds, and so helps to keep down numbers.

Other soil pests (see Soil Pests p.64)
Digging and hoeing also exposes other soil pests – notably millipedes, cutworms and leatherjackets – to birds.

Destroy any pests you come across yourself. Many soil pests, for example wireworms, cutworms and millipedes, can be attracted to traps made from scooped-out potatoes or carrots fixed on skewers just below the soil surface. Examine the traps daily and destroy any pests that have been caught. Investigate casualties. If a lettuce plant has suddenly keeled over, dig it up. You may catch the guilty wireworm or leatherjacket 'red-handed', so preventing damage to adjacent plants. Cutworms, like slugs, can often be found at night, feeding on plants at ground level.

Alternative methods for controlling flying insect pests
Use of fleece and net barriers
Apart from soil pests, most insect pests which attack vegetables fly or have a flying stage. At the risk of stating the obvious, caterpillars, for example, are the larval stage of butterflies and moths. The various horticultural films which have become available in recent years, such as the fleeces (see Crop

Covers p.90) and the very fine nets, form excellent barriers against flying pests *provided there are no holes and they are anchored in the ground so insects cannot get inside.*

They can either be laid directly on to the plants, readjusting them as becomes necessary as the plants grow, or laid over wire hoops. The hoops used for low polytunnels are ideal (see Protection p.85). An-chor the films either by burying the edges in the soil or by weighting the edges with stones, piping, or small polythene bags filled with soil or sand. The fine nets, which are much the same mesh size as mosquito netting, are the most satisfactory for insect control as they can be left in place permanently. An exception is insect-pollinated crops. Fleeces, in most cases, are only suitable for early stages of growth; they have to be removed when the temperatures created become too high beneath them. All the flying pests below, as well as birds, can be kept out by fleeces and nets.

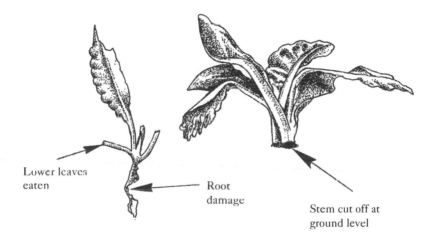

Lower leaves eaten

Root damage

Stem cut off at ground level

Typical Soil Pest Damage

Aphids
Keep plants well watered as attacks are less frequent on turgid plants. Try squashing aphid colonies by hand. Encourage their natural predators – ladybird adults and larvae, hoverfly and lacewing larvae, by *not* spraying with harmful chemicals, and by growing flowers which attract them and supply nectar, such as pot marigolds and *Phacelia tanacetifolia* (see Green Manures p.32). In greenhouses a certain number of aphids can be caught on sticky yellow traps, suspended above the plants.

Caterpillars
The best method of control is to pick them off by hand.

Cabbage root fly (see below right)

The adult fly can be prevented from laying eggs, which hatch into damaging maggots, by protecting the stems of newly transplanted plants with a physical barrier. These are best made with a 15cm (6in) diameter circular disc of carpet foam underlay. Make a small hole in the centre, then cut from the central hole to one outside edge and use this slit to place the disc around the stem of the plant at ground level. Alternatively use a plastic pot, bottle or carton as a protective collar around the plant's stem. Make a hole in the bottom of the pot large enough to slip the cabbage root through from above, plant it, and bury the pot rim 1cm (½in) deep in the soil.

Organic gardener Jack Temple recommends planting brassicas in the bottom of shallow V-shaped trenches, which are filled in as the plants grow with a good mix of well-rotted compost. This encourages the growth of secondary roots higher up the stem, which take over if the lower roots are damaged for any reason.

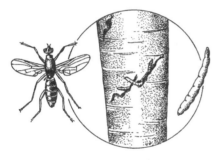

Carrot fly larvae feeding on
carrot root, with adult fly
(left) and larvae *(right)*

Cabbage root fly maggots attacking
a young plant. Damaged plants
normally wilt and die

Carrot fly (see above left)

The most successful measure against this devastating pest is to surround the carrot bed with a barrier of heavy duty polythene or netting, at least 60cm (2ft) high, buried 5cm (2in) deep in the soil. The bed should be no more than 1m (3ft) across. One method of doing this is to put posts at the corners of the bed, staple wire to the top of the posts, then to fold a metre wide sheet of polythene or net over the wire.

Animal pests

Mice Their main target is peas, and mouse traps the best remedy. Some people cover pea seeds with holly leaves or something prickly to deter mice. I remain unconvinced that it works.

Moles Unfortunately moles find the high earthworm population in an organic garden very inviting. They can be caught with traps set in their runs, or, if you have no objection to using them, chemical fuses. Other products on the market merely drive moles away – presumably to your neighbour's garden. Mothballs pushed into their runs, or pieces of foam rubber soaked in paraffin and set on fire, are also said to frighten them away. The traditional remedy of planting caper spurge is, in my experience, quite useless.

Cats Hawthorn twigs laid on the surface help to protect seeds and seedlings from cats, as do pea guards. Unfortunately cats love playing in and on fleecy films and fine nets.

Birds Small birds such as sparrows, which can be very damaging to plants, are best deterred with single strands of black cotton alongside or above seedlings, about 5cm (2in) above ground. Use strong cotton; button thread is ideal.

Of the larger birds, pigeons, and sometimes jays, are the most serious pests. Wire netting 60-90cm (2-3ft) high around a vegetable patch usually keeps them away, although it is a nuisance for cultivation and access. It can be made fairly mobile by anchoring it with bamboo cases. Cages, made from nylon, wire, or plastic netting, are increasingly being used where bird damage is serious; 10 or 15cm (4 or 6in) square mesh will be sufficient to keep off pigeons. This sort of device, of course, also keeps out cats and dogs, but prevents birds from scavenging for pests. Better, perhaps, to give temporary protection to vulnerable crops with netting over the wire hoops used for low polythene tunnels (see p.85).

If possible, use smooth hoops that won't entangle the net. The various types of 'humming wire' which 'sing' in the wind can be good deterrents. They need to be at least 60cm (2ft) above the ground, with lines running at different angles to catch the wind from various directions.

Other common deterrents include:

~ Windmills of many types, often incorporating a jangling sound.
~ Plastic sacks with edges cut into fringes, or rags strung in lines over the rows of vegetables.
~ Milk bottle tops suspended on string or wire.
~ Upturned bottles painted red, placed over sticks, or even ordinary wine bottles, stuck, necks down, into the ground.
~ Low protective wire guards, such as pea guards.
~ Aluminium discs cut into shapes.
~ Hawthorn and other sharp twigs placed around growing crops.
~ Lifelike hawks or other birds of prey, which are attached to fence posts or nylon lines.

The scope is endless, but ring the changes as much as possible. Birds become used to anything!

Birds are particularly attracted to young seedlings and newly planted greens such as lettuces. It always pays to put up protection when sowing or transplanting. Tomorrow is often too late!

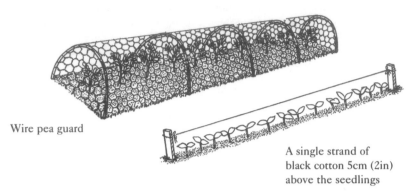

Wire pea guard

A single strand of
black cotton 5cm (2in)
above the seedlings

Methods of Deterring Birds

Beneficial and related creatures

The soil is inhabited by a number of beneficial creatures and care should be taken not to destroy them by mistake. As a general rule, fast moving grubs and related creatures are beneficial. They need to be fast as their prey, small slugs and insects, is mobile. Plant eaters, pests from our point of view, tend to be more 'sluggish'.

Beneficial creatures living mainly in the soil include centipedes, carabid and ground beetles and, of course, earthworms. Above ground the devil's coach horse beetle and other beetles, ladybirds, the parasitic ichneumons which lay their eggs on caterpillars, lacewings, wasps, frogs and toads are beneficial, though wasps, of course, are a pest if you have fruit trees.

WEEDS

Weeds are a serious problem in any garden. They compete for plant nutrients and water in the soil, and for space and light above ground. The weight of a barrow load of weeds is proof of how much they take from the soil. Weeds are very vigorous and will take over completely if unchecked. A row of vegetable seedlings can be smothered by weeds, which generally germinate and grow faster than cultivated plants. As already mentioned, some weeds harbour pests and diseases during the winter. So one way and another, weeds must go.

One of the advantages of a small garden is that controlling weeds is not an impossible task. The problem falls into two parts: annual weeds, which germinate, flower and die in one year, and perennials, which go on from year to year and develop very vigorous, persistent root systems.

Annual weeds

The annuals, groundsel, chickweed, fat hen, and so on, are easily dealt with by hand weeding or hoeing. Start as early in the year as you can, to minimize the competition to the crops you are trying to grow. With most vegetable crops, weed competition starts to become really serious about three weeks after the seedlings have germinated. So start weeding then if you haven't already done so. Interestingly, research has shown that it is the weeds between rows, rather than within rows, that are the most competitive. So work on them first.

At all costs, annual weeds must be prevented from going to seed. It's a much quoted and somewhat depressing statistic, that one large fat hen plant can produce 70,000 seeds! Even small, insignificant weeds can produce a fair number of seeds. Take heed of the old proverb 'one year's seed is seven years' weed'. There's a lot of truth in it.

One of the most satisfactory ways of keeping weeds under control is to abandon the idea of growing plants in rows with wide spaces between them, in favour of growing plants in blocks or patches, at equidistant spacing (see Patches p.106). When fully grown the leaves of neighbouring plants will touch and form a blanketing canopy over the soil, which effectively prevents most weed seeds from germinating. Here again, research supports the practice: apparently the filtered light created by a canopy of leaves actually makes the weed seeds dormant! This system won't work with narrow-leaved vegetables like onions and leeks, and it will be necessary to weed or hoe between plants in the early stages – or even better, mulch with dry lawn mowings, mushroom composts, or some well-rotted organic material. Some weeds inevitably find their way through the mulch but they are relatively easy to pull up. A snag is that the mulch itself can be a source of weeds; even so, it is worth using.

Mulches of black plastic film can be a valuable way of keeping down weeds and conserving moisture in the soil – though they are unsightly. Either plant first, then unroll the film, cutting cross-like slits in it over the plants and pull the plants through, or lay the film on the ground, cut slits in it, and plant through the slits. Use whichever method you find easiest. The type of film that is white above and black beneath is useful for mulching crops like tomatoes that produce fruit in summer. The black side keeps down the weeds, while the white surface reflects heat and light up onto the plant and ripening fruit.

Weed seeds remain viable for many years and ground that has not been cultivated for some time holds a huge reservoir of seed. Much of this will germinate on cultivation. In this case it is advisable to prepare the ground for sowing or planting, leave it for a week or so to allow the first flush of weeds to germinate, and hoe them off before sowing or planting. You can speed up germination by covering the ground with clear polythene film. In the first season try to avoid deep cultivation, as this will only bring up more weed seeds from the lower layers. Just hoe shallowly, or pull up weeds by hand – or mulch! All annual weeds can be put on the compost heap – unless they have gone to seed.

Perennial weeds

Perennial weeds are more of a problem. The most common are couch grass, dandelion, ground elder, docks, nettles, marestail or horsetail, and bindweed. There are others, and occasionally a 'cultivated' plant runs riot in a vegetable plot and becomes a weed – Japanese knotweed for example.

With most of these weeds, the answer is to learn to recognize them, both by their leaves and by their roots, and to dig them out. Use a good wild flower book to identify them (see Further Reading p.248). As a rule the perennials either have long deep roots (dandelions, thistles), or rambling extensive roots (couch grass, ground elder, bindweed). Annuals generally have shallow roots and are easily pulled up. If in doubt, pull it out!

With thistles, bindweed, ground elder, couch grass and dandelion even small pieces of root can sprout, so it is important to remove the plant as completely as possible. The best time is during winter digging. In summer try not to hoe perennials off at ground level, which may encourage them to resprout, but extract them by the roots. One piece of good news: docks will apparently die if you chop off the top 10cm (4in) of root.

The roots of perennials should either be burnt or dried out in the sun before being put on the compost heap. Some of them have remarkable powers of recovery in second-rate compost heaps!

Perennial weeds can be very discouraging to anyone tackling a new or neglected garden. This is where the use of a chemical weedkiller (herbicide) is tempting. The organic alternative is to blanket the ground so that all light is excluded. Good materials for this include heavy gauge black polythene film or carpeting. How long it needs to be left down depends on the weeds, soil and situation. I would suggest a minimum of three months in the growing season, and up to a maximum of a year. Lift the covering from time to time and dig down to see to what extent the plants and roots have been weakened. If you can get most of the remaining weeds out, start cultivation. It is advisable to plant through black polythene film initially.

Remember also that all weeds manufacture food through their leaves: if you continually remove the leaves the plants will eventually be considerably weakened.

One way of tackling a weedy situation in an overgrown garden, after chopping back the growth with a hook, is to rotovate the ground. It may be necessary to do this several times, as the first and second rotovations may simply cut the roots up into pieces that will regenerate.

CHAPTER SIX

Protection

Anyone wanting maximum returns from a small garden should invest in some kind of protection – whether it be cloches, frames, a small greenhouse, low or walk-in polythene tunnels, or the newer 'crop covers', such as perforated and fleecy films. With protection, the growing season can be extended by at least three weeks in spring and as much again in autumn. Almost as important, the quality of many vegetables can be improved, especially during the winter months, by protecting them from the elements. Lastly, protection enables the more tender vegetables to be grown successfully in colder parts of the country. In a small garden there is no question that any form of protection is worth its weight in gold, for the reasons below.

RAISING THE TEMPERATURE
Plants normally start growing when the average daytime temperature reaches approximately 6°C (43°F) in the spring. The date this happens varies from year to year, but can be any time from late winter in warmer areas, to the beginning of mid-spring in colder regions. Similarly growth stops again when the temperature falls below 6°C (43°F) in the autumn. The days between these two points are considered 'growing days' for your plants. For example, the warmest parts of England get over 300 growing days; the coldest fewer than 250. Quite a difference! Temperature also affects the rate of growth: provided plants have moisture, the higher the temperature reaches above 6°C (43°F), the faster they grow. Evidently, it makes sense to give your plants as many 'growing days' as possible.

As a general rule, protection raises the temperature of the soil and air around plants, and slows down the rate at which heat is lost from the soil at night. This amounts to increasing the number of 'growing days'. Protection is therefore most valuable in cold, high and exposed areas where the growing season is shortest.

When the sun shines in mid-winter, temperatures can soar under glass or polythene, allowing plants under cover to grow when those outside are still gripped in arctic conditions.

FROST PROTECTION
Some vegetables withstand frost satisfactorily, but many are killed or damaged by frost. So protection against frost is useful. Cloches and other unheated forms of protection can be relied upon to give protection only against slight frost. They will not keep out severe frost. On cold clear nights, the air temperature under cover can fall as low as the temperature outside, although the soil temperature may be warmer than the exposed soil's temperature.

Where there is suitable protection for plants, frost causes less damage, for several reasons:

~ The plants are dry, and frost damage is worse on wet plants.

~ They are protected from wind, and wind greatly increases damage to plants at low temperatures.

~ Frost penetrates less deeply and does not remain so long in the soil.

Incidentally, if there has been a heavy frost on unprotected plants, frost damage, which is caused by rapid thawing, can be lessened by spraying the plants with water the following morning before the sun reaches them. This helps to thaw them more slowly.

PROTECTION FROM WIND AND HEAVY RAIN

It is now known that plants give much higher yields if they are protected from even the lightest of winds. The damage that is caused by gales and the bitter winds which can occur in the spring time is enormous. Winds dry out leaves, batter and tear them, and make it a struggle for the plant to survive, let alone grow. Even the most rudimentary protection is of value. In coastal areas it is well worth protecting the plants from the salt spray in the wind. Protection from heavy winter rains, which wash nutrients out of the soil, and heavy spring rain, which can wash out seed and even seedlings, is also beneficial. Cloches also give protection against birds.

CLOCHES

Cloches, because they are small and easily moved, are probably still the most popular form of protection for small gardens, though perhaps less so than they used to be. There are various types.

Glass

Traditionally cloches were made of panes of glass, held together in a wire frame. 'Tent' cloches were made of two panes, low and high 'barn' cloches of four (see diagram opposite), and the flat-topped 'tomato' or 'utility' cloches of three panes.

Glass has two important qualities. Firstly, it is an effective heat trap. During the day soil absorbs heat in the form of short waves but some of this heat is subsequently lost from the soil as long-wave radiation. While glass transmits incoming short waves, to some extent it holds back outgoing long waves, which therefore warm up the air above the soil instead of being lost. Most plastic materials, on the contrary, transmit long waves as well, so there is less build up of heat under the cloche, particularly at night.

Secondly, provided it is kept clean, glass transmits a great deal of light. This is extremely important in winter, where poor light is one of the major factors limiting the growth of plants.

Glass cloches have several disadvantages. They are expensive, easily broken, heavy to handle, many people find them awkward to erect single-handed and they are potentially dangerous to children.

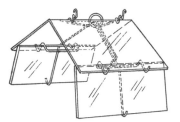

Glass 'Barn' Cloche
When in use the ends should
be closed with panes of glass

*Cloche made from
Corrugated PVC*

Plastics

The supremacy of glass cloches is now being challenged by cloches made of plastics and related materials. Most of these are considerably cheaper than glass, give more or less the same protection against wind and rain, do not pose so much of a danger to children, and are lighter and easier to handle. On the other hand, they do not last as long and few conserve heat as well as glass.

Many of the transparent plastics transmit light as effectively as glass, and plants seem to grow surprisingly well in the diffused light created by some translucent cloches. A drawback of plastics is that they discolour with time, due to exposure to ultra-violet light. This limits the light they let in. Treatments against ultra-violet light will make them last longer. Plastic cloches are very often semi-circular in shape (see diagram left). Improvements in the different materials used for cloches, and in their design, are continually being made. The following are some of the most common materials in use at present.

Rigid materials

Corrugated PVC sheeting transmits plenty of light, retains heat well, is strong and should last at least five years.

Acrylic sheeting (originally known as 'Perspex') is at present mostly used in frames; it has good qualities of heat retention and light transmission, and is very durable.

Glass fibre is very strong and durable, although opaque, but plants grow satisfactorily under it.

Semi-rigid materials

Polypropylene is a double-layered woven form of plastic with a corrugated appearance. It has the effect of double-glazing; the thermal insulation is higher than glass. Light transmission is considerably lower than glass, but this is a case where plant growth is good in the diffused light. The cloches last at least four or five years.

Wire reinforced plastics of several types are used to make cloches. Within limits the cloches can be bent into higher, narrower shapes or wider lower shapes as required for your particular situation. With care they will last three or four years.

Homemade cloches (see diagram below)

DIY cloches can be perfectly satisfactory. Most of the materials mentioned above are now sold in suitable lengths and widths for making cloches. They can be tacked, nailed or screwed onto a wood frame. Polythene film is best fixed between two pieces of wood, and you will find that a tent shape is the easiest to construct. Make the supporting frame as narrow as possible, so that maximum light is admitted.

Clips Odd panes of glass can be converted into cloches with wire links or special clips, such as the 'Rumsey' clips.

Plastic bags Medium weight plastic bags can be made into low cloches. Cut the bottom off the bag, bend two pieces of fairly heavy wire (coat hangers can be used) into a semi-circular or barn outline. Slip one into each side of the bag to support and anchor the plastic. These cloches are extremely useful for protecting tender herbs and salads in winter. They can be straddled over an insulating layer of bracken, straw or dried leaves.

Side shelters These, rather than roofed cloches, can be made by fixing rigid PVC, polypropylene, wire-reinforced plastic or polythene film onto a wooden frame. They can be supported between upright canes to make shelters for tomatoes, leant against runner beanpoles to make a protective tent over young beans, propped against a fence as a lean-to, or used as a 'light' transparent roof on a frame.

What to look for in cloches

The following factors are of importance when buying or making cloches:

Light

Cloches should let in as much light as possible and be easy to clean. If they are translucent, the light should be gently diffused. The light factor is most important (a) where cloches are used during the winter to grow, rather than merely protect, vegetables, and (b) in industrial areas where smoke in the atmosphere reduces the light.

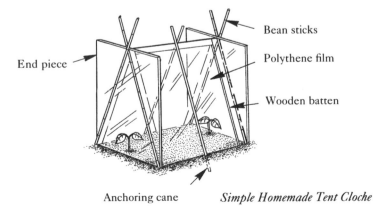

End piece

Bean sticks

Polythene film

Wooden batten

Anchoring cane

Simple Homemade Tent Cloche

Heat

The more cloches prevent heat loss from the soil, the better. Here one has to rely on available technical information about the materials. Note that there is less heat loss from a double layer of material, although this reduces the light. Scientists are uncertain at present as to whether the value of the heat gained outweighs the light lost! An interesting point is that the layer of moisture which condenses on the underside of a clear plastic film helps to prevent heat radiation from the soil.

Strength and stability

Cloches are very vulnerable to wind. Avoid sharp angles which catch the wind and make sure there is a secure means of anchorage, such as strong steel pins which protrude into the soil, flanges which can be pinned or weighted down, or overhead wire stays.

Ventilation

Cloches should not be completely airtight; in summer ventilation is essential. Glass cloches have gaps in the top which can be adjusted for ventilation. In some cloches roof panels can be raised for ventilation. Small ventilation holes can be made in the roof of rigid and semi-rigid plastic and glass fibre cloches. If there is no built-in ventilation, leave small gaps between the cloches when erecting them.

Draughts

The ends of a single cloche or of a row of cloches must be closed, otherwise a wind tunnel is created, with disastrous results. Ends which interlock securely over the cloche, or are self-anchoring with steel pins, are very useful. Otherwise sticks or canes have to be used to keep it in place. Glass or transparent ends are preferable to pieces of wood or slate.

Storage

Cloches which stack on top of each other or fold flat when not in use are an asset in small gardens.

Size

When choosing cloches bear in mind the main purpose for which they will be used. Large cloches are usually more expensive. Tent cloches and low tunnels are fine for seed raising and for low crops such as lettuce. Low barns, with sides 15cm (6in) high, are adequate only for the young stages of tall crops such as tomatoes, sweet corn, peppers and peas, but high barns, with sides 30cm (12in) high, and flat-topped cloches are needed for the later stages. Some cloches have side extensions to increase their height, while in others the top pane can be raised slightly or removed to give more height. The height-width ratio of the semi-rigid cloches can be adjusted within certain limits. Several brands of cloche are available in varying widths.

Cloche techniques
Soil
To make the most of cloches, always put them on the best soil where you can expect to grow top quality vegetables. Work as much organic matter as possible into the top 15cm (6in) or so.

Anchoring (see diagram right)
High winds are deadly. Glass cloches and brittle plastics may break, and lighter cloches be blown away in exposed positions – where, of course, cloches are most valuable. In such conditions cloches need additional anchorage, for example by running twine through the handles and tying it to canes or stout sticks at either end. Putting pea sticks alongside cloches is another useful trick for additional anchorage. Tent cloches can be anchored with pairs of bamboo canes, which are stuck into the ground on either side. Tie them together, above the ridge, if necessary.

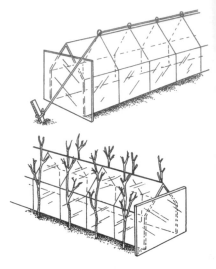

Methods of Anchoring Cloches
Above: with twine run through the handles and tied to sticks at either end *Below:* with pea sticks pushed into the ground alongside

Cloches can also be weighted down. With plastic cloches, empty wine bottles serve the purpose well. Tie them together at the neck with heavy string or baler twine, so they can hang on either side of the cloche ridge.

Where glass cloches are used, it pays to rub all edges with a carborundum stone when first putting them up. This cuts down breakages.

When securing the end panes of glass cloches, use a cane or stick placed at an angle, rather than upright. This is much less likely to work loose and cause friction against the cloche.

Watering
Rain water runs off the sides of cloches and, provided there is plenty of organic matter in the soil, will percolate through to the roots of plants under the cloches, which tend to grow outwards. Apart from watering small seedlings (which have not had time to develop an extensive root system), there is normally no need to remove cloches for watering; they can be watered overhead with hoses or cans. This indirect form of watering helps to conserve the tilth of the soil. Check to see if the soil is sufficiently moist by poking your finger into the soil in the middle of the cloche. If it feels dry 2.5cm (1in) or so below the surface, it may be necessary to remove the cloche to water more thoroughly.

In light soils a shallow drill alongside the cloche helps the water to go straight to the roots.

Ventilation
On hot spring days and in summer plenty of ventilation is required. When it is very hot it is a good idea to remove every other cloche in a row to provide ventilation.

Coverage
In frosty weather glass itself can become so cold that plants touching it will be frost-bitten. Make sure the plants are not in contact with the cloche sides to prevent this occurring.

Cloches can be raised to cover growing crops by standing them on bricks or wooden blocks, by using side extensions where available, or by planting the crops in trenches about 15-23cm (6-9in) deep. The cloches straddle the trench. This is only practicable in light well-drained soils, otherwise the trench is apt to turn into a waterlogged ditch.

Planting distances have to be adjusted to some extent to take advantage of the width of a cloche.

Side protection
Some cloches can be stood on their side and then wrapped around tall plants to act as a windbreak. Anchor them by having a cane put through the handles, or with canes pushed into the ground alongside.

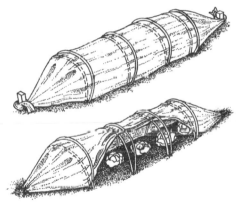

Low polythene tunnels
The cheapest form of protection must, without a doubt, be the low polythene tunnel, which is made from lightweight (which is

Above: low polythene film tunnel, laid over wire hoops, and kept down with fine wire hoops
Below: film pushed up for ventilation

usually 150-gauge) polythene film stretched over galvanized steel wire hoops pushed into the ground about 1m (1yd) apart. Flexible polythene piping can also be used as hoops. As the film is flimsy it generally only lasts one, or, at the most, two seasons, though tears can be mended with tape. Heavier polythene films can be used for low tunnels but are harder to manipulate than the lightweight films. Film can be bought in rolls and then cut to the lengths required. Width and height can be varied. I like my tunnels to fit snugly over my 1m (1yd) wide beds, the height at the centre being up to 45cm (18in).

The film is kept in place over the hoops with fine wire or strings, running over the top and hooked or tied to the base of the hoops. The ends of the film are either dug into the ground, or knotted around canes or pegs in the ground 60cm (2ft) or so beyond the end hoop. In windy situations, or in winter, it may be necessary to anchor the sides. Use clods of soil, pieces of wood, metal piping stones, or plastic bags filled with sand or earth; alternatively, bury one side in a slit made in the ground with a trowel. Leave the other side free for access.

For watering, ventilation and other operations, the film is simply pushed up on one side. In hot weather the combination of high temperature and humidity under the film is conducive to pests and diseases – in which case push up both sides for maximum ventilation. On the continent, where low polythene tunnels are extensively used for early outdoor tomatoes, melons and other crops, square or round 'peep holes' are cut along the lengths of the tunnels, so plants are sheltered but still get plenty of air. Low tunnels can also be made with perforated films (see p.91), creating a very well-ventilated tunnel.

Bearing in mind the limitations of their height, low polythene tunnels can be used for the same purposes as cloches, as outlined below.

All year round use of cloches
As temperatures vary widely from one season to the next and from district to district, references to specific months are for general guidance in the UK only.

Spring
1 *To prepare for sowing* Cloches can be used to: dry out the soil before preparing the seed bed, preserve a tilth on a prepared seed bed if sowing is delayed and to warm up the soil before sowing (to do this leave them in position several days to a week beforehand).
2 *For earlier crops of hardy vegetables* (late winter to mid-spring). These can be sown or planted under cloches; some can remain under cloches until mature or nearly mature.
   eg beans (broad); beetroot; calabrese; carrots; cauliflower (summer and autumn); chicory ('Sugar Loaf'); kale (for unthinned small crop see p.180); lettuce; onions (spring and bulb); parsley; peas (early and maincrop); potatoes (early); radish; salad seedlings (see p.121); spinach/spinach beet/Swiss chard; Texsel greens; turnips.
3 *To raise seedlings which can be started under glass to give them a longer growing season* (late winter to mid-spring). They can be sown in boxes under cloches, or directly in the ground and transplanted later. The cloches will also protect them from birds and cats.
   eg Brussels sprouts; cabbage (summer and winter); cauliflower (summer and early autumn); celeriac; celery; leeks; lettuce (summer).

4 *For early stages of half-hardy vegetables* (mid- and late spring). By using cloches sowing or planting can be done several weeks earlier. Sow in boxes or pots under cloches and transplant when large enough into permanent position under other cloches, or else in the open after any danger of frost is past. Alternatively sow *in situ* under cloches, removing the cloches when they are no longer needed after the weather becomes a little warmer:

eg aubergines; both French and runner beans; cucumbers; courgettes/marrows; iceplant; peppers; spinach (New Zealand); sweet corn; tomatoes.

5 *Hardening-off tender seedlings and young plants raised in heat indoors* (mid- and late spring). These can be put under cloches in boxes or pots. Harden them off gradually by moving cloches a little further apart each day, then by leaving them off during the day. Finally remove them at night unless frost threatens.

Summer

6 *Crops suitable for growing under cloches in summer.* These are usually transplanted under cloches late spring/early summer, or sown *in situ* two or three weeks earlier:

eg aubergines; cucumbers (bush types); peppers; tomatoes (either the bush type, or cordons grown horizontally).

Autumn

7 *Extending the season by protecting late summer sowings in early autumn.*

eg beans (dwarf forms of runner and French beans); carrots; chicory (red and 'Sugar Loaf'); endive; lettuce; peas (early types); oriental greens (Chinese cabbage, choy sum, pak choi, mibuna, mizuna); salad seedlings (see p.121).

8 *For ripening off tomatoes and onions in early autumn.*

Winter

9 *For autumn sown crops which will over-winter under cloches and mature the following spring and summer:*

eg beans (broad); cabbage (spring, in cold areas); cauliflower (the early summer types); chicory ('Sugar Loaf' seedlings); peas (the hardy types); lettuce; onions (spring, and also as a maincrop in cold areas); spinach/spinach beet/Swiss chard.

10 *For mature crops which will be used during the winter, but will benefit from additional protection:*

eg chicory (red); chicory ('Witloof', earthed up under cloches to mature earlier than fully exposed plants); corn salad; endive (hardiest cultivars); land cress; lettuce (winter hardy cultivars); oriental greens (komatsuna, mizuna, mibuna, hardy mustards); purslane (winter); salad seedlings (hardy types such as cress, mustard, salad rape – see p.195); Texsel greens; turnip tops.

To make the most of cloches it is advisable to draw up a simple plan so that there is always something in the garden which will benefit from cloche protection at any given time. This will ensure that you get the fullest use from your cloches and that there is always something that will benefit. The plan should be flexible enough to allow for the vagaries of the weather. Sowing dates, cultural details and recommended cultivars for cloches are given in Chapter 9.

Strip cropping

The ideal way of using cloches is 'strip cropping'. This means cultivating two (or more) adjacent strips of ground each about 1m (1yd) wide, and planning the cropping so that the cloches are simply moved backwards and forwards between the strips with the minimum of effort.

The possible alternatives in strip cropping are endless. With a little gardening experience you will be able to work out your own plans, devising schemes to enjoy your favourite vegetables for a longer period.

The basis of strip cropping is as follows:

Vegetables are divided roughly into four groups according to the months during which they will be under cloches. There will inevitably be some overlapping of groups.

The cloches are used first for a Group 1 crop during the winter months. In late spring, when the Group 1 crop is cleared or no longer requires cloche protection, cloches are moved on to a Group 2 crop, ideally sown or planted alongside. This would be a half-hardy crop requiring cloche protection at least during the early stages of growth.

By early summer, when the Group 2 crop will have outgrown the cloches, the first strip of land will have been cleared and replanted with a Group 3 crop, which can stay under the cloches all summer.

When this crop is finished in autumn, the cloches can be moved back to the second strip, where a crop either maturing in late autumn or over-wintering, will have been sown or planted.

As before, the months mentioned are for general guidance. There is considerable variation from one region to another.

A simple strip cropping plan is given on page 122.

Group 1
Hardy spring crops under cloches mid-winter to mid-spring.
Some are cloched the previous autumn.
(a) Crops normally cleared from the ground as late spring approaches, allowing others to be sown or planted:
    eg spring cabbages (planted and cloched in mid-autumn; usually in cold districts only).
        lettuce (sown mid-autumn, mid- or late winter).
        radish (sown early spring).
        carrots (mid-winter sown in mild districts).
        corn salad; land cress; winter purslane (sown previous summer

or autumn).

hardy chicories; endives; hardy oriental greens (late summer/ autumn planted).

(b) Crops which will not be cleared from the ground until early summer or later though cloches are removed in mid-spring:

eg cauliflower (mid-autumn planted).

broad beans (sown late autumn or mid-winter).

carrots (sown late winter).

peas (sown late winter).

beetroot (sown early spring, ready early summer).

spinach (autumn sown).

peas (spring sown).

sowings of brassicas, leeks, celery, oriental bunching onions, among many possibilities, for planting out later.

Group 2

Late spring crops.

These are half-hardy vegetables either sown *in situ* under cloches in mid- or late spring, or raised indoors and planted out under cloches in mid- or late spring:

eg French beans, marrows/courgettes, runner beans, sweet corn, cucumbers, tomatoes.

Group 3

Tender crops which can be grown under cloches all through the summer season:

eg aubergines; cucumbers (bush types); peppers; tomatoes (bush types, or cordon types trained horizontally).

Group 4

Autumn crops using cloches:

eg dwarf French and runner beans – sown early summer; will be killed by the first frost if not under cloches. (Normally cleared by late autumn.)

dwarf early peas – sown mid-summer.

carrots; corn salad; hardier endive; land cress; winter purslane; lettuce; oriental greens (such as Chinese cabbage, pak choi, mizuna, mibuna, komatsuna); spring onion; radish; seedling salads (see p.121), spinach/spinach beet/Swiss chard – mainly sown late summer, cloched during early autumn/mid-autumn for use in cooking in late autumn/early winter.

spring cabbage – (sown mid-/late summer; cloches required for protection in cold areas).

potatoes – early cultivars planted mid-summer, cloched early/ mid-autumn. Will need extra protection against frost.

tomatoes – covered with cloches early autumn to ripen. Must be brought in before frost.

INTERCROPPING

Often two or three crops can be sown together under cloches to make the most of the space, for example:

~ Radishes with most crops.

~ Peas with lettuce and radish on either side.

~ Dwarf French beans either side of sweet corn.

~ Carrots and radishes on either side of French beans.

~ Carrots, salad onions or cos lettuces intercropped with small lettuce.

~ Turnips, lettuces, carrots or radishes alongside peas.

~ Seedbed sowings of brassicas, onions, leeks and lettuces alongside a row of carrots.

~ Quick maturing salad seedlings such as cress, salad rape, Mediterranean rocket and oriental green such as pak choi or mizuna alongside tomatoes, sweet corn, French or runner beans.

CROP COVERS

'Crop covers' is the term for various types of light films which can be laid directly on a crop to give protection. Originally known as 'floating' mulches, cloches or films, they are either perforated with slits or holes, or made of fabrics with considerable natural 'give'. This accounts for their main characteristic – an ability, within certain limits, to expand as plants grow, supported by the plants beneath. They can be very useful in small gardens where there is no space for a greenhouse, polytunnel or frames.

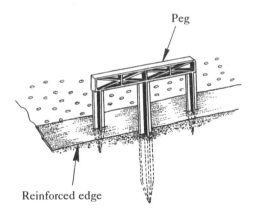

Crop covers raise the soil and air temperature around plants, and have a sheltering, windbreak effect. As a result crops can be ready a couple of weeks earlier, will yield more heavily and be of better quality. Crop covers also give some protection against flying pests. They are most valuable early and late in the year.

Perforated films *(above)* and fleecy films can be anchored with plastic pegs. Reinforced edges extend the useful life of the films

Think of covers primarily as a way of *shortening the growing season* and improving quality. Except where heavy fleece films are being used, don't plant out much earlier than would otherwise be the case. Once planted, crops will grow much faster than they would in the open. Covers are a good method of capitalizing on the advantages of naturally early sites.

This is a rapidly developing field, so watch out for potentially useful new products.

The main types of crop cover currently available are clear perforated polyethylene films, and the much softer fleecy films which are made from polypropylene combined with other compounds.

Clear perforated films

These light films are either perforated with many small holes of 1cm (½in) in diameter, or with myriads of tiny slits. The latter type is much more expensive but more 'elastic'. Use types with reinforced edges where available. Perforated films will last for two seasons if handled with care.

Buy UV treated films wherever possible to extend their useful life. You can make your own perforated film by burning holes in 200 gauge film with a hot poker. Aim to make the holes about 1cm (½in) in diameter, spaced about 4-5cm (1½-2in) apart, so there are roughly 200 holes per square metre/yard. Burning seals the edges so the film won't tear, as it is likely to do if the edges are cut.

Characteristics of perforated films

~ Soil warms up rapidly beneath the films: in hot spells temperatures can rise very high and damage plants. They offer very little protection against frost but will protect against the chill winds which increase the potential damage of frost.

~ Although watering can be done through the films, they are relatively impervious to rain and overhead irrigation; so, if left on too long there is a risk of plants being short of water, and possibly being chafed and damaged by the relatively harsh film.

~ For every crop there is a critical point at which the film must be removed, either because of chafing or temperature rises. For this reason they are generally used in the first few weeks or months of growth.

~ Although normally laid directly on the crop, they can also be laid over low tunnel hoops, to cover taller crops such as tomatoes in their early stages.

Using perforated films

The films are put on immediately after sowing or planting. If sowing, sow in slightly sunken drills, so that the seedlings can get going before they 'hit' the film. Lay the film over the bed so that it is reasonably taut, but not over-stretched or sagging. Allow a little slackness so the film can stretch. Anchor it in slits about 5cm (2in) deep in the soil on either side of the bed, pushing the soil back against the edge of the film to keep it in place. The ground must be as weed free as possible, as weeds will thrive in this cosy protected environment.

The trick in using perforated film is knowing when to remove it. This varies from crop to crop. With radishes, for example, it can stay in place until they are ready; with carrots it should be removed after about ten weeks, when the plants have about seven leaves. Details for the different vegetables are given in Chapter 9 but, as a rough guide, if the film looks as if it is restricting growth, remove it – sooner rather than later.

As growth under perforated films is rather soft, plants should be 'weaned' carefully when the covers are removed. Ideally remove covers towards the evening on still, overcast or damp days, when there is no risk of frost. Weaning can start by slitting the covers several days beforehand, although this means the film cannot be used again, (see diagram p.234). First make intermittent slits along the cover, subsequently slitting the entire length. Water gently just after the covers are removed if the ground is dry, as will often be the case. (For cultivation of bush tomatoes under covers see Tomatoes p.233.)

Fleecy films

These spun fibre, 'non-woven' films have a soft, cheese-cloth texture and drape easily over plants. They are made of varying thicknesses, the number after the trade name, for example 'Agryl P 17' or 'Envirofleece 30', being the weight of the film in g/m^2. So the higher the number, the heavier the film.

The recently introduced '60' films give considerable protection against frost and can even be used as a form of double-glazing inside a greenhouse. Films with reinforced edges are longer lasting and more easily anchored.

Characteristics of fleecy films

~ Fleecy films are more expensive than perforated clear films but gentler in action, so that there is less chafing of plants and more flexibility in use. They are, however, more easily torn and less durable than plastic films; depending on the film thickness, they may last a couple of seasons or perhaps more if handled carefully.

~ They are more permeable to air and water, so less subject to temperature fluctuations. The ground is less liable to dry out and they can be watered from above.

~ The films give protection against several degrees of frost: the heavier the film, the greater the protection.

~ They can be left on plants much longer than perforated films, sometimes until harvesting. These films are especially recommended for early and late sown crops and over-wintering leafy crops. They improve the growth of the plants and the quality of the vegetables.

~ The films give protection against birds and flying insect pests, such as aphids, cabbage root fly, carrot fly, flea beetle, butterflies and moths, *provided* they are securely anchored at soil level with no gaps between the film and the ground, and there are no holes in the fabric. Japanese radishes, for example, can be protected against cabbage root fly by covering them with fleecy films until shortly before lifting.

Unless very hot weather is experienced, carrots can be grown under fleecy films until near maturity; the fleece will protect them against carrot root fly.

Using fleecy films

On the whole fleecy films are best laid after planting rather than after sowing. This is because heavy rain after sowing tends to make them drape on the ground, damaging emerging seedlings.

Lay the film so it is fairly taut, but fold the edges of the film at the sides, so it can be released in stages as the crops grow.

Anchor the edges with any of the methods suggested for low tunnels (see p.84), or use the purpose-made pegs.

As with perforated films, it is important to make sure the ground is weed free before being covered. Any weeds will flourish under covers and weeding is awkward once they are in place. Removing the covers is less critical than with plastic films, but watch plants carefully and remove them as soon as plant growth seems to be slowing down or the plants look stressed. In most cases they should be removed after three or four weeks. They should be removed from insect-pollinated crops such as tomatoes and courgettes when the flowers appear. Again, removing the covers in dull conditions is recommended.

MAIN USES OF CROP COVERS

There is enormous scope for experimenting with the use of crop covers in small gardens. Many of the previously suggested uses for cloches can be applied to crop covers. Here potential uses are summarized.

Spring and early summer

~ For the early stages of many vegetables, including early potatoes, lettuce, outdoor bush tomatoes, beetroot, celery, spinach, cabbage, parsley, French beans, endive, red chicory and other leafy salad crops. Fleecy films will give some protection against frost.

~ To grow radishes and carrots to maturity (under fleecy films only).

Autumn and winter

~ As extra protection for over-wintering lettuce, corn salad, spring cabbage, late sowings of beetroot, spinach, radish, oriental greens and cut-and-come-again seedlings.

~ Emergency frost cover. If heavy frost is forecast, drape films over outdoor crops and also over crops under cover – as extra protection against frost.

FRAMES

Like cloches, cold frames are a useful means of providing extra protection. They retain heat better than cloches, are less affected by wind, but are less flexible to use. They can be portable or permanent, lean-to or free-standing, with a flat roof facing in one direction or a tent-shaped span roof.

The roof is usually sloping to catch the maximum sunlight. A shallow frame for salad crops would be about 17cm (6½in) high in the front, 23cm (9in) at the back. A deeper frame for cucumbers would be about 30cm (12in) in front, and 45cm (18in) at the back.

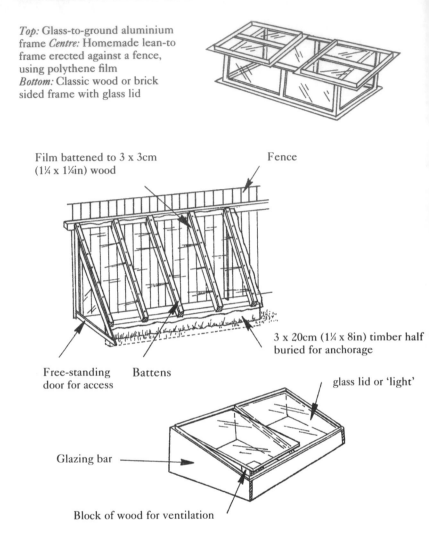

Top: Glass-to-ground aluminium
frame *Centre:* Homemade lean-to
frame erected against a fence,
using polythene film
Bottom: Classic wood or brick
sided frame with glass lid

Film battened to 3 x 3cm
(1¼ x 1¼in) wood

Fence

3 x 20cm (1¼ x 8in) timber half
buried for anchorage

Free-standing
door for access

Battens

glass lid or 'light'

Glazing bar

Block of wood for ventilation

Traditionally the sides of frames were built of bricks, wood or concrete.
The glass roof (known as a 'light') was held in a wooden frame. Many modern frames have steel or aluminium frames and glass to the ground on the
sides. The lights may be hinged or slide backwards: bear this in mind if
selecting a frame to fit into a small area. Most of the synthetic materials dis-
cussed can be used in the construction of homemade frames.

A solid-sided frame retains heat best, especially if built against another
wall. The glass-to-ground frames let in more light, an important factor

where crops are being grown in winter and early spring. The scope of frames for winter and spring crops is increased enormously if they can be heated. The simplest method is with electric soil-warming cables. An alternative is the old-fashioned 'hotbed' method, using rotting manure.

Siting a frame

Frames should be in an unshaded position, facing south if single span, or in a north/south direction if double span. As with cloches, make the soil in the frame as fertile as possible. Replace the top 15cm (6in) with really good soil or compost if necessary.

Frame techniques

Ventilation Frames are relatively airtight, so ventilation is very important to prevent a muggy atmosphere which encourages disease. Ventilate by propping up the lights or by sliding them open. In summer they can be removed completely.

Watering In winter try to keep the leaves dry and water the soil only, again to prevent disease. And, according to gardening lore, it is best to use warm water if possible.

Frost In very cold weather give additional protection by covering frames with sacking or other insulating material at night.

Light If seeds are raised in boxes in a solid-sided frame, stand them on bricks or blocks to bring them nearer the light. Otherwise the seedlings become drawn and leggy.

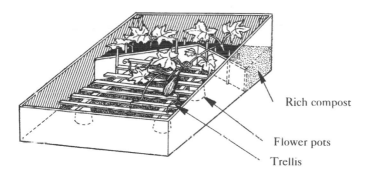

Rich compost

Flower pots

Trellis

Horizontal trellis on frame to keep cucumbers off the ground

Use of frames

Frames can be used for the same purposes as cloches, though the lights have to be removed for taller crops. They are particularly useful for raising seeds in boxes and pots, for hardening-off seedlings, and for salads such as lettuce, radish, beet and young carrots. In summer they are ideal for cucumbers, though these do better if they can be raised off the ground, for example with a horizontal trellis (see p.95). In winter, endives, chicories and dandelion can be transplanted into frames for blanching under straw; or they can be used for storing white cabbage. Mice soon track down any goodies, so set a few traps!

GREENHOUSES

A greenhouse can be used to good effect for growing tomatoes, cucumbers and peppers in summer, for raising plants in spring and, from winter to spring, for growing the hardy salad vegetables and oriental greens that were suggest-ed for winter cloches. A greenhouse glazed to soil level to allow in maximum light is the most suitable for vegetables.

One of the disadvantages of using a permanent greenhouse is that, if tom-atoes and cucumbers are grown every year in the soil, there is a high risk of 'soil sickness' diseases building up in the soil, making it impossible to grow further crops unless the soil is sterilized or replaced annually. The most practical alternative is to grow plants in fresh soil in pots or growing-bags. On economic grounds it is hard to justify building even an unheated greenhouse for growing vegetables – but use one if you have it. Heated greenhouses are a luxury outside the scope of this book.

Walk-in Polythene Tunnel

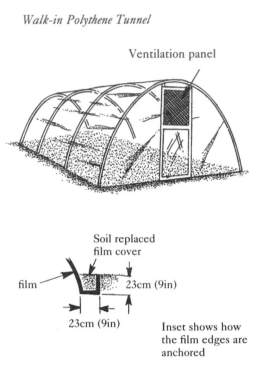

Ventilation panel

Soil replaced
film cover

film

23cm (9in)

23cm (9in)

Inset shows how the film edges are anchored

POLYTHENE STRUCTURES

The archetypal polythene structure is the 'walk-in' tunnel, made from galvanized tube hoops, generally 1·5-1·8m (5-6ft) at the ridge, covered with heavy, ultra-violet inhibited film of 500 or 600 gauge. The hoops are sunk in the ground, a trench is taken out around the perimeter, and the edges of the film are then buried in the trench (see diagram above).

It may seem absurd to suggest this sort of structure for a small garden but, *if* the space exists, they are without equal for increasing productivity at a low cost. 'Off-the-peg' tunnels –3 x 6m (10 x 20ft) is a typical size – are a fraction of the cost of a greenhouse, but small structures can be made any shape or size by battening film to a wooden frame, or anchoring it into the soil over a metal framework. Flowers and herbs can be grown around the edge to soften the harsh appearance of the tunnel. In summer they can be screened off completely with climbing beans or cucumbers trained up poles or on a trellis positioned along the sides of the tunnel, or with several rows of giant sunflowers, planted 23cm (9in) apart each way. The light shade will be beneficial to the plants inside the tunnel.

The film lasts two or three years, when the structure can be re-covered or moved to a fresh site, so avoiding the soil sickness problem of permanent greenhouses. Walk-in tunnels are really giant cloches without the fiddly inconvenience of cloches. They can be in use all year round, for traditional greenhouse vegetables in summer and the many hardy crops suggested for winter cloches from autumn to spring. They are a wonderful haven for the winter gardener.

Hints on erecting and managing polytunnels

1 The film should be as tight fitting as possible. Put it on the frame on a hot day when the film is supple and very much easier to pull taut.
2 Bind any rough corners or edges on the frame with tape or cloth to prevent friction, which leads to tears and shortens the life of the film. Mend tears with adhesive tape sold for the purpose.
3 Batten the film firmly to the door frame.
4 Extra ground space can be gained at a doorless end by pulling the film out to a point (as in low tunnels) and burying it in the ground.
5 Temperatures and humidity build up rapidly even in winter, so always err on the side of over-ventilation. If possible, build a permanent ventilation panel into the door. Rigid plastic windbreak 'net' is ideal for the purpose. If necessary, cut a few, semi-circular, dinner plate size 'portholes' in the sides of the polytunnel in summer, 30cm (12in) or so above ground level. They can be taped down again in winter.
6 Watering is usually done by hand, so keep the soil generously mulched to conserve moisture. This applies equally in winter, when frost can have quite a desiccating action.

For more information on polytunnels see *Salads for Small Gardens*, Further Reading p.248.

Polytunnel orientation

With organic systems, far and away the greatest problem in using polytunnels is a build up of pests and diseases in summer as temperatures soar. Where there is an option, it is therefore advisable to site a polytunnel in a north/south, rather than east/west direction. The summer sun then falls on the narrower ends, rather than the body of the tunnel, making a surprising difference in temperature.

CHAPTER SEVEN

Space Saving

VERTICAL GROWING
Climbing vegetables

The most obvious way of saving space is to grow plants vertically. Several vegetables are climbers by nature and can be trained up a fruit cage, fencing, trellis, arch, pergola or up netting – 5, 7·5, or 10cm (2, 3, or 4in) mesh is suitable. Marrows and climbing beans will cling very well to willow fences or hurdles. So if a small garden is enclosed with a fence of strong wire netting or willow, the potential area for growing vegetables can, in fact, be increased enormously.

Where the existing walls or fences are smooth surfaced brick, cement or wood, some additional climbing support will be needed, either right against the wall, or a foot or so away leaning towards the wall. Trellis work, or any kind of wire or nylon netting can be used (see diagram below). A simple way of doing this is to construct a frame with galvanized pipes and 'Kee Klamp' fittings. They are easily erected and dismantled. (Beans don't cling very easily to plastic-coated wire but can be encouraged to do so.) Alternatively run a few parallel wires along the wall as supports.

Extending Low Wall with 'Kee Klamp' Construction

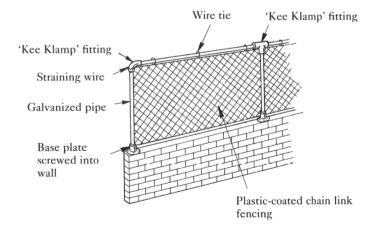

Wire tie 'Kee Klamp' fitting

'Kee Klamp' fitting

Straining wire

Galvanized pipe

Base plate screwed into wall

Plastic-coated chain link fencing

The height of low walls can be increased with a strip of trellis, rigid fencing or rigid windbreak material along the top. Avoid north facing walls which get very little sun but don't overlook the walls of the house. Why not

98

pick beans from a bedroom window? Grow them up strings attached to screws set in wall plugs.

Ground at the foot of walls dries out rapidly, so work plenty of humus into the soil and keep it well mulched to retain the moisture. Extra watering may be necessary in the lee of walls.

The classic method of supporting climbing runner and French beans is on structures made from long, criss-crossed bamboo canes or poles (see Beans, p.139). Equally picturesque, and taking up less space, are 'wigwams' or 'tepees' made with anything from three to a dozen bamboo canes or poles. They need to be up to 2·4m (8ft) long. Push them well into the soil so that they are secure, tying them together near the top. Beans, trailing marrows and cucumbers grow up them well. Another simple way of supporting the same vegetables is to take lengths of supple young wood, such as hazel or willow, pushing both ends into the ground to make an arch. Overlapping arches look particularly effective edging paths; they can be of any height. Rigid polythene hoops can be used in the same way. For this and other supports for climbing beans, see Chapter 9.

Climbing beans and trailing marrows can become very weighty plants, and may well reach a height of 2·4m (8ft). So any supports must be very strong to prevent them collapsing under the weight of the plants. Pinch out the growing points when the plants reach the top of the supports. Beans may need to be tied to supports in the early stages; cucumbers and marrows usually need a little tying throughout their growth.

Smaller wigwams can be made for growing and securing peas. They require a little more grip, so either wrap netting around the canes, or run extra strings from top to bottom, buried in the soil or pegged down firmly. The plants will then successfully grow up the structure.

Backs to the wall

Several non-climbing vegetables do well planted against a sunny wall, basking in the extra heat. Obvious candidates are tomatoes, peppers, aubergines and sweet corn, and sun-loving herbs such as basil and rosemary. If there is room, plant sweet corn in double rows to assist pollination.

Homemade lean-to frames and small greenhouses can be built against a wall or fence, saving space and materials. Window boxes or other containers can be hung on walls or railings, provided they are attached securely. They can also be stood on low walls, though if they can be set into the wall, they will be less exposed to drying winds.

Vegetables as screens

Vegetables can be used to screen off unsightly compost heaps, rubbish bins, domestic oil storage tanks, or to mark boundaries. Climbing vegetables, as mentioned above, need some support. Tall free-standing vegetables may need staking in exposed situations. Jerusalem artichokes, cardoons (if you have space), red orache and sweet corn are all good screening vegetables. So are sunflowers which, for screening, can be planted in rows two to three deep and as close as 15cm (6in) apart each way. If you need to justify this theatrical extravagance, remember that the seeds are edible. Runner beans, French beans, trailing marrows and pumpkins can all, in different degrees, scramble over hedges, fences, low buildings, even up trees. Marrows and pumpkins can make excellent ground cover, concealing ugly bits of ground and dreary corners.

On a smaller scale, the leafless and semi-leafless peas can be grown as low hedges. The tendrils of neighbouring plants twine together so they become virtually self-supporting – a green barbed wire fence. Grow them in a band at least 30cm (12in) wide. From summer to late autumn, when it loses its colour, the delicate fern of asparagus makes an attractive screening hedge 90cm-1.2m (3-4ft) high.

VEGETABLES IN FLOWER BEDS
Many vegetables are pretty enough to be grown in flower beds if they are positioned carefully. Except where being used as edgings, plant them in small groups or irregular shaped patches, rather than in rows. The exception is large plants like courgettes, which can be planted singly. Vegetables are much more demanding than flowers, so if grown in flower beds, make sure they have enough space and light to develop, and that the soil is reasonably fertile. Here are a few suggestions.

Taller vegetables for the back of the border
Climbing beans These make a wonderful feature, growing up any of the supports already mentioned. Runner beans were originally introduced for their decorative qualities. Most cultivars have bright orange flowers, but some are white flowered, 'Painted Lady' has beautiful apple blossom pink and white flowers, and 'Sunset' has warm pink flowers. The purple flowered forms of climbing French bean are equally striking.

Sunflowers These can be used as a natural support for climbing beans. Get the sunflowers well established and, when they are about 75-90cm (2½-3ft) high, plant pot-raised beans at the base. It can be a dramatic combination – though extra staking may be needed to keep them all upright!

Climbing marrows and other squashes These can be grown similarly at the back of a bed, provided strong enough supports are erected. The less vigorous cultivars, such as 'Table Dainty', 'Rolet' and 'Little Gem' are recommended. Climbing outdoor cucumbers can be grown in the same way. The outdoor Japanese cultivars are the best climbers.

Sweet corn Decorative at every stage, clumps can look very handsome in a border. For pollination and visual impact, sweet corn is best grown in groups of at least three plants.

Asparagus Best grown as a single plant, as it becomes quite bushy. Asparagus is perennial, so make sure it is planted in a suitable position as it can't be moved once established. It makes a lovely foil for flowers. Cut it down in the autumn and, from the third season onwards, enjoy a few delicious spears in late spring.

Red orache The leaves of this continental spinach can be anything from a purple bronze to deep red, depending on the strain. The seedlings and young leaves make excellent spinach in spring and early summer, when the plants shoot up dramatically to 2.4m (8ft) or so. It is worth keeping a few for the rich autumn colour. But in a small garden it is wise to grow only a few, as they can become very woody and greedy for soil moisture, and will self-seed shamelessly.

Cardoons and globe artichokes Handsome, thistle-like perennial plants with magnificent, deep blue flower heads and blue green foliage, often with a 90cm (3ft) spread. Best grown as single specimens. The cardoon flower spikes may grow up to 2.4m (8ft) tall; artichokes are more modest. The flower buds of artichokes and the blanched stems of young cardoons are edible. Globe artichokes need protection in severe winter weather.

Chicories All the chicories – including red, 'Witloof' and 'Sugar Loaf' – throw up magnificent spikes of sky blue flowers in their second season. Leave a few plants at the back of a border to run to seed in early summer. They may need some support.

Medium height, mid-border vegetables

Ornamental cabbages and kales These variegated forms of cabbage and kale have brilliant colours deepening in cold weather, often with the bonus of attractively shaped, serrated and fringed leaves. The kales are the hardiest but neither plant will survive very cold weather. Standard curly kale, however, is very much hardier, and both tall and dwarf forms look very pretty in flower beds.

Dwarf beans With their colourful flowers, both the dwarf forms of French beans and the reintroduced dwarf forms of runner beans take on the air of bedding plants in a flower bed. The cultivars with purple-podded beans generally have attractive, purplish foliage and so are particularly suitable. All seem to look best planted in groups.

Swiss chard This glossy-leaved vegetable with contrasting white stems is very handsome in flower beds, and remains looking good over many months. The red leaves and stems of the 'Ruby Chard' forms are a brilliant colour, unforgettable when seen with the light behind them. However, they are very prone to premature bolting.

Scorzonera and salsify Quite an ornamental pair of root vegetables with attractive narrow, upright leaves followed, in their second season, by pretty yellow and mauve flowers respectively and wonderful fluffy seedheads. The flower buds are edible – and quite a delicacy.

Tomatoes Small bush types can fit into borders well. If possible choose cultivars with attractive foliage, such as 'Pixie'.

Leeks Commonplace, but clumps of the purple-blue leaved, hardy cultivars like 'Blue Solaise' look pretty in winter. Leave a few to run to seed early the following summer: the pale mauve and white, globular flower heads are magnificent.

Oriental greens Several are very striking plants in their different ways: the brilliantly coloured purple-leaved mustards and the purple-stemmed choy sum; mizuna with its deeply serrated, rich green leaves and the closely related, strap-leaved mibuna; the unbelievably symmetrical rosette pak choi; and the loose-headed Chinese cabbage 'Ruffles', with its creamy heart set in a fringe of emerald green.

Asparagus pea Not the most productive of plants, but the clover-like leaves and deep red vetch-like flowers are a pretty combination. They make a neat edge to a path.

Lower growing vegetables for the front of borders, or as edges

Lettuce The 'Salad Bowl' types are the most suitable as they don't form hearts, so are slower to run to seed. Individual leaves can be cut over many months. Many have exceptionally pretty, indented leaves; the red forms, particularly of the deeply curled 'Lollo' types, are outstanding from the decorative point of view.

Purslane The gold and green forms of summer purslane make very pretty patches or edging; in addition they can be sown as 'cut-and-come-again' seedlings in patches or strips.

Beetroot Long used in park bedding schemes, some of the cultivars with deep red foliage look particularly superb in flower beds. My favourite is 'Bull's Blood'. It keeps its colour well into mid-winter, and besides, produces very nice beetroots.

Parsley Both the herb parsley and the dual-purpose Hamburg parsley with its edible root make excellent edging plants for beds and borders. They also look well grown in patches.

Carrots The foliage is very delicate. Mix seeds of any types of carrot with the seeds of annual flowers or ornamental grasses and broadcast them together. Thin both to at least 2·5cm (1in) apart. The carrots benefit from the light shade provided by the annuals and, for some reason, carrot fly seems to be deterred. One year my best carrots were grown among ornamental grasses, dried for winter decorations.

Other low growing vegetables suitable for flower beds include iceplant *Mesembryanthemum crystallinum* – a sprawling, Mediterranean plant with sparkling 'dewdrops' on its fleshy leaves and stems; winter purslane *Montia/Claytonia perfoliata* which has pretty heart-shaped leaves; curly endive; and the edible oriental chrysanthemum *Chrysanthemum coronarium*.

Herbs and edible flowers

Although outside the scope of this book, common culinary herbs – especially their more colourful and variegated forms – along with the many edible flowers, are perfectly suited to being grown in flower beds. Chervil, chives, basil (in warm areas), green and bronze fennel, and the countless varieties of thyme, marjoram and sage are some of the most appropriate. *Calendula* (pot marigold), all pansies and violas, *Bellis perennis* daisies, borage, anchusa, roses, pelargoniums and nasturtiums are just a few of the flowers which have a culinary use, mainly in adding colour and flavour to salads. The buds, flowers and leaves of nasturtiums can all be used in salads, while the young green seedheads can be pickled as a caper substitute.

Chinese, or garlic chives, a longstanding favourite of mine, is ideally suited to flower beds or the decorative vegetable garden. Its leaves have a pleasant, mild garlic flavour and its dainty white flowers add a lovely touch to a salad. As it can also be used as a vegetable, its cultivation is described briefly on p.176.

DIFFICULT SITUATIONS
Shade
Most vegetables like to grow in an open sunny site, so shady corners of the garden, where the soil is often dry and poor, tend to be wasted. Ideally such corners should be used for the compost heap. If that is impractical, build up their fertility and try the following vegetables, which will tolerate light shade and will grow reasonably provided they are well watered: spinach, land cress, sorrel, chrysanthemum greens, Hamburg parsley, Jerusalem artichokes, red chicories and spring sown endive. Lettuces, radishes, cucumbers and peas will tolerate light shade in mid-summer. Of the herbs, mints, parsley, chives, angelica, lovage and chervil are all tolerate shade.

Early in the year most of these vegetables and herbs can be grown under fruit trees or ornamental trees such as flowering cherries, before the tree foliage becomes dense. The exceptions are the tall growers: Jerusalem artichokes, lovage and angelica.

Dry situations
New Zealand spinach, pickling onions, and winter and summer purslane all perform reasonably in fairly dry positions. 'Sugar Loaf' chicory, though it needs moisture in the early stages, has a deep root and will tolerate dry situations better than many leafy vegetables. Once established, Swiss chard also withstands dry conditions remarkably well. The same is true of mature rhubarb plants, again, presumably, on account of the deep root system they develop.

Moist situations
Celeriac, celery, red chicory, corn salad, land cress, fennel and leeks tolerate fairly damp positions, provided they are not waterlogged.

SPACE SAVING TECHNIQUES
Cut-and-come-again (CCA) systems
I am convinced that the secret to getting the maximum out of a very small garden is to use cut-and-come-again (CCA) techniques. These depend on the fact that many leafy vegetables will regrow after they are first cut, giving two, three or occasionally more cuts from one sowing. CCA can be done at the seedling stage or with semi-mature or mature plants for a successive supply of leaves.

Seedling CCA

To appreciate what CCA seedlings are about, think back to the mustard and cress we all grew on moist blotting paper during schooldays. The seedlings were cut when about 2·5cm (1in) high and that was it. But if the same cress had been sown in soil, it could grow eventually up to 30cm (12in) high before running to seed. If cut repeatedly when 4-5cm (1½-2in) high, it might resprout two or three more times over a few weeks – producing a surprising amount of 'greenery' in all, in a very short time, in a very small space.

Patch of CCA seedlings; those on the *right* are ready for cutting, those on the *left* for resprouting

Apart from being a highly productive system, at this young stage seedlings are at their most nutritious and tastiest, making them ideal for use raw in salads. Salad rocket, 'cutting' lettuces, cress, salad rape, endive and 'Sugar Loaf' chicory are a few of many which make delicious salad seedlings. After a cut or so, a number of others can be left to grow a little larger for cutting between 10-15cm (4-6in) high. They will be a little coarser but will still be excellent as cooked greens. Spinach, leaf radish, Texsel greens and many of the oriental greens such as pak choi are suitable for this treatment. For a complete list of vegetables which can be grown as CCA seedlings, see p.121.

CCA seedlings can be sown in single drills, broadcast, or in wide drills – the latter probably being the most efficient method (see p.45). As the seedlings will not be thinned, aim to space seeds about 2-2·5cm (¾-1in) apart. Never sow on weedy ground, as weeding among the seedlings will be almost impossible.

To maintain a high level of productivity over several weeks, or in some cases months, the soil must be reasonably fertile and the seedlings must always have plenty of water. On the whole, mid-summer sowings in hot weather should be avoided, as seedlings are liable to bolt prematurely. They are best value outside from spring to early summer, and late summer to early autumn; and under cover in very early spring and autumn. Cut the seedlings with scissors or a sharp knife about 2cm (¾in) above soil level, and always above any tiny seed leaves that are visible.

Mature CCA

There are several vegetables for which, if the mature head is cut just above the lowest leaves, rather than pulling the plant up by its roots, a secondary head or heads will develop later in the season. This is the case with spring and summer cabbage. To encourage the process, make a shallow cut in the top of the remaining stalk. Sometimes as many as four or five medium-sized cabbages will develop from the edges of the cuts. Similarly, if an over-wintered lettuce is cut in spring, leaving a few basal leaves, a slightly misshapen second head will develop four or five weeks later. This is far quicker than starting from seed, which can take three months. (In my experience the secondary heads of summer lettuce do tend to be bitter – but it is worth experimenting.) For these systems to work, the soil must be fertile and the plants must have plenty of water.

More frequently when a head is cut, the stump will throw out a second crop of loose leaves rather than forming another head. It can continue to do this over many months. Chinese cabbage and pak choi, 'Sugar Loaf' and red chicory, broad and curly-leaved endives are typical of plants that act this way. Apart from the inherent productivity, the reduced head size seems to give the plants increased tolerance of low temperatures and more resistance to frost. Whereas a heavy frost would kill a large, leafy plant of 'Sugar Loaf' chicory, a relatively bare stump will survive winter, ready to produce further leafy growth the following spring.

This characteristic can be utilized by planting these crops in poly-tunnels in late summer or early autumn. They may well remain productive throughout winter (especially in mild winters) but, even if they merely remain stagnant in winter, they will survive, ready to burst into growth as soon as temperatures rise on warm spring days – a time of year when vegetables are most scarce.

Semi-mature CCA

Many other vegetables respond well to CCA treatment at a semi-mature stage. Either cut across the plant before the head has formed or, in the case of naturally loose-headed plants, simply harvest single leaves, leaving the plant to resprout. Besides those mentioned in the previous paragraph, the following respond well to this CCA treatment: 'Salad Bowl' lettuces, curly kales, salad rocket, chrysanthemum greens, Texsel greens, all the purslanes, and most of the oriental greens including oriental mustards, mizuna and mibuna.

Cutting the head of a 'Salad Bowl' lettuce. The cut stump almost immediately starts producing more leaves

Successional sowing

Small gardens cannot afford to waste space on gluts, unless the surplus can be frozen or dried for winter. Rather than sowing large quantities of any one vegetable, it is more economic to maintain a succession by sowing little and often. The following are some of the vegetables which can be sown at fortnightly or three weekly intervals for much of the year and can be eaten young to give quick returns: carrots, radishes, lettuces, turnips, kohl rabi, beetroots, spinach, spring onions and Texsel greens. For cutting as CCA seedlings grow the following: cress, mustard, salad rape, salad rocket, 'Sugar Loaf' chicory, curly endive, Texsel greens, pak choi and 'oriental saladini' (see pp.202-3).

Catch cropping

'Catch cropping' means getting a quick crop off a piece of ground which is intended for a main, later crop. The later crop could be a tender summer crop such as tomatoes or sweet corn, or the winter brassicas, which are not planted out until early to mid-summer. Any of the vegetables suggested for successional sowing could be used as a catch crop. (For Quick Maturing Vegetables, see p.119.)

Gap filling

Sometimes gaps appear in the winter greens, usually due to pest damage. There may still be time to transplant one of the faster growing brassicas, such as calabrese or one of the oriental greens, into the gap. The practice of sowing a few spares in modules comes in very handy for this purpose. Alternatively sow a few seeds of kohl rabi, autumn lettuce, spinach beet or spring cabbage (in this last case it is best to wait until late summer in warmer areas).

Patches

The practice of growing vegetables at equidistant spacing, rather than in the traditional widely spaced rows with a lot of wasted space between them, is highly recommended for small gardens. It lends itself to the 'narrow bed' system (see p.38). When converting spacing recommendations for widely spaced rows into equidistant spacing, add the in-row and inter-row spacings together and halve them. For example, instead of planting 20cm (8in) apart in rows 30cm (12in) apart, plant 25cm (10in) apart each way. As a general rule, the leaves of adjacent plants should be just touching, or slightly overlapping, when mature. Some can stand being more crowded than others.

Almost all vegetables, apart from the climbers, can be grown in patches at equidistant spacing – even peas. These will need a little support but the perimeter of the pea patch can be ringed with wire netting to keep them in place. As explained earlier (see Weeds p.76), another benefit from equidistant spacing is that the vegetable leaves eventually blanket the soil, suppressing the weeds. The exceptions are narrow-leaved vegetables

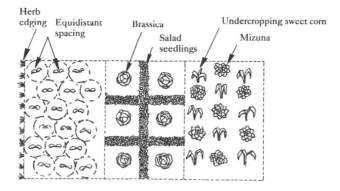

Space Saving Systems

like onions and leeks. They can certainly be grown in patches but it is necessary to mulch well between the plants to keep down weeds.

Garden operations such as thinning, weeding and picking can be a little more awkward in patches. So limit any patch to a size you can reach comfortably from the edges.

Double cropping in rows

A slow and fast maturing crop can often be grown in the same row. The fast growing crop is out of the way before the slowest one requires the space. They are normally sown together but can sometimes be planted together (having module-raised plants helps here), and there are occasions when one is sown between established plants of the other.

Root vegetables are among the slowest developers: parsnips, Hamburg parsley (and parsley herb, which also has a substantial root), salsify and scorzonera, can all be 'station sown' (see p.44) with faster maturing seed sown between the stations. Ideal quick growers include radish (often used as a marker for slow germinating seeds), small lettuces such as 'Tom Thumb' which are only about 10cm (4in) diameter, small types of pak choi and almost any of the salad seedlings mentioned earlier.

Radishes and small drills of seedling crops can also be sown between brassicas, or widely spaced leeks or celeriac, when they are first planted. Salad seedlings can also be sown above potatoes when they are planted: they will normally be ready for cutting before the potatoes have come through the ground to disrupt them!

Mixed patches

Another variation on the double cropping theme is to mix and sow together various seeds that will develop at different rates. The companions have to be chosen carefully so that the more vigorous will not smother the weaker. Sow fairly thinly for this reason. The following are some successful collaborations but there is plenty of scope for experimenting with your own combinations. They make good use of limited space.

~ Carrots plus annual flowers (see p.102).

~ Carrots plus pak choi. (This is a Chinese practice. It worked well for me when I mixed two teaspoons of carrot seed with one of pak choi.)

~ Leeks and spring onions. Sow together in spring. Start to pull the spring onions in mid-summer, leaving the leeks to mature.

~ Radishes and/or spring onions with, say, carrots, turnips, parsnips or parsley. Sow very thinly and pull the carrots and onions carefully when large enough to use, so the remaining crop is not disturbed.

~ A mixture of salad seeds, as in the classic continental salad mixtures known as 'misticanza', 'mesclun' and, more recently, 'saladini'. They may contain over a dozen different species, emerging and developing in turn over a twelve-month period.

~ 'Oriental saladini'. A mixture of six oriental brassicas (see pp.202-3 for further details).

Intercropping between rows

The principle is the same. A quick-growing crop is sown or planted alongside, or between, the rows of a slower maturing one.

The quick crop is cleared before the space is required for the later stages of the main crop. This system, of course, is less applicable where equidistant spacing has been adopted but, nevertheless, can be very useful in small gardens. Take care not to overdo it. Remember both crops must have enough space, light and moisture to develop, and there must be room to cultivate and pick.

For these reasons it may be advisable to sow or plant the main crop rows a little farther apart than usual. To sustain both crops, the soil must be fertile and more watering than normal may be required. Water generously when the plants are being established, and mulch to preserve moisture in the soil and minimize the need to weed. Generally speaking, avoid intercropping sprawling and spreading vegetables, such as potatoes and globe artichokes.

Here are some suggestions for intercropping:

Between rows of shallots – carrots, small lettuces like 'Little Gem' and 'Tom Thumb', small cultivars of pak choi, chrysanthemum greens, corn salad, turnips for pulling young and spring onions.

Between and alongside dwarf cultivars of French, runner and broad beans – any of the above, as well as standard lettuces, winter brassicas (which will continue to develop when the beans are finished), spinach and chard.

Between rows of winter brassicas – carrots, small summer cabbages, lettuces, corn salad, winter purslane, land cress, red chicory (which seems to enjoy being overshadowed), small cultivars of pak choi, chrysanthemum greens, kohl rabi and beetroot (see 'intercropping brassicas' opposite).

Between bands of peas – preferably the dwarf types – winter brassicas, turnips, carrots, spinach and chard, lettuces, beetroot and oriental mustards.

In addition, there are other useful variations on intercropping:
~ Rows or bands of radishes, lettuces, corn salad and salad seedlings can be intercropped successfully with almost any vegetable throughout the growing season.
~ Space between rows can almost always be used as a seedbed, for raising ,say, brassicas, leeks or lettuces that will later be transplanted.
~ Parallel rows of two or three crops can be grown close to one another in order to get maximum diversity of vegetables in a small area of the garden, for example lettuce and beetroot or carrots and onions.

Here is an example of successional intercropping which proved successful in my vegetable garden:
1 Mid-spring, two bands of peas sown 75cm (2½ft) apart.
2 Mid- to late spring, a row of Brussels sprouts planted between the two bands of peas spaced 60cm (2ft) apart.
3 At the same time, radishes sown between half the sprouts and land cress between the other half.

Intercropping brassicas
Mature brassicas such as purple sprouting broccoli and Brussels sprouts require a lot of space so, even when grown at equidistant spacing, there is plenty of room around them when they are first planted. I have found this best utilized by weaving 5-10cm (2-4in) wide bands of CCA seedlings or radishes among them. (If you use, say, red 'Salad Bowl' lettuce, you can make some lovely colourful patterns.) It is often possible to take a couple of cuts of the seedlings before all the space is needed by the developing brassicas. Resist any temptation to leave them longer, or the brassicas will suffer from the competition.

Undercropping: the long, the short and the tall
Vegetables of different, but complementary, growth habits can be grown together. Sweet corn is one of the most accommodating. Although tall, its leaves are flimsy and create little shade, allowing a wide range of plants to grow beneath. Marrows, cucumbers, even pumpkins can trail between them. Dwarf French beans, salad crops such as lettuce and red chicory, orientals such as mizuna and chrysanthemum greens, all thrive planted among sweet corn. The hardier ones will continue cropping long after the corn has been harvested. Sweet corn itself can be planted successfully between rows of brassicas.

Where climbing beans are grown up criss-crossed poles or canes, there is often room in the early stages, before the maturing bean plants block out the light, to grow a catch crop down the centre. Vegetables that tolerate shade are suitable, and I've had reasonable results with 'Sugar Loaf' and red chicory, land cress, spinach and corn salad.

In the past I've planted trailing marrows between rows of early potatoes. They are vigorous enough to hold their own until the potatoes are lifted.

Dwarf cultivars

Space can often be saved by growing dwarf cultivars, which can be planted closer than standard cultivars. Dwarf peas, for example, will take less space than tall peas, require less netting or fewer pea sticks, and are easier to intercrop. The drawback is that most dwarf cultivars are lower yielding, though this is an area in which a lot of plant breeding is taking place so improvements are likely. Some excellent dwarf cultivars of tomatoes, peppers and aubergines have been introduced recently. They are mentioned in Chapter 9, but watch in the seed catalogues for new introductions. Bush forms of trailing plants, most notably the bush courgettes, marrows and cucumbers take up less space than the trailing forms, so are excellent in small gardens. Remember, however, that trailing plants can be trained around in circles to make them much more compact. Peg down the leading shoots with sticks or bent pieces of wire. You may have to do it daily to keep up with them as shoots can grow very quickly indeed.

Reducing paths

In very small gardens paths can take up valued space. Replace them with occasional stepping stones, to give a solid base from which to work in wet weather. I once saw some very neat concrete stepping stones, which had been moulded in seedtrays.

Raised beds and mounds

Raised beds (see p.39), increase the area that can be cultivated. So do raised mounds, an idea originating in China but taken up in Germany (see Further Reading, *Forest Gardening*, p.249).

CONTAINER GARDENING

Precious space in small gardens is often taken up with paths and paved areas around the house, garage and shed. These, along with windowsills, patios, balconies, flat roofs and low walls can be made productive by growing vegetables in pots, boxes or other containers. Useful supplementary crops can be grown this way, although it is hard work and fairly expensive to do on a large scale.

Types of container

Almost anything can be used: traditional clay and plastic flower pots, wooden, plastic, polystyrene or concrete window boxes, plain wooden boxes, barrels – whole or cut in half – coal scuttles, picturesque old wheelbarrows, cattle troughs, rubber tyres piled on top of each other, or cut in half and suspended from a balcony, 9 litre (2 gal) plastic cans with the tops cut off . . . the scope is endless.

Makeshift boxes can be made by boarding up an area with a piece of wood, using the existing foundation as a base. A shallow border against a wall can be 'built up' with soil if a wooden or brick edge is made. I have seen a beautiful crop of runner beans growing on a concrete path against a house. The box they were in was made from two wooden drawers with the bottoms knocked out, standing on top of each other. Around them a loose wall had been built of rounded bricks, washed up on a nearby beach. They kept the boxes in place and added a decorative touch.

A board can be fitted across a windowsill and plants grown in pots behind it, to give the impression of a window box

Whatever the container, it must be strong enough to withstand the weight of damp soil, the effects of watering and the weight of a crop. If it is to stand on a balcony or flat roof, it must be fairly lightweight.

Size

For vegetable growing the bigger the container the better. A minimum soil depth and width would be 15cm (6in); a depth and width of 20-25cm (8-10in) would enable a much wider range of vegetables to be grown.

Drainage

Good drainage is essential in any type of container. Wooden boxes can have holes drilled in the bottom, or burnt with a poker. They should be at least 1cm (½in) in diameter and seem to be more efficient if sloped at an angle. Containers should be raised off the ground on bricks, blocks or small pieces of wood to allow water to drain away (but see also Preventing moisture loss p.112). Or drill drainage holes in the side of the container, 2.5cm (1in) or so above the base. Window boxes on sloping sills can be made level with wooden wedges.

Containers on balconies or window sills should have some sort of drip tray underneath to prevent water dripping down walls or even on to people below.

To ensure good drainage fill the bottom layer of a box or pot with at least 1cm (½in) of broken crocks, pieces of brick, small stones, charcoal, or coarse ashes. If, for any reason, there are no drainage holes, increase this to 2·5cm (1in). This layer can be covered with 2.5cm (1in) or so of dry leaves, or pieces of moss or turf (face downwards) before putting in the soil – again to help drainage.

The soil

The soil should be as 'open' and porous as possible. Either use good quality potting compost (see pp.55-6), or good garden soil, lightened with handfuls of all or any of the following: well-rotted garden, potting or worm compost; any peat substitutes; vermiculite; coarse sand. Using fresh manure is inadvisable.

If you are within easy reach of seaweed, an equal mixture, by volume, of seaweed, straw and garden compost makes an excellent growing medium.

Put it in the containers two or three months before planting and leave it to rot down well.

Maintaining fertility

With the frequent watering that is unavoidable with container growing, the soil tends to become stale, compacted and impoverished, so is best renewed annually. During the growing season, an occasional top dressing of 2·5cm (1in) or so of well-rotted manure or compost is beneficial, particularly for hungry vegetables like tomatoes, oriental greens or any of the beans. Always make sure that you top dress to cover any roots that appear on the surface of the soil.

Most vegetables will also require regular feeding: seaweed or liquid comfrey are suitable. Always dilute strong feeds before use.

Contrary to popular belief, earthworms are beneficial in pots, boxes, or any other containers, but they will only remain if the soil is kept moist.

Preventing moisture loss

In dry weather and in areas of low rainfall, the biggest problem with all containers is preventing them from drying out. If they are against a wall they may be effectively shielded from rain. A lot of moisture is lost through evaporation from the sides and the soil surface. To offset this, containers can be lined with heavy-duty polythene with drainage holes punched in the bottom, and the surface covered with as much as 5cm (2in) of fine stones or gravel chippings. Stand pots in dishes or trays of gravel, and water through the gravel. A useful tip I was once given was to put narrow strips of cloth in the bottom of the pot, coming out through the drainage hole into the gravel. They act as wicks, making it easier for moisture to be taken up. A pot can be placed inside a larger container, filling the gap between them with soil or pebbles to minimize evaporation. Be prepared to water plants in all containers twice a day in really hot weather.

Protection

Plants in windows boxes in exposed positions, for example on high buildings or balconies, can be torn to shreds by wind. Rig up small windshields across the ends with hessian, netting, matting or even twigs; this will break the force of the wind.

To give extra protection in early spring or late autumn, window boxes or long containers can be fitted with small low cloches, or a polythene film cover anchored over small wire hoops. Wire framed bell-shaped cloches can be made for round containers. Inverted glass jars can be used in spring as mini cloches for seed sowing.

Purpose-built containers

From time to time, new containers for vegetable growing in a confined space are designed. The 'vertical polytube' is one example. Invented and patented by Maurice Howgill in the 1970s, it consisted of polythene tubes approximately 1m (1yd) high and 30cm (12in) diameter, supported on a frame. The tubes were filled with compost. There were holes or 'pockets' all around the tube at every level and in these almost any vegetable could be grown, simply planted through the hole into the compost. From roughly the equivalent of 1sq m (1sq yd) of ground space Mr. Howgill produced 100 leeks, 100 sticks of celery, 10 Brussels sprout stalks, 9kg (10lb) of tomatoes and so on. As far as I know the vertical polytube was never marketed, but it illustrates the principle that growing plants vertically is a means of increasing the productivity of small gardens.

Compost-filled 'growing-bags'

The various types of growing-bags, made from heavy-duty plastic filled with prepared compost, have been a feature of home gardening in the last twenty years. The average size is about 1m (3½ft) long, 30cm (12in) wide and 15cm (6in) high. Vegetables are planted directly into the bags. The original bags used chemical fertilizers and peat-based compost, but organic growing-bags are now available.

Growing bags are most useful where space is limited and soil scarce.

Compost-filled growing-bag. Plant through the small holes to minimize evaporation

Growing-bag pannier and sloping support for climbers

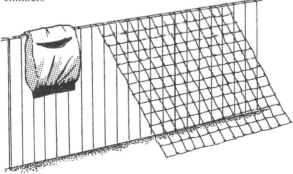

They are simply laid on a path, balcony, patio, roof or low wall, or against a wall or fence, in which case tomatoes and climbing plants like cucumbers and beans can be trained upwards. Some types are supplied with supporting frames for this purpose. Growing-bags are also widely used in greenhouses where the soil has become diseased. In this instance the base of the bags must not be perforated for drainage or they will become infected with the soil diseases. Otherwise they can be perforated.

The compost can generally be used twice, first for a demanding crop like tomatoes, then for a less demanding follow-on crop, like salad seedlings. Plants, of course, have to be fed regularly, following the supplier's instructions where appropriate. The spent compost can eventually be used as a garden mulch or for seed raising.

You can make your own growing-bags from strong plastic sacks. Ideally open them initially down the middle rather than across the ends, and fill them with good-quality compost or soil mixture as recommended for standard containers.

All growing-bags dry out rapidly. For this reason, wherever possible, plant through small holes cut in the upper surface, rather than slitting the whole bag open as is often recommended (see diagram p.113). Water carefully, so they neither dry out nor become waterlogged.

Growing-bag panniers (see diagram p.113)
An ingenious 'growing-bag pannier', which can be hung over a fence, branch or any horizontal rail, was devised by tomato grower Terry Marshall. Hold an unopened growing bag in the middle, shake the contents so they divide evenly between the two ends, and place it straddled over the supporting fence or rail. Make a slit on each side about 7.5cm (3in) below the centre, and plant in the slits. The cascading 'Tumbler' tomatoes look most effective grown this way.

Vegetables for containers
It is surprising what a range of vegetables can be grown in the relatively confined conditions of pots and boxes, provided there is plenty of humus in the soil mixture and they are kept well watered. Taking the cost of the containers and compost into account, it is fairly hard to justify on economic grounds, but who can put a price on the satisfaction of cutting a lettuce or picking a few spinach leaves from a window box?

Tomatoes are the most popular container crop, but peppers, cucumbers, chard, beet, dwarf beans (and in suitable situations climbing beans), salad plants like lettuces, endives, spring onions, corn salad, land cress, purslane, radishes and the many CCA seedlings, are all among the possibilities. Courgettes can be grown in large boxes or troughs; early potatoes in boxes, bags or tubs; carrots in deep boxes. Where ground is short, a deep box standing on a path will serve as a good seedbed for brassicas, leeks or lettuce.

Colour can always be added by planting a mixture of vegetables and flowers – such as trailing lobelia and hanging petunias – or edible flowers like pansies and nasturtiums. Use either dwarf cultivars of nasturtiums, or the less rampant trailing forms such as the variegated 'Alaska'.

Many perennial herbs such as thyme, marjoram, and savory tolerate dry conditions and do well in containers, while fine specimens of rosemary and bay can be grown in large tubs. On the whole, culinary herbs such as parsley, chives and chervil, which require plenty of moisture do not do as well in containers.

VEGETABLES IN THE HOUSE
Windowsill gardening
Indoor windowsills are not the easiest place to grow vegetables. Most likely to succeed are cut-and-come-again salad seedlings. Spring sowings are probably the best bet and a useful means of filling the famous 'vegetable gap'. Sow in seedtrays filled with good potting compost: it should be possible to get at least one, often two cuttings. Give the boxes a half turn daily so seedlings are not too drawn towards the light. (See Mustard, Salad Rape, Garden Cress p.195.)

Seed sprouting
Seed sprouting is the technique of germinating seeds in some kind of domestic container and eating the first, small green shoots, normally within a few days of starting them off. No soil is required. An enormous range of vegetable seeds can be sprouted, making a valuable contribution to the diet, particularly in winter. To germinate successfully, the seeds must have warmth and moisture – but, as the combination of warmth and moisture encourages the growth of moulds, the germinating seeds must be cooled down regularly to keep them fresh and healthy. This is normally done by rinsing them frequently with cold water. Always purchase seeds that are intended for sprouting. Many seeds today are treated with chemicals, and it would be dangerous to sprout and eat them. See also Bean sprouts, p.140. For further reading see *Salads for Small Gardens* p.248.

Forcing indoors
Several vegetables that are forced into growth in the dark can be grown indoors. Mushrooms, for example, can be grown successfully in commercially prepared kits. Results can be variable.

'Witloof' chicory is very easily potted up and forced in a cupboard indoors, as are some cultivars of red chicory. (For cultivation see p.163.) Another candidate for forcing is rhubarb. Lift a mature plant in late autumn, expose it to frost for a few days, then plant it in a large container, such as an old-fashioned ash can, in ordinary garden soil. To keep out the light, cover it with an inverted ash can of the same size, or with black polythene firmly secured over a wire frame. Keep it at a temperature between 7-16°C (45-61°F) and in mid- or late winter it will produce beautiful fresh pink stalks.

CHAPTER EIGHT

Planning

Even in a small garden it is worth drawing up a plan each year with the aim of making the best use of all available space. It should be a very flexible plan and treated as such. All sorts of unforeseen factors – early seasons, late seasons, bumper crops or failures – will drive a coach and horses through a rigid plan. But an unplanned, haphazard approach will inevitably result in a waste of precious resources.

The main questions to sort out are *what* to grow, and *where*. In both cases there are a number of factors to consider.

WHAT TO GROW

Family preferences In many gardens vegetables are wasted because it turns out that the family does not like them. Whoever grows the vegetables either has to convert the family to wider tastes (the best course), or alter his or her plans.

Setting priorities It is rarely possible to keep an average family in vegetables from a small garden, so decide on your priorities and plan accordingly. The main purpose could be one of the following, or a combination of two or more of them:

'Feed the Family Plan', where the aim is to produce as much food as possible all year round.

'Gourmet Plan', where the emphasis is on vegetable delicacies, or especially well flavoured cultivars of ordinary vegetables, which are difficult or very·expensive to obtain through normal channels.

Suggested plans for a basic 'Feed the Family' garden and a 'Gourmet' garden are given on pp.124-7.

The plans are drawn up for gardens of 15 x 7m (50 x 22ft) and 10 x 5m (30 x 16½ft) respectively, as these are typical of the space devoted to vegetables in many gardens.

The plans are for fairly intensive use of the plot but, as mentioned earlier, it is more than likely that factors beyond one's control will mean that some changes have to be made during the course of the season. The point to remember in making an 'Feed the Family' plan is that most of the vegetables we grow mature naturally between early summer and mid-winter. Between late winter and late spring there is the 'Hungry Gap', which is only filled with careful planning. Remember also that the use of protected cover will increase the output and extend the season enormously.

In making a plan for an 'Economic' garden, root vegetables (except possibly young carrots), onions, Brussels sprouts and cabbages would probably be cut out, as they are almost always cheap, and one would concentrate instead on salad crops, peas and beans, maybe sweet peppers and aubergines, which tend to be expensive. The 'Value for Space Rating' (see

Planning Information Table pp.128–9), helps to evaluate which vegetables give the best returns for the space they occupy.

Getting a balance Other factors being equal, aim for a balance between the main types of vegetables – brassicas (cabbage family), legumes (peas and beans), roots, salads and onions.

Climatic factors Don't waste space on vegetables which don't do well in your area. In cold parts of the country, outdoor tomatoes and cucumbers, sweet corn, and even runner beans are risky. Grow extra salads, roots or greens instead.

Freezer If you have a freezer modify your plan accordingly. It may be worth growing more peas, beans or calabrese – all of which freeze well – to give greater variety during the winter months. (For other vegetables recommended for freezing, see p.120.)

Storage space Most root vegetables can be stored outside, either in the ground or in clamps. But onions and garlic should be under cover by early autumn, so only grow them if you have space to store or hang them.

WHERE TO GROW WHAT

Unless you plan to convert the whole garden into a decorative vegetable garden or 'potager', it is probably best to set aside part of the garden for vegetables. If you feel it necessary the vegetable patch can be separated off with a low ornamental hedge, a trellis covered with decorative climbers, or with a flower border.

The traditional textbook vegetable garden might have been an open, square or rectangular plot, but in practice a small modern garden often consists of odd shaped pieces of ground, parts of which are heavily shaded. Planning has to take all its idiosyncracies into account. Don't be afraid to make small odd-shaped beds – round, triangular or semi-circular – if that will enable you to utilise available space more fully. The following are some other factors to consider when making a basic planting plan:

Permanent or semi-permanent features Greenhouses, frames, compost heaps, water butts are the most common. Choose a place for these first when you start making your plan. Greenhouses and frames should be placed to catch the maximum sun, preferably facing south. (For siting polytunnels, see Polytunnel Orientation p.97.) Compost heaps can successfully utilize awkward or heavily-shaded areas. A rain butt which catches water off a roof near the vegetable garden is a boon in dry summers.

Direction Where there is a choice, arrange rows to run north and south, so they do not shade each other. This applies particularly to tall growing vegetables like runner beans. In steeply sloping gardens it is easiest to cultivate across a slope, which also helps to prevent soil erosion.

Walls Use walls, fences, trellises or fruit cages for climbing vegetables (see Vertical Growing p.98). Fences are preferable to hedges in vegetables gardens as they do not compete with plants for moisture or soil nutrients and nor do they harbour pests.

Wet, shady, dry areas Select suitable vegetables for these positions. (For suggestions see p.121.)

Flower beds, paths, paved areas Decide what vegetables can be grown in flower beds, or in pots or boxes on paths, patios and so on.

Access Have herbs as near the house as you can, or along edges. Where possible, put winter crops where they can be reached easily without treading over too much ground.

Intercropping, catch cropping, intersowing, 'cut-and-come again' Use these techniques as much as possible (see Chapter 7).

GROUPING FOR CONVENIENCE

Within the limitations of rotation (see below), it is useful to group together vegetables that are likely to (a) mature at roughly the same time, or (b) be sown or planted at roughly the same time.

In the first case this makes it easier to clear a patch of ground from time to time, dig it over thoroughly and possibly sow a green manure; the second case enables a cleared piece of ground to be put immediately to maximum use. Typical groupings could be:

~ Spring sown salad crops such as spring onions, early carrots, lettuce and CCA salad seedlings.

~ Crops which over-winter in the ground, such as leeks, celeriac, kohl rabi, Brussels sprouts and kales.

~ Half hardy summer vegetables, such as courgettes, tomatoes, sweet corn and peppers.

Rotation

Closely related vegetables should never be grown continuously in the same piece of ground. The main reason for this is that the soil pests and diseases which attack that group of vegetables can build up to serious levels if their 'host' plants are always present. If, however, there is a break of a couple of years with completely different kinds of vegetables (from the botanic point of view) being grown, their numbers decline – or fail to build up in the first place. The traditional practice of rotating the main groups of vegetables around a garden on a three to four-year cycle is very sound, though in reality a cycle of six or seven years is needed to rid a garden of pests like eelworm and diseases like clubroot.

Operating effective rotation systems in small gardens is notoriously difficult. There just isn't enough space to manoeuvre; and to make matters worse, both soil pests and diseases are to some extent mobile themselves.

However, it makes sense to *try* and rotate, and certainly to avoid planting vegetables from the same group in the same area in consecutive seasons. Organizing the garden as a series of narrow and/or small beds certainly gives more flexibility than is found in the traditional layout of three or four large plots.

The most important groups for rotation purposes are the brassicas (cabbage family), legumes (peas and beans), onion family, and potato family (which includes tomatoes). See p.124 for examples of those vegetables which come in each group.

A very simple, three-year cycle rotation plan is given below.

	Plot A	Plot B	Plot C
Year 1	Legumes	Brassicas	Roots
Year 2	Brassicas	Roots	Legumes
Year 3	Roots	Legumes	Brassicas

In this rotation the nitrogen fixing root nodules of the legumes enrich the soil for the nitrogen-hungry brassicas which follow, ensuring that the plants thrive. The main root vegetables would be potatoes and carrots, but not turnips, swedes or radishes, which are brassicas. Members of the onion family, salad plants and miscellaneous vegetables like celery are fitted in to the plots wherever possible. See the plans on pp.124–7 for ideas for planting sequences.

In very small gardens, where only the most limited rotation is feasible, growing a diversity of crops, intercropping, and growing some flowers among vegetables should all help prevent serious pest and disease problems arising.

The Planning Information Table on pp.128-9 summarizes key facts on some of the vegetables suitable for small gardens – including weeks to maturity, the spread of the plant, its 'value for space' rating, the season of use, whether the season can be extended with cloches, and whether the vegetables can be stored successfully. The lists which follow are intended as supplementary aids to planning and give at-a-glance information, indicating vegetables suitable for specific purposes and specific situations, as well as indicating rotation groups.

QUICK MATURING VEGETABLES
(Note: Many of these vegetables are also suitable for intercropping, see Space Saving p.108.)

Under 8 weeks
Chrysanthemum greens; land cress; pak choi; radish; salad seedlings (see p.121); Texsel greens; turnip greens.

Under 12 weeks
Asparagus pea; beans (dwarf French); beetroot (young); calabrese; carrots (early); cabbage, (Chinese); cauliflower (mini); choy sum; Chinese broccoli; corn salad; courgettes; cucumber; endive; fennel; iceplant; komatsuna; kohl rabi; land cress; lettuce (summer); mibuna and mizuna greens; mustards (oriental); onions (spring); peas (spring sown); purslane (summer and winter); radish (oriental); spinach (all types).

CROPS IN GROUND ALL WINTER

(Very cold areas excepted; the plants recommended below will normally survive temperatures of -5°C (23°F)).

Brassicas Broccoli, purple sprouting; Brussels sprouts; cabbage, spring, savoy & hardy winter types; kale; komatsuna; mizuna greens; pak choi, rosette; oriental mustards eg Green-in-the-Snow and purple; radish, winter; Texsel greens; turnips (for tops).

Roots Artichoke, Jerusalem; parsley, Hamburg; kohl rabi; parsnips; salsify; scorzonera.

Others Beans, broad (autumn sown); celeriac; celery (leaf types); chicory, 'grumolo' and red; chrysanthemum greens; land cress; leeks; onions (Welsh, hardy autumn sown bulb onions and oriental bunching onions); peas (autumn sown); purslane, winter; spinach; Swiss chard.

Salads see Winter Salad Crops.

WINTER & EARLY SPRING SALAD CROPS

(Note: Success outdoors depends upon the severity of the winter, choosing the hardiest and most suitable cultivars and, in some cases, on crops being grown as CCA rather than mature crops (see Space Saving Techniques p.103) and the use of protection such as cloches or films wherever possible; * = the more vulnerable plants.)

Celeriac; chicory, 'grumolo', red and *'Sugar Loaf'; celery, leaf; oriental mustards, hardy cvs above; *mibuna and mizuna greens; corn salad; *endive; land cress; *lettuce; onion, Welsh and hardy oriental bunching; *purslane (winter); radish (hardy oriental types); salad rape; salad rocket; Senposai; Texsel greens.

Indoors: sprouted seeds and salad seedlings (see p.115 and p.121).

FRESH VEGETABLES FOR THE 'HUNGRY GAP'

(Roughly late winter to early spring in the UK)

(Note: Not all cultivars of the vegetables below are suitable for this period; * = better results if cloched at some stage.)

Artichoke, Jerusalem; broccoli, purple sprouting; Brussels sprouts; cabbage, savoy and spring;*carrots (early); celeriac; chard, Swiss; chicory: grumolo,*red, *'Sugar Loaf', 'Witloof' (forced); *chrysanthemum greens; corn salad;*endive; kale; komatsuna; land cress; leeks; *lettuce; mizuna greens; mustard: ordinary, 'Green in Snow', purple; parsley, Hamburg; parsnip; radish: leaf, ordinary and Chinese over-wintered types; salad rocket; salad seedlings (see opposite); Senposai; *sorrel; *spinach; Swiss chard; Texsel greens; turnips; turnip tops.

VEGETABLES SUITABLE FOR FREEZING

(Note: Some, for example aubergine and tomatoes, are probably best frozen in mixtures such as 'ratatouille'. Some cultivars are more suited to freezing than others; consult current seed catalogues.)

Beans (all types); beetroot (young); broccoli, purple sprouting; Brussels sprouts; cabbage, spring and savoy; calabrese; carrots (young); cauliflower; kale, curly; peas; peppers; spinach; Texsel greens; tomatoes.

SALAD SEEDLINGS
(Suitable for cut-and-come-again)
All (except for summer purslane), are moderately hardy; those marked * normally require some protection for cropping in the late winter to late spring period.
Cabbage, Chinese; chicory,'Sugar Loaf'; corn salad; cress; kale, curly; mustard: ordinary, red, Green-in-the-Snow; komatsuna; *lettuce, 'Salad Bowl' and 'cutting' types; *mibuna; mizuna; *orache; oriental saladini; *pak choi (all types); *purslane, winter; radish, leaf cvs; salad rape; salad rocket; Senposai; spinach; Texsel greens; turnip tops.

VEGETABLES FOR PARTICULAR SITUATIONS
Lightly shaded
(Note: There must be reasonable moisture.)
Artichoke, Jerusalem; chicories: grumolo, red and 'Sugar Loaf'; Chinese cabbage (mid-summer); Chinese chives; chrysanthemum greens; cress; endive (spring sown); fennel; Good King Henry; parsley, Hamburg; kohl rabi; land cress; lettuce (mid-summer); mizuna greens; pak choi (mid-summer); peas (mid-summer); purslane, winter; radish (mid-summer); salad rocket; sorrel; spinach.

Fairly dry
(There must be enough moisture to get the plants established so you will need to water seedlings regularly; and some further watering will probably be necessary for the plants to continue to do well.)
Chard, Swiss; chicory,'Sugar Loaf'; Good King Henry; iceplant; onions, pickling; purslane, summer and winter; spinach, New Zealand.

Fairly damp
Celeriac; celery; chicory, red; corn salad; fennel; land cress; leeks; lettuce, stem; mizuna greens; sorrel.

Climbers
Beans, runner and French; cucumbers; marrows; peas (to some extent).

VEGETABLES SUITABLE FOR FLOWER BEDS
Artichoke, globe; asparagus; asparagus pea; beans, French and runner (both climbing and dwarf forms); beetroot (red-leaved forms); cabbage: Chinese, red and ornamental; carrots; chicory, red; choy sum; chrysanthemum greens; fennel; iceplant; kale, curly and ornamental; lettuce (especially 'Salad Bowl' types); mibuna; mizuna; mustard, red; onions, oriental bunching; orache; parsley, Hamburg; salsify; scorzonera; sweet corn; Swiss chard; tomatoes (dwarf cvs); purslane, summer and winter.

SEEDS FOR SPROUTING

(Note: The following are the most commonly sprouted, but there are many other possibilities, see *Salads for Small Gardens*, Further Reading p.248.)

Alfalfa (lucerne); beans, azuki, mung and soya; brassicas (all can be sprouted); fenugreek; lentils; radish.

MAIN GROUPS FOR ROTATION PURPOSES

Brassicas (all types of the following): Broccoli; Brussels sprouts; cabbage; calabrese; cauliflower; kale; kohl rabi; oriental greens eg Chinese broccoli, Chinese cabbage, choy sum, komatsuna, mustards, pak choi, Senposai; radish; salad mustard; salad rape; Texsel greens; turnips; swedes.

Legumes Beans (broad, French and runner); peas; leguminous green manures, for example field beans, tares, clover (see pp.32-3).

Onion family Garlic; leeks; onions; shallots.

Potato family Aubergine; peppers; potatoes; tomatoes.

STRIP CROPPING PLAN

Season	Strip 1	Strip 2
October to April	**Cloched** Winter hardy *lettuce* or *'Sugar Loaf'* chicory planted under cloches down each side. Oct; narrow band of *peas* sown down middle, Nov	
end April to May	*Peas* and *lettuce* unprotected	**Cloched** *Dwarf French beans* sown under cloches late April
June to October	**Cloched** *Peppers* or *bush tomatoes* planted under cloches early June	*Dwarf French beans* unprotected
October to April		**Cloched** Mixture of oriental greens such as *rosette pak choi*, *mizuna*, *mibuna*, *leaf radish* and *hardy salad seedlings*

Note: See Season and Month Conversion Chart p.245.

GOURMET PLAN (see pp.126-7)

The plan is for a 5 x 10m (15 x 30ft) garden. It is divided into four narrow beds, A-D, each 1m (3½ft) wide and 7m (22ft) long, separated by 30cm (1ft) wide paths. At each end of the garden 1.5m (5ft) strips are used for perennial and climbing vegetables, compost bins and frames.

The plan is for a year round supply of vegetables chosen for their flavour and quality when homegrown.

Cropping within the beds is planned in 1m (3½ft) strips, numbered i-vii. For rotation, abbreviations see Feed the Family Plan.

FEED THE FAMILY PLAN (see diagram pp.124-5)

General notes

All measures are approximate. Months are given for UK conditions (please see p.245 for Season and Months Conversion Chart).

The plan is designed to grow as much food as possible for a family over a year.

The plan is for a rectangular garden 15m (50ft) long x 9m (28ft) wide. Assume it is a north/south direction.

The main bed area is divided into four 9m (28ft) long x 1m (3½ft) wide beds, A-D, divided by 30cm (1ft) wide paths.

Each bed is planted mainly with one rotation group, for example legumes or brassicas, but crops from other groups are included. The brassica bed sometimes breaks rules by following a quick-maturing brassica with another brassica. (Gardening rules are made to be broken, especially in small gardens!)

The beds are rotated over a four-year cycle. Bed A in year 1 becomes bed B in year 2 and so on.

Cropping within the beds is planned in 1m (3½ft) strips, numbered i-ix. Some sowing, planting and clearing dates are included to make the plan easier to follow.

A garden this size could include:

~5m (15ft) x 2m (6ft) wide polytunnel at the south end. Suggested cropping: summer – tomatoes, peppers, aubergines. Winter to spring – oriental greens, winter salads, calabrese, spinach or Swiss chard.

~5.5m (17ft) x 2m (6ft) area for compost heaps and frame at the north end.

~1m (3½ft) border along eastern edge for permanent beds of asparagus and rhubarb, and a three-year bed of perennial broccoli.

~0.6m (2ft) border along western edge, to include a seedbed, some globe artichoke plants interplanted with herbs and perennial vegetables such as sorrel and Good King Henry. (Alternate the globe artichokes and perennial broccoli on a three-year basis.)

~Jerusalem artichokes planted as a hedge along one of the boundaries.

Key for plans (see pp.124-9)

CCA = cut-and-come-again; o/w = over-wintering; sdlgs = seedlings

FEED THE FAMILY PLAN

	BED A (Legumes)	BED B (Brassicas)	BED C (Potatoes/Roots)	BED D (Onion family)
i	1 BROAD BEANS (o/w), cleared late spring/early summer 2 KALE planted early/mid-summer, in ground all winter	1 EARLY TURNIPS intercropped with CCA SENPOSAI sow early spring/clear early summer 2 LETTUCE plant early summer cleared early autumn	1 MINI CAULIFLOWER sow early spring cleared early summer 2 MAINCROP CARROTS sow early summer, lift autumn	1 SHALLOTS plant late winter/early spring lift mid-/late summer 2 CCA SDLGS ROCKET/RADISHES for rest of summer 3 BROAD BEANS sow mid-/late autumn to overwinter
ii	1 BROAD BEANS sow early/mid-spring, cleared late summer 2 SPRING CABBAGE planted late summer to o/w	1 SPRING CABBAGE (o/w), cleared early summer 2 'WITLOOF' CHICORY sow/plant early summer, lift early winter	1 EARLY POTATOES plant early/mid-spring lift early summer 2 RED CHICORY sow/plant early summer	1 STORAGE ONIONS plant late winter/early spring, lift late summer 2 BROAD LEAVED ENDIVE plant late summer, use until winter
iii	1 SHELLING PEAS sow early/mid-spring, cleared mid-summer 2 LETTUCE sow/plant mid-summer	One half: RED CABBAGE plant early spring, lift by autumn One half: SUMMER CABBAGE plant mid-/late spring, clear late summer/early autumn	1 SECOND EARLY POTATOES plant mid-spring, lift mid-summer 2 FLORENCE FENNEL plant mid-summer	1 EARLY LEEKS plant late spring; use autumn/early winter 2 HARD WINTER SALADS eg LAND CRESS, CORN SALAD, WINTER PURSLANE interplanted between leeks in late summer
iv	1 SPRING ONIONS (o/w), use in spring 2 DWARF FRENCH BEANS sow/plant late spring/early summer (can plant among spring onions)	One half: MUSTARD, CRESS, SALAD RAPE CCA sow sdlgs early spring 2 CALABRESE OR ROMANESCO CAULI sow/plant late spring, clear early autumn One half: SWEDES sow/plant late spring	1 SECOND EARLY POTATOES plant mid-spring, lift mid-summer 2 SUGAR LOAF CHICORY sow/plant mid-/late summer. interplant with hardy 'TREVISO' CHICORY	1 'LEAF LETTUCE' patch Early successional sowings mid- to late spring for crops late spring to late summer 2 SPRING ONIONS sow late summer to overwinter, intercrop with WINTER SALADS as iii

v	1 MANGETOUT PEAS sow mic-/late spring, crop until early autumn. 2 SWISS CHARD sow/plant late summer between peas, (crops until following spring)	1 SALAD ROCKET & RADISHES sow early/mid-spring. 2 CHINESE CABBAGE plant early summer, intersow with ORIENTAL CCA SDLGS cropping until winter	One half: 1 SELF-BLANCHING CELERY Plant late spring, clear early autumn. 2 TURNIP TOPS sow mid-autumn. One half: HAMBURG PARSLEY sow mid-spring, in ground all winter	1 CCA SPINACH sow mid-/late spring. 2 SWEET CORN plant late spring/early summer intercrop early summer with SUMMER SALADS eg ICEPLANT, SUMMER PURSLANE
vi	1 PEAS (as v). 2 CCA SDLGS SPINACH sow late summer between PEAS or MOOLI RADISHES; sown/planted late summer between peas	1 CHRYSANTHEMUM GREENS & LETTUCE sow/plant early spring, clear mid-summer. 2 ORIENTAL GREENS eg BROCCOLI, CHOY SUM, PAK CHOI, MIZUNA plant mid-summer	1 EARLY CARROTS sow early spring, cleared early summer. 2 STORAGE BEETROOT sow/plant early summer, lift autumn	1 CCA CURLY ENDIVE sow mid-/late spring, intercrop with radishes. 2 COURGETTES AND MARROWS plant early summer, crop until frost
vii	1 FRENCH BEANS, RUNNER BEANS, OUTDOOR CUMCUMBERS growing on supports on vii, viii & ix. sow/plant late spring/early summer, crop until frost	1 CCA KALE SDLGS sow early spring. 2 HARDY ORIENTAL GREENS plant late summer/early autumn eg MUSTARDS, KOMATSUNA, MIZUNA	PARSNIPS sow/plant early spring in ground all winter	1 LETTUCE plant early spring, clear early summer. 2 HARDY LEEKS plant early summer, use until mid-/late spring following year
viii	1 o/w ONIONS us ng early summer. 2 See vii	1 TEXSEL GREENS CCA SDLGS sow early spring. 2 MID & LATE BRUSSELS SPROUTS plant late spring /early summer, interplant late summer, see iii D	1 CCA SDLG LETTUCE sow early spring. 2 CELERIAC plant late spring/early summer, in ground all winter	1 SWISS CHARD plant early spring, clear early/mid-autumn. 2 BULB ONIONS plant early/mid-autumn to overwinter
ix	See vii	One half: 1 CCA SPINACH SDLGS sow early spring. 2 SAVOY CABBAGE plant early/mid-summer. One half: 1 kohl rabi sow/plant early/mid-spring, ready early summer. 2 PURPLE SPROUTING BROCCOLI plant early/mid-summer for spring	1 EARLY BEETROOT sow/plant early spring, cleared late spring. 2 OUTDOOR TOMATOES plant early summer, cleared by frost. 3 GARLIC plant mid-/late autumn	1 GARLIC o/w, lifted mid-/late summer. 2 'LEAF LETTUCE' patch successional sowings in late summer to crop early autumn to winter

GOURMET PLAN

	BED A (Legumes)	BED B (Potato Family/Roots)	BED C (Onion Family)	BED D (Brassicas)
	(Top end) PERENNIAL BROCCOLI, 3 or 4 plants alternating with globe artichokes every 3 years	(Top end) GLOBE ARTICHOKES, 2 plants alternating with perennial broccoli every 3 years	(Top end) ASPARAGUS BED	(Top end) RHUBARB
i	1 BROAD BEANS (o/w), cleared late spring/early summer 2 CALABRESE planted early/mid- summer, finished autumn	1 EARLY POTATOES successional planting in i, ii & iii from early spring, lifting starts early summer 2 FLORENCE FENNEL plant early/mid-summer	SWISS CHARD sow/plant early/mid-spring, cut until winter	1 RED CABBAGE plant early spring, cleared autumn 2 CCA SALAD SDLGS eg CRESS, SALAD RAPE, ROCKET, MUSTARD sow autumn
ii	1 BROAD BEANS as i 2 LETTUCE or CCA SALAD SDLGS or mooli radish sow/plant early summer	1 EARLY POTATOES lifted mid-summer 2 RED CHICORY plant mid-summer	1 EARLY LEEKS plant late spring, used autumn/early winter + CORN SALAD, LAND CRESS interplanted between leeks in summer for winter use	1 TEXSEL GREENS sow spring or CCA salad sdlgs 2 BRUSSELS SPROUTS plant early summer; interplant with RED CHICORY
iii	1 DWARF MANGETOUT PEAS sow late winter/early spring, finished mid-summer 2 CHINESE CABBAGE plant mid-/late summer, lasts until frost	1 EARLY POTATOES lifted mid-/late summer 2 ENDIVE & SUGAR LOAF CHICORY plant mid-/late summer for use autumn	1 SALAD ROCKET, RADISHES sown spring 2 LATE LEEKS plant early summer, use until mid-/late spring next year	1 EARLY LETTUCE plant early spring 2 PURPLE SPROUTING BROCCOLI plant early/mid-summer, interplant with SUGAR LOAF CHICORY

iv	1 TALL PEAS several bands, sow mid-/late spring, finished early autumn 2 SWISS CHARD or SPINACH inter-sow or plant between peas late summer	CELERIAC plant late spring/early summer, in ground until following spring	1 SPRING ONIONS sown late winter/early spring, cleared by early summer, and/or CCA SDLGS 2 SWEET CORN plant early summer, interplant with MIZUNA & MIBUNA GREENS	1 MINI-CAULIFLOWER sow/plant early spring, cleared early/mid-summer 2 LETTUCE or BROAD LEAVED ENDIVE sow/plant early/mid-summer
v	as iv CHARD and SPINACH crop until following spring	PARSNIPS sow or plant early/mid-spring, in ground until spring	1 SHALLOTS plant late winter/early spring, lifted early autumn + WINTER PURSLANE intersow or plant in summer	1 SUMMER ENDIVE plant early/mid-spring, cleared early/mid-summer 2 ORIENTAL BRASSICAS interplant hardy & less hardy (see vi)
vi	DWARF FRENCH BEANS for use fresh, sow/plant late spring/early summer, crop until early autumn	1 EARLY CARROTS sow/plant late winter/early spring, lifted early summer 2 BUSH TOMATOES plant early summer, cleared by frost 3 GARLIC plant mid-/late autumn	1 GARLIC planted previous autumn; lifted late summer 2 HARDY RED CHICORY &/or CHRYSANTHEMUM GREENS plant late summer	1 ORIENTAL SALADINI, CCA SALAD sdlgs sow spring 2 ORIENTAL BRASSICAS (see v) eg hardy: MUSTARDS, MIZUNA, KOMATSUNA, SENPOSAI; less hardy: PAK CHOI, CHOI SUM, FLOWERING RAPE, CABBAGE
vii	DWARF FRENCH BEANS for use dried, sow/plant late spring/early summer, lifted early autumn	1 EARLY BEETROOT sow/plant early/mid-spring, lifted by early summer 2 PEPPERS/AUBERGINES plant early summer 3 ONIONS (o/w) plant mid-/late autumn	1 o/w ONIONS planted previous autumn, lifted early/mid-summer 2 COURGETTES plant early/mid-summer 3 SPRING CABBAGE plant early autumn	1 SPRING CABBAGE planted previous early autumn, cleared early summer 2 'WITLOOF CHICORY' sow/plant early summer, interplant with SUMMER PURSLANE
	(Lower end) COMPOST HEAP/FRAME	(Lower end) COMPOST HEAP/FRAME	(Lower end) Climbing MARROWS & CUCUMBERS, alternating with climbing beans every year	(Lower end) Climbing FRENCH and RUNNER BEANS, alternating with climbing beans every year

PLANNING INFORMATION – ANNUAL VEGETABLES

	Jan	*Feb*	*Mar*	*Apr*	*May*	*Jun*	*Jul*	*Aug*	*Sep*	*Oct*	*Nov*	*Dec*	*Av. weeks to maturity*	*Av. spread*	VSR
Artichoke, Jerusalem	■	■	■							■	■	■	28-32	30-60(12-24)	*
Asparagus pea						■	■	■					10-12	45(18)	*
Aubergine								■	■	■			21	60(24)	*
^Bean, broad (autumn sown)					■	■	■						28-32	38-45(15-18)	*
^Bean, broad (spring sown)						■	■	■					12-16	38-45(15-18)	**
^Bean, French						■	■	■	■	■			8-10	30(12)	***
^Bean, runner							■	■	■	■			8-10	30(12)	***
Bean sprouts	■	■	■	■	■	■	■	■	■	■	■	■	few days	–	****
^Beetroot, salad					■	■	■	■	■	■			9-11	15(6)	***
Beetroot, storage	•	•	•	•				■	■	■	•	•	12	24-30(10-12)	**
^Broccoli, Chinese						■	■	■	■	■	■		7-9	25-37(10-15)	**
Broccoli, sprouting		■	■	■	■								38	68(27)	*
Brussels sprouts	■	■	■	■					■	■	■	■	30-36	60(24)	*
^Cabbage, Chinese~								■	■	■	■		9	23-30(9-12)	**
^Cabbage, spring				■	■	■	■	■					32-36	30(12)	*
Cabbage, summer							■	■	■	■			14-20	30-37(12-15)	*
Cabbage, winter	•	•	•	•					•	•	•	•	20-25	45(18)	*
^Calabrese		■	■	■		■	■	■	■	■			12-16	28(11)	**
^Carrots, early					■	■	■	■	■				10-12	5-8(2-3)	***
Carrots, main	•	•	•	•			■	■	■	•	•	•	20-24	20-25(8-10)	***
Cauliflower, mini						■	■	■	■	■			12-16	15-20(6-8)	*
Celeriac	■	■	■	■	■				■	■	■	■	28	45(18)	*
Celery, self-blanching					■	■	■	■	■	■			14	30(12)	**
^Chicory, red	■	■	■	■			■	■	■	■	■	■	12-14	15-25(6-10)	**
^Chicory, Sugar Loaf~	■	■	■					■	■	■	■		12-14	15-30(6-12)	***
Chicory, Witloof	■	■	■	■							■	■	24	25(10)	*
^Choy sum, hybrid rape								■	■	■	■		7	15-30(6-12)	**
^Chrysanthemum greens~				■	■	■	■	■	■	■	■	■	4-8	15-20(6-8)	***
^Corn salad~	■	■	■	■	■	■	■	■	■	■	■	■	12	10(4)	***
^Cucumber, outdoor							■	■	■	■			12	45(18)	*
^Endive~	■	■	■	■		■	■	■	■	■	■	■	13-16	30(12)	**
^Fennel							■	■	■	■			8-12	30(12)	*
Garlic	•	•	•	•	•	•	■	■	•	•	•	•	36-42	16(6)	*

CCA = cut-and-come-again seedlings
VSR = Value for Space Rating see p.131
^ = season can be extended and/or quality improved with cloches
▪ ▪ ■ ▪ ▪ = fresh and stored

Vegetable			
(row above cut off)		10-13(4-6)	**
^Kohl rabi	5-10	23-30(9-12)	**
^Komatsuna~	8	30-45(12-18)	**
Land cress	8	25(10)	*
Leek	25-28	15(6)	*
^Lettuce, summer (outdoor)~	12	23-30(9-12)	**
^Marrows/courgettes	8-12	60(24)	***
^Mibuna greens~	10	25-30(10-12)	**
^Mizuna greens~	7-10 days	25-30(10-12)	***
Mustard, rape, cress	12	dense	****
^Mustard, 'Amsoi' type	25	30-37(12-15)	**
^Onions, maincrop (sets)	8+	10-15(4-6)	**
^Onions, spring	3-4	2.5(1)	*
^Oriental saladini	6-7	2.5(1-2)	****
^Pak choi (medium size)~	28	25(10)	***
Parsnip	13-14	25(10)	*
^Peas (maincrop)	21-24	variable	**
^Peppers, sweet	16	38-45(15-18)	*
^Potatoes, early	8	38-45(5-18)	*
^Purslane, summer~	10-12	15(6)	****
Purslane, winter~	20-30 days	15(6)	***
Radish, ordinary	10-12	10-13(4-5)	**
Radish, winter	20-30 days	25-30(10-12)	**
^Salad rocket (CCA)	24-28	dense	****
Salsify/Scorzonera	4-5	23-30(9-12)	*
^Senposai~	20-24	5-8(2-3)	***
Shallots	4-6	23(9)	**
^Spinach beet(CCA)	6-8	5-8(1-3)	**
^Spinach, NZ	16-17	18(45)	*
Swiss chard	18-20	38-50(15-20)	*
Swede	17-20	15-18(38-45)	**
^Sweet corn	3-4	60(24)	*
^Texsel greens (CCA)	17-20	5-8(2-3)	***
^Tomatoes (outdoors)~	6-12	50(20)	**
Turnip (for roots)~	6-12	25-30(10-12)	***

~ = Can also grow as CCA seedlings; assume the CCA VSR rating would be one or two stars higher
▬▬▬ = months available fresh
••• = months available stored

CHAPTER NINE

Annual Vegetables

The second part of this book describes the cultivation of more than 70 vegetables. It is largely in note form, which I hope will make it easier for you to find information quickly. I'm thinking of those particular occasions when you are in the middle of sowing or planting and need to pop into the house to check up on spacing or whatever! Sometimes alternative ways of growing things are suggested: try them out, and stick with whatever seems to suit your situation best. There are no absolute rights and wrongs in gardening, and it is quite possible that you will devise systems that are better, in your circumstances, than anything I have suggested. The aim here is to grow vegetables for ordinary household consumption, not to produce enormous, prize winning specimens for exhibition purposes. That's another story altogether.

Most of the vegetables covered are well known, but a number of less common ones are included because they are particularly suited to small gardens and easy to grow. Corn salad, summer and winter purslane, salad rocket, and the relative newcomer Texsel greens all come in this category. This revised edition also gives more space to the oriental greens, which seem to me to be so productive and to give excellent returns in small spaces. I hope you will feel tempted to try some of these more unusual vegetables. They deserve to be more popular.

Vegetables which occupy a good deal of space are only included where they have particular merits. For example, the tall Jerusalem artichokes can be effective screens or windbreaks, and will grow in rough pieces of ground. Purple sprouting broccoli takes up quite a lot of room but a few plants can produce an extraordinary number of 'helpings' at a time of year when vegetables are scarce and expensive.

All sowing dates, planting dates, and so on in these notes should be treated as approximations. There is a world of difference, gardening wise, between cold and warm areas (and between one year and the next), and it is impossible to be dogmatic. I have tried to indicate the variations as far as possible. Be guided by practice in your own locality.

Similarly planting distances, pot sizes and other measurements need not be followed slavishly. They are there as guidelines. Where the term manure is used, this includes garden compost and other substitutes for animal manure.

Choosing between the many cultivars (cvs) of any vegetable is no easy task for the amateur. Those suggested here have been selected primarily because they are reliable, but also bearing small gardens in mind, because of qualities like early or quick maturity, high yields, dwarf habit and good flavour – although that is always a subjective judgement. As far as possible, they are cultivars I have grown successfully myself. But there are certainly others that are equally good, and new improved cultivars are continually being introduced. Unfortunately, with the combined pressures of modern marketing and European Union (EU) legislation, cultivars (including some good ones), seem to come and go at an increasing rate. I apologise now for the fact that some I recommend may no longer be available in a few years' time. If only one knew which!

It is still quite difficult to buy seeds of the more unusual vegetables, or the more unusual cultivars, from general outlets such as stores and garden centres. They can, however, be obtained from the specialist mail order seed companies, who advertise in the gardening press. They offer an excellent service. When buying seed, the smallest quantity sold is normally sufficient for small gardens – except where required for cut-and-come-again purposes, which requires more seed.

VALUE FOR SPACE RATING (VSR)

The yields one can expect from any particular vegetable vary tremendously according to the district one is in, the season, the fertility of the soil and the cultivar – to name but a few of the variables. So instead of quoting yields which in practice are often meaningless, I have worked out a 'value for space rating' for each vegetable. This is an attempt to evaluate which vegetables will give the best returns in a small garden. In calculating the index the two principal factors considered were:
~ The length of time the vegetable is in the soil before it can be eaten or harvested.
~ The number of helpings yielded per m^2 (yd^2) by the vegetables under average conditions.

So quick growing, high yielding vegetables scored most points and slower growing, lower yielding vegetables fewer points.

ADDITIONAL POINTS WERE ALSO GIVEN FOR:
~ vegetables which are available fresh, in winter and in times of scarcity.
~ vegetables which are of far better quality when homegrown.
~ vegetables which are normally difficult or very expensive to buy.

GUIDE TO THE VSR
*	worth growing in most cases provided they can be intercropped at some stage
**	worth growing provided you have space
***	very good value
****	best returns of all

PP = 'Potager potential'. Indicates plants with decorative qualities, such as good colouring or pretty foliage. (See pp.6-7 and 99-102.)

Throughout this chapter refer to earlier chapters for special sowing techniques, such as sowing in modules; methods of pest and disease control; and crop protection. The term 'under cover' indicates cold greenhouses or polytunnels, cloches or frames.

AMERICAN CRESS see Land cress

ARTICHOKE, JERUSALEM *Helianthus tuberosus*
Very hardy plant with nutritious, sweet-flavoured and non-starchy tubers. Can grow 3m (10ft) tall.

Site and Soil
Open or shady site; tolerates most soils unless waterlogged or very acid.
Useful for breaking in rough ground because of fibrous root system.
In small gardens use as screen, windbreak or in odd corners.

Cultivation
Plant tubers from late winter to mid-spring, 10-15cm (4-6in) deep, 30cm (12in) apart (or wider spacing for heavier crops), rows 90cm (3ft) apart.
Egg-sized tubers best; can cut very large tubers so each section has three 'eyes' or buds.
Earth up stems when 30cm (12in) high for extra support.
Pinch out tops (and flower buds) in mid-summer to keep height down to 1·5-2m (5-6ft).
Irrigate in very dry weather in order to prevent tubers becoming excessively knobbly.
In late summer it is advisable to stake plants individually, or support groups with strong canes and twine: yields are lower if plants damaged by autumn gales.
Cut stems down to a few centimetres when leaves wither in late autumn.
Leave tubers in soil during winter months, lifting as required, or clamp them like swedes.
Remove *all* tubers eventually; any tiny tubers remaining in the soil will spread uncontrollably, usually leading to deterioration in quality.
Save good tubers for replanting.

Harvesting
Tubers ready when foliage is withered, from mid-winter to early autumn.
Can be boiled, steamed, fried or baked. Make excellent soup.
Very knobbly so scrub, then boil or steam in skins (20-25 minutes) and peel just before serving.

Cultivars
Fuseau – long, narrow, smooth tubers.
Dwarf Sunray – dwarfer in some circumstances.
In practice named cvs are not widely available.

VSR*

ASPARAGUS PEA *Tetragonolobus purpurens*
Ornamental, somewhat bushy plant, with delicate foliage, pretty scarlet-brown flowers, odd-shaped triangular, winged, pods. Grows up to 45cm (18in) tall with up to 60cm (2ft) spread.

Site and Soil
Open sunny site, rich light soil. Effective lining paths.

Cultivation
Sow outside *in situ* mid to late spring.
Thin so that plants 30–38cm (12-15in) apart.
Or start indoors in boxes mid-spring, transplanting outside when about 7.5cm (3in) high.
Give some support with twigs; protect against pigeons.

Harvesting
Ready early to late summer.
Must pick pods when no longer than 2.5cm (1in) long or they become tough. Not a heavy bearer, but keep picking to encourage further growth. Boil pods in minimum water; serve with sauce or butter. Or eat cooked and cold in salads. Interesting and rather unusual flavour.

VSR*

AUBERGINE *Solanum melongena*
Bushy tropical plant, normally 60-75cm (24-30in) high with spread of up to 60cm (2ft). Standard fruits glossy, long, deep purple, but white, pink and green fruits, of varying shapes and sizes occur.

Site and Soil
Will only mature outdoors in warm parts of UK; needs warm sheltered site unless grown under cover. Requires fertile soil, and slightly higher temperatures than peppers to do well.

Cultivation
For plant raising, planting, pests and diseases, see peppers. Remove growing point when plants 40cm (16in) high to encourage bushiness. Advisable to allow only one fruit per stem and a total of four per plant unless growth exceptional. Remove surplus flowers once a fruit has set on a stem; remove new sideshoots once four fruits are developing on plant. Can feed with organic tomato fertilizer every ten days or so once fruits start to set.

Harvesting
Pick when fruits look glossy. Plants very susceptible to frost; protect if frosts imminent in late autumn.

Cultivars
Bambino – recently introduced, very compact cv with small round purple fruits (PP).
Easter Egg – original white fruited cv; more productive forms may be introduced in future; less prickly than some cvs.
Any of the F1 hybrid cvs are reasonably productive in good seasons.

VSR*

BEAN, BROAD *Vicia faba*
Very hardy bean. Most types over 90cm (3ft) high; but dwarfer, smaller podded 'fan' or dwarf types generally 30-38cm (12-15in) high. Recommended for small gardens.

Site and soil
Well-dug soil, preferably manured previous winter.

Cultivation
Sow: 1 Outdoors from mid-autumn to early winter in fairly sheltered position (in warm areas only). Plants need be no more than 2·5cm (1in) high before the onset of winter.
   2 Outdoors from late winter to mid-spring.
   3 In boxes under glass or in cold frame from early to mid-winter, planting out in early spring. Useful method for early crops in cold districts, or where over-wintered beans attacked by soil pests.
Sow 4-5cm (1½-2in) deep. Highest yields from two plants per 30cm^2 (12in^2): space plants 23-30cm (9-12in) apart each way. Sow some 'spares' to fill gaps.
Can be protected with cloches or crop covers from late autumn until early spring to ensure plants thrive.
Pull soil around stems of autumn sown beans for extra protection.
Pinch out tops when in full flower to help pods swell and prevent infestations of blackfly.
After picking put plants on compost heap; or cut off stems at ground level and dig in roots, as nodules on roots return nitrogen to the soil.

Pests and Diseases
Blackfly Young shoots often covered with masses of black aphids. Pinch out tops, or spray with liquid derris. Burn infested shoots.

Harvesting
Small immature pods can be eaten whole, boiled or sliced.
Young green tops also edible.
Beans are ready late spring to late summer, depending on sowing date.
Eat when *young and tender*. Pick frequently.
Mature beans can be dried for winter use.

Cultivars
The Sutton, Bonny Lady – dwarf.
Feligreen – semi-dwarf.
Aquadulce Claudia Express – recommended for autumn sowing.
Red Epicure – reddish beans, good flavour.

VSR **Spring sown.
      *Autumn sown.

BEANS, FRENCH (Kidney) *Phaseolus vulgaris*

Tender, climbing or dwarf, bushy annual. Many types of pod. Pod colour includes green, yellow, purple and flecked: bean seeds can be brown, beige, red, flecked, white. Standard round podded and very fine, pencil thin 'filet' types, up to 15cm (6in) long. Newer short, round podded types up to 10cm (4in) long; ideal for cooking/freezing whole. Flat podded cvs mostly longer pods and white seeded. Yellow waxpod types very succulent. In my view waxpods, 'filets', purple and flecked types best flavoured. Most modern cvs are stringless when young.

Mostly eaten in green/coloured pod stage; but semi-mature 'shelled' beans (*flageolets*) excellent in cooking. Mature shelled beans (haricots) can be dried successfully for winter use. Some cvs more suitable for some purposes than others.

Most cvs dwarf bushy plants about 45cm (18in) high with 30cm (12in) spread, but several climbing forms growing over 2.4m (8ft) high. Dwarf forms crop earlier; taller forms crop over longer period and potentially give higher yields; dwarf cvs recommended in cold areas. Both excellent value and decorative in small gardens. Purple podded cvs have beautiful deep purple flowers.

Site and Soil
Avoid exposed sites; otherwise open unshaded site.
Fertile, well-prepared, slightly acid, moisture-retentive and well-drained soil is preferable. Advisable to rotate around garden.
For climbing cultivars can trench soil beforehand (see runner beans p.137 for appropriate method).

Cultivation
Never sow or plant in cold or wet soil; beans will rot or succumb to pests and diseases. In adverse conditions better to start indoors (see p.136).
Can sow in stale seedbed (see p.67) to deter bean seed fly.
Germination of seeds is very poor at temperatures below 10°C (53°F). Warm soil beforehand with cloches if it is necessary. Note: White seeded types require slightly higher temperatures to germinate than dark seeded ones.
Sow: 1 Early spring (warm areas only)or in mid-spring under cloches for a good crop in early summer.

Give plenty of ventilation; remove cloches during day late spring, completely by early summer. Alternatively use crop covers.

2 Outdoors late spring to mid-summer

Sow 4-5cm (1½-2in) deep. For highest yields space plants 23cm (9in) apart each way.

To start indoors:

~ Put beans on moist paper towelling until they swell; discard any that fail to plump out.

~ Then sow in modules or seedtrays and plant out after hardening-off, *or* sow swollen seeds *in situ* outside.

For extra 'guarantee' can wait until tiny shoot emerges from plumped seed, then sow in modules, seedtrays, or *in situ*, handling seed very carefully to avoid damaging shoot.

In small gardens two small sowings, three weeks apart, ensure a long season and good yield.

French beans are self pollinating, so there are no setting problems as with runner beans.

Prop up plants with brushwood or small sticks to prevent them flopping over and getting muddied.

Prolong cropping of later sowings by covering plants with cloches in early autumn.

Pests and Diseases

Slugs Likely to attack young plants.

Broad bean aphid blackfly For control measures see Broad beans.

Harvesting

Ready 60-70 days after sowing.

Pick young beans regularly to get a heavy crop; otherwise beans soon become stringy and cease cropping. Edible at pod stage as long as pods can be snapped in half.

Beyond 'snap pod' stage you can continue to shell and eat young beans at green, *flageolet* stage.

To dry beans for winter: preferably leave plant unpicked until end of season so pods dry on plant. Pull up entire plant and hang in airy place to dry. When pods brittle, shell beans and store in airtight jars.

Note: Beans contain toxins which are broken down by cooking; don't eat them raw.

Cultivars

Dwarf cvs

Masterpiece Stringless, Deuil Fin Précoce – for early crops.

Nerina (filet), Tendercrop, Purple Tepee, Processor, Montano – give heavy yields.

Aramis, Delinel (filets); Kinghorn Wax (yellow waxpod); Purple Tepee, Royalty (purple-podded) – for flavour.

Chevrier Vert, Limelight – for *flageolets* and drying.
Dutch Brown, Processor, Coco de Prague – for drying.
Pros – short for freezing whole.

Climbers
Blue Lake (multi-purpose); Hunter (flat podded); Kingston Gold (yellow); Purple Podded (purple); Rob Roy (speckled).

VSR*** PP

BEAN, RUNNER *Phaseolus coccineus*
Tender, vigorous prolific bean, most types climbing – up to 3-3·6m (10-12ft); some dwarf types. Dwarf types crop earlier but lower yielding.
Used to be grown for ornamental flowers; useful for screening.
Beans long, flattish, more pronounced flavour than French beans.

Site and Soil
Likes well-cultivated, rich light soil, with plenty of organic matter; not too acid. Advisable to rotate around garden. Sheltered position best, sun or partial shade. Dwarf cvs excellent in flower beds. Must be able to root deeply – needs at least 38cm (15in) topsoil.

Cultivation
Prepare ground previous autumn if possible. Dig trench one spit deep, 38-45cm (15-18in) wide; put in layer of straw-manure, garden compost or equivalent, before replacing topsoil.
Allow ground to settle thoroughly before sowing.
Can work in general fertilizer before sowing, but normally unnecessary.
Never sow in cold or wet soil. Can start germination indoors if necessary.
(See French beans.)
Sow: 1 For main crop outside mid-spring (warm areas) and in late spring (cold areas).
2 For later crop, cloched in early autumn, sow dwarf cultivar in early summer.
Sow seeds 5-7·5cm (2-3in) deep, 15cm (6in) apart; highest yields from two plants per 30cm^2 (1ft^2).
Climbers can be grown in double rows 30-38 (12-15in) apart.
Best to erect supports before beans sown or planted.
Beans will climb horizontally, vertically or at an angle; will cling to bean sticks, canes, heavy string, wire, plastic coated wire, 10-15cm (4-6in) mesh net and so on.
Essential to erect strongly anchored supports for climbing cvs; many systems used (see diagram p.139). Wigwams and criss-crossed poles or canes are typical. Stretch taut wires between them 30cm (12in) and 2m (6ft) above ground. Attach netting or strings firmly to top and lower wires.
For end supports of double rows use 5 x 5cm (2 x 2in) timbers or piping.

Can be trained over archways, willow hoops, trellis work, up supports against walls. (See also Space Saving pp.98-100.)

If growing near a wall, make sure the roots are in fertile soil with plenty of moisture.

If growing by hedge, slope the canes towards hedge to minimize competition for moisture.

Young growths may need twisting or tying around supports initially.

Water copiously in dry weather as roots should never be allowed to dry out; mulching with well-rotted manure or compost valuable.

Water well when flower buds first showing if weather dry.

Pinch out leading shoots when top of supports reached.

Flower setting problems

Seem to be increasing, especially in dry summers; high night temperatures may be cause.

Flowers mainly pollinated by bees. Early crops may fail to set if weather cold and bees not flying.

White flowering cvs appear to set better in hot climates and where pollination difficult.

Planting in groups to provide more shelter for insects may help. Conflicting evidence that syringing flowers with water, as sometimes advocated, helps setting; however, watering the soil at the base of the plants when the buds first appear seems to encourage flowering as well as setting.

Artificial dwarfing

To convert climbing cvs into earlier flowering, dwarf cultivars 'pinch' plants ie nip out growing point when plants about 20cm (8in) high.

Secondary side shoots will now develop. Nip out their tips above the second leaf.

Pests

Slugs and black bean aphid (see French beans).

Pollen beetle May attack open flowers, but spraying inadvisable as will damage bees.

Harvesting

Ready from mid-summer till frost.

Keep picking young beans to ensure continuous cropping and reduce stringiness. Don't be put off by 'bumpy' look; can still be quite tender.

Old cvs generally develop 'stringy' pieces along pod edges which have to be peeled off; some modern cvs less stringy, but most develop strings when ageing.

Runner bean seeds can be dried for winter use (see French beans), but very long cooking required.

White seeded 'Czar' beans can be dried and used as lima or butter beans.

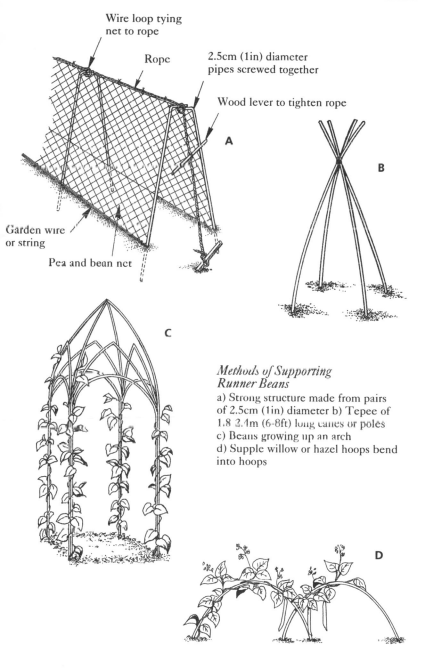

Wire loop tying net to rope

Rope

2.5cm (1in) diameter pipes screwed together

Wood lever to tighten rope

A

B

Garden wire or string

Pea and bean net

C

Methods of Supporting Runner Beans

a) Strong structure made from pairs of 2.5cm (1in) diameter b) Tepee of 1.8 2.4m (6-8ft) long canes or poles c) Beans growing up an arch d) Supple willow or hazel hoops bend into hoops

D

Cultivars
Gulliver and Pickwick (both 'stringless'), Hammonds's Dwarf – dwarf cvs; can be grown under cloches.

Climbers
Butler, Desirée, Polestar, Royal Standard – 'stringless'.
Czar, Desirée, Mergoles, White Emergo – white seeded.
Red Rum – exceptionally early.
Achievement, Enorma, Liberty, Scarlet Emperor – old but superbly productive cvs.
Painted Lady, Sunset – lovely bicoloured and pink flowers respectively.

VSR*** PP

BEANS, SPROUTS (Mung Beans) *Phaseolus aureus*
Mung beans are small (rarely over 6mm (¼in) long), round and normally green in colour.
Germinated seedlings (sprouts) widely used in Chinese cookery; probably world's most popular 'fast food'.
Highly nutritious, rich in minerals, protein and vitamins; very tasty.

Cultivation
Can grow indoors all year round, but most valuable in winter months.
Only sprout a few at a time; 56g (2oz) enough for three to four helpings; beans undergo sevenfold increase in weight and bulk during sprouting.
Key to producing good crunchy sprouts is growing under pressure; this can be achieved by weighting them down.
Ideal temperature for sprouting 20°C (68°F); avoid markedly higher or lower temperatures.
Sprouts are whiter and more attractive if sprouted in the dark, so either put them in a cupboard, or cover them with tinfoil to exclude light.
Commercial sprouters can be used; but homemade sprouters are just as successful.
Following is my own 'cheap and simple' loose sprouting method:
Make container by punching holes roughly 1cm (less than ½in) apart in base of plastic carton such as ice cream tub. This allows water to drain through easily.
~ Soak beans in water overnight so they swell; remove any discoloured or unheathly looking seeds.
~ Following morning drain beans, and refresh by putting in a strainer and rinsing them through with water until just moist.
~ Put drained beans in a layer at the bottom of the container. Layer 6mm-1cm (¼-½in) deep normally sufficient in small carton.
~ Cover with damp piece of cloth (to retain moisture) and tinfoil (if necessary to exclude light).
~ Put weight on top. Experiment with suitable weight for the container.

I use a roughly 900g (2lb) weight on a 13cm (5in) diameter carton. If the weight does not fit easily on the container, put it on a saucer on top of the beans so as to distribute the weight evenly. (It is hard to believe the sprouts can push up such a weight in order to grow: but they will!)

~ Put the sprouts in a cupboard, or somewhere dark and moderately warm to sprout.

~ Every morning and evening remove weight and coverings, hold the container under the tap, and run cold water through to rinse the sprouts. Allow water to drain through the container without dislodging the beans; they should be just moist after rinsing.

~ Re-cover with cloth, weight (and foil if used).

~ Repeat until ready for use.

Alternative method:
The following method will not produce such long or crunchy sprouts, and is a little more awkward. The sprouts root into the base
For the base use several layers of paper towelling or flannel laid in a dish.

~ Prepare the sprouts as opposite.

~ Cover the dish with foil to exclude light if necessary.

~ Rinse by carefully pouring water in and out.

~ When ready the sprouts will have to be cut from the base.

Harvesting

Depending on the temperature, sprouts will be ready within three to six days.

Ideal length for eating 5-7.5cm (2-3in) long; quality deteriorates when larger and seed leaves starting to develop.

If not eaten immediately keep in fridge in water, rinsing daily. Best to eat within a couple of days.

Green seed coats may sometimes still be attached to sprouts. No harm in eating them, but they are easily removed by tipping sprouts into a bowl of water, allowing seed coats to rise to the surface and then skimming them off with a spoon.

Sprouts can be used raw or very lightly cooked. They should not be eaten raw in very large quantities.

For further reading see *Oriental Vegetables* (see p.248).

VSR****

BEETROOT *Beta vulgaris*

Slightly hardy plants, grown primarily for roots.

Roots are round, obelisk or cylindrical in shape, and red, white or yellow in colour.

Longer rooted types slower maturing, considered well flavoured; often grown for storage.

Leaves normally reddish, quite pretty in flower bed.

Site and Soil
Open, shade-free site; prefers rich, light, sandy soil, though grows in any
fertile soil, preferably manured for previous crop; lime soil if acid.

Cultivation
On poor soil can apply tomato fertilizer (high in potash) ten days before
sowing to encourage plant growth.
Small beet ready 9 to 11 weeks after sowing; useful catch crop and good
for intercropping.
Beet 'seeds' are a cluster of seed, so several seedlings liable to germinate
close together; pelleted and 'monogerm' seed are single, therefore
require less thinning; worth getting if available.
Beetroot normally sown *in situ* as only very young seedlings can be transplanted; however responds well to being sown in modules and transplanted when 5cm (2in) high.
Germination poor at temperatures below 7°C (45°F); delay sowing or
warm soil beforehand with cloches/crop covers.
Sow about 2cm ($^3/_4$in) deep.
Early beetroot liable to 'bolt' (run to seed) if sown early in cold conditions; use bolt-resistant cultivars.
Make several sowings for continuous supply, for example:
Sow: 1 Bolt-resistant round cultivar late winter/early spring under cover
or in cloches or frames, for small beet ready in late spring/early
summer. Can remove glass mid-spring. Space seed 2·5cm (1in)
apart, rows 20cm (8in) apart; or sow in patches, spacing seeds
5cm (2in) apart either way, or in 18-23cm (7-9in) wide flat drills
as for peas. These are traditional spacings. Research has shown
that *early* beet can also be spaced much further apart to encourage very rapid growth. Recommendation is to grow in rows 23cm
(9in) apart, thinning to 8cm (3½in) apart, or spaced 15cm (6in)
apart each way.
Yields from early sowings can be doubled by growing under crop
covers; remove after four to five weeks (see p.90).
Early sowings require little thinning if roots pulled young and
eaten small.
2 Bolt-resistant round cultivar outside in early/mid-spring for small
beet in early summer, spacing as above, thin to 7·5-10cm (3-4in)
apart.
Optimum spacing for pickling beet 20 plants per 30cm^2 (1ft^2).
3 Round or long cultivars, late spring or early summer outside, for
main summer supply and winter storage.
'Station sow' 7·5cm (3in) apart, rows 20cm (8in) apart, or at
equidistant spacing 13-15cm (5-6in) apart.
Lift storage beet in early/mid-autumn, to prevent them from
becoming tough.
4 Round cultivars, outside early/mid-summer, to leave in soil for

pulling during winter in mild areas. Thin to 7·5-10cm (3-4in) apart; can protect with thick layer of bracken or straw.

Note: Round types beetroot can be multi-sown in modules (see p.56). Sow three seeds per cell; if numerous seedlings germinate, thin to four to five seedlings. Plant group of seedlings out 'as one' about 10cm (8in) apart each way.

Keep beet weed free. Water sufficiently to prevent soil drying out.

Pests

Sparrows Very attracted to small seedlings. Take protective measures to prevent damage to crops (see p.76).

Harvesting

Beets mature 60-90 days after sowing, but can more or less be eaten at any size.

Pull salad beets from late spring to mid-autumn; maincrop beets can be pulled from mid-summer onwards.

Can leave beet in soil for winter in mild areas with well-drained soil; otherwise lift for storage mid-/late autumn.

Lift carefully, twist off stems (cutting will cause bleeding), gently rub off adhering soil and put in boxes of sieved ashes, sand or soil in shed; or store in clamps outdoors.

Beetroots eaten cooked – hot or cold – and grated raw. Small beets are delicious pickled.

Young leaves and stems cooked like spinach.

Cultivars

Bikores, Boltardy, Regala – bolt-resistant, round (many excellent new cvs are being introduced).

Detroit Little Ball, Monopoly (monogerm) – round maincrop,

Cylindra, Cheltenham Green Top, Cheltenham Mono (monogerm) – long types.

Burpee's Golden – lush edible foliage; yellow roots (which don't bleed).

Albina – white roots (which don't stain).

Bull's Blood – decorative deep red foliage; fairly hardy.

Chioggia – old cv with attractive white rings in beet. Good flavour.

VSR ***young, early beet; **maincrop beet; PP

For LEAF and SPINACH BEET see Spinach

BROCCOLI, CHINESE *Brassica oleracea* var. *alboglabra*
Rather stout brassica growing about 45cm (18in) high; also known as Chinese kale, but in reality far more akin to western sprouting broccoli; grown for very succulent and well-flavoured flowering shoots which are excellent cooked.

Site and Soil
Fertile, moisture-retentive but well-drained soil. Tolerant of both fairly high temperatures and – once beyond seedling stage – slight frost.

Cultivation
Can sow from late spring to early autumn but, like most oriental greens, naturally crops best from mid- to late summer sowings, maturing in towards the end of summer and autumn.
Can plant late summer-sown crop under cover for winter pickings.
Can grow as:
– small plants harvested whole.
– large plants cropped over a longer period.
In both cases plants require plenty of moisture throughout growth to retain their succulence. Keep well watered and mulched, especially in dry weather.
1 Small plant method
    Sow broadcast or in rows about 10cm (4in) apart, thinning to about 13cm (5in) apart. Use small plants whole when the flowering shoots start developing.
2 Large plant method
    Sow *in situ*, or in modules, or in a seedbed. When seedlings about 7·5cm (3in) high transplant to permanent position, spacing plants about 30cm (12in) apart. (If sown *in situ* thin in stages, using intermediate plants at young stage.) In good soil closer spacing of plants may be equally successful.
    Pick main central head first, then sideshoots as they develop.

Pests and Diseases
See Cabbage. Pollen beetle can be a pest in some areas.

Harvesting
Mature plants ready within 10 weeks; young plants two weeks earlier. Pick shoots while still in flower bud stage. Peel stems if outer skin has become tough. Steam, use in stir fries, or cook like sprouting broccoli.

Cultivars
F_1 Green Lance.

VSR**

BROCCOLI, SPROUTING *Brassica oleracea* **Italica group**
Reasonably hardy brassica, purple forms growing up to 90cm (3ft) high, with similar spread in good soil. White forms somewhat smaller, less prolific and are less hardy, but have an excellent flavour. Grown for flowering shoots. Traditional standby in 'vegetable gap', though may not survive severe winters.

Site and Soil
See Cabbage. Avoid very exposed site. Well-drained soil advisable.

Cultivation
Sow mid- to late spring, in seedbed or in modules. Sow early maturing cvs first to get succession of vegetables. A few plants sufficient for most households.
Plant out firmly early to mid-summer, spacing 60cm (2ft) apart each way.
Advisable to earth up and stake as plants grow. (See Brussels Sprouts.)

Pests and Diseases
See Cabbage. Pigeons and similar birds are the most likely pest, especially in spring when greens are scarce.

Harvesting
Season extends from late winter to late spring; individual plants may crop over two months.
Snap off shoots before buds open, when about 10cm (4in) long.
Keep picking regularly to encourage further cropping; inadvisable to strip a plant completely at one go.

Cultivars
There are early and late strains of both purple and white forms, but sometimes there seems little difference between them.
Quality appears to have deteriorated in recent years, but improved selections are becoming available.
Red Arrow, Red Spear – recent introductions.

VSR*

BRUSSELS SPROUTS *Brassica oleracea* Gemmifera Group
Very hardy winter brassica, 45cm-1m (18in-3½ft) high.

Site and Soil
See Cabbage. Soil must be fertile but not freshly manured.

Cultivation
Firm ground and long growing season keys to success.
Sow: 1 Under cover late winter/early spring; thin to 7·5cm (3in) apart; plant out mid-/late spring. Excellent method.
2 In seedbed in open early/mid-spring; thin to 7·5cm (3in) apart; plant out late spring (ideally) or early summer.
3 If space available sow two or three seeds *in situ* early/mid-spring; remove superfluous seedlings.
Note: Brussels sprouts that have been raised in modules show a tendency to 'lodge' or keel over, possibly due to forming a compact root at the

expense of a deeper anchoring tap root. The problem seems to be overcome by planting module raised plants very deeply.

Sow early manuring cvs first, followed by later maturing cvs.

Planting

See Cabbage (general cultivation); can be planted directly into ground vacated by peas, beans, or any other early crops without having to dig over first.

Plant dwarf types 60-75cm (2-2½ft) apart, tall types 90cm (3ft) apart.

To save space interplant between other crops, provided plenty of light.

Draw soil around stems month after planting to increase stability.

Keep weed free.

Stake tall sprouts (and dwarfs in exposed areas) during summer to preventing 'rocking'; two ties often necessary.

If not growing well in mid-summer top dress with general fertilizer.

Remove yellowing leaves to improve air circulation and prevent sprouts from rotting.

'Stopping' sprouts: practice of removing top-most sprout in mid-summer to encourage sprouts to mature at same time, rather than in succession. Useful where sprouts required for freezing.

Only 'stop' early maturing cvs; 'stop' them when lowest sprouts are roughly 1cm (½in) in size.

Pests and Diseases

See Cabbage. *Mealy aphids* are a particular problem with Brussels sprouts as they get right inside the sprout.

Harvesting

Ready for harvesting from early autumn to early/mid-spring; most crop for a period of two to three months. Pick the lowest sprouts first; eat sprout tops, which are delicious, last; some weigh up to nearly 2kg (4lb)! Pull out the stumps when finished as aphids have a tendency to over-winter in them.

Cultivars

F_1 hybrids are far more productive than the open pollinated cvs. Recent trials have indicated that the following cvs are especially suitable for organic gardeners:

F_1 Oliver – very early.

F_1 Richard – early mid-season.

F_1 Lunet – late mid-season.

F_1 Stephen – late.

The old cvs 'Noisette' and 'Rubine' (red sprouts) are low yielding but exceptionally well flavoured.

VSR*

CABBAGE *Brassica oleracea* Capitata Group

The most widely grown brassica of all, cabbage ideally suited to a cool maritime climate. Most types of cabbage form dense heads, but loose-headed cvs and immature spring cabbage can be used as 'spring greens', which are excellent for cooking. Cabbages divided into broad groups according to main season of maturity; in practice considerable overlap between groups. With appropriate choice of cvs, can be cut fresh from garden all year round. Generally used fresh, but 'Dutch Winter White' type and some red cabbages can be stored for winter.

Site and Soil
Open, unshaded site; rich, moisture-retentive soil. Acid soils should be limed to reduce risk of clubroot.
Rotate over minimum three-year cycle to avoid build up of clubroot and brassica cyst eelworm.
Has high nitrogen requirement; excellent crop to follow nitrogen fixing green manure.
Needs to be planted in firm soil, and will not grow so well in freshly manured or freshly dug ground.

General cultivation – all types
Sowing options:
1 Sow in seedtrays, prick out, transplant to permanent position at three to four leaf stage.
2 Sow in modules. Plant out as above.
3 Sow in seedbed. Thin to required spacing.
4 Sow *in situ.* Thin to required spacing. Mainly used for spring cabbage, mini-cabbage and cut-and-come-again greens.

Planting
Only plant sturdy, straight-stemmed plants.
Must be planted in firm ground. Can normally just rake dug-over ground before planting. If necessary dig ground several weeks ahead of planting and leave the soil to settle. For summer plantings sufficient to clear previous crop, rake soil and plant without forking over soil.
In very light soil plant in shallow furrows, 10cm (4in) deep; earth up soil around stem to fill in furrow as plant grows. This also helps secondary roots to develop, which may overcome initial cabbage root fly attacks. (See p.74 for preventive measures for cabbage root fly.)
Plant with lower leaves just above soil level.
Size of cabbage can be controlled by spacing: the wider the spacing, the larger the head. Cabbage grows well at equidistant spacing.

General care
Keep plants weed free; remove dead and rotting leaves.
Cabbage growth poor if checked through lack of water.

In dry weather can water at rate of 22 litre/sq m (4gal/sq yd) per week; most critical period for watering is 10-20 days before crops mature. One heavy watering at this point very beneficial.

Harvesting
Cabbages normally pulled up when required. Some cvs bolt soon after maturing; others stand in good condition for weeks or months.

Intensive systems
Double cropping: with spring and early summer cabbages can get two crops from each plant. Instead of uprooting plant when harvesting cut head across stalk, leaving a couple of basal leaves attached to stalk. Make a shallow cross in the cut surface of the stalk to encourage development of new growths. Several months later you will find as many as four or five secondary heads may develop.

Ground must be fertile and plants well-watered for this to succeed. Give organic feed to boost growth when new growths start to grow.

Mini-cabbage: tiny cabbages with no wasted outer leaves. In trials by Dobies Seeds most suitable cv was 'Protovoy' (savoy type).

Sow *in situ*, or in seedtrays, or in modules, from early to late spring. Space or plant out 12cm (5in) apart each way.

Double Cropping Cabbage

Cabbages sprout at these points

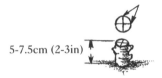

5-7.5cm (2-3in)

A cabbage can produce a secondary crop of five heads after initial head has been cut

Neat little heads ready about 20 weeks after sowing.
(Promising experiments under way with red cabbage 'Primero', grown closely spaced for using at tennis ball size.)
Cut-and-come-again greens catch crop: for quick returns from small area in summer/early autumn.
Use spring cabbage cv. Sow spring to early summer.
Sow *in situ*, spacing few seeds per station 10cm (4in) apart each way.
Thin to one seedling per station after germination.
Within eight weeks leaves 10-13cm (4-5in) high.
Cut across stems to use as young greens. Then either:
– leave all plants to resprout to give second cutting.
– leave every third plant to heart up.
– pull up completely and use ground for follow on crop.

Spring cabbage (for use mid-spring until early summer)
Sow in mid-summer in cold areas and in the first two weeks of late summer in warm areas.
Plant early to mid-autumn.
(For succession sow under cover, for example, in cold frame or cloches, in early autumn, planting out in spring.)
Plant in shallow drills, 30cm (12in) apart each way.
Or space plants 10cm (4in) apart, rows 30cm (12in) apart. Leave one plant in three to heart up; use others young as spring greens in cooking.
Pull soil around stems few weeks after planting to give extra protection. In very cold areas protect with cloches until early/mid-spring. When growth starts in spring hoe round plants; can apply a nitrogenous top dressing in spring to boost growth.

Cultivars
Mostly small, pointed heads, though a few cvs are round headed.
Avoncrest, Dorado, Duncan, Durham Early, Pixie, Spring Hero (don't sow until late summer or may bolt prematurely) for headed cabbage.
Greensleeves, Sparkel (and cvs above) – for spring greens.

Summer cabbage (for use early summer to late autumn)
Sow: 1 Late-winter (warm areas), early spring (cold areas) in heated propagator, at roughly 13°C (55°F). harden-off well before planting out mid-/late spring. Use early summer cv.
2 Early to late spring in open, planting late spring to mid-summer for succession.
Space plants 35-45cm (14-18in) apart, according to the size of head required.

Cultivars
Mainly round, medium to large heads.
F_1 Hispi and F_1 Kingspi (both pointed), F_1 Golden Cross, F_1 Spitfire, Derby Day, F_1 Spivoy (crinkled savoy leaves) – all suited to early sowing.
F_1 Stonehead, F_1 Castello, F_1 Minicole – all reasonably compact cvs which stand well.

Autumn cabbage (for use mid-autumn and into early winter)
Sow mid- to late spring.
Plant by early summer 50cm (20in) apart.

Cultivars
Typically dense dark heads which stand well into late autumn/early winter – F_1 Rapier, F_1 Hawke.

Dutch winter white cabbage (for use mid-autumn until moderate frost, then stored until following spring) Sow mid-spring.

149

Plant early summer 50cm (20in) apart.
Lift remaining plants before heavy frost for storage.
Pull up by roots; hang in frost-free shed or cellar.
Examine the plants regularly during winter months and gently roll off diseased outer leaves.
Can also store in garden frames, raised off ground on wooden slats and covered with straw, but must ventilate on sunny days to discourage pests and diseases.

Cultivars
Typically smooth round heads with thin leaves; which are excellent raw as 'cole slaw'. F_1 Hidena, F_1 Polinius.

Hardy winter cabbage (for use mid-autumn until following spring)
Sow late spring.
Plant by mid-summer 50cm (20in) apart.
Can earth up stems to give extra protection in winter; remove all the rotting leaves.

Cultivars
'January King' type – flattish heads, blue-red tinge, generally stand until mid-winter: January King Hardy Late Stock 3.
White x savoy hybrids – with crisp white leaf; some cvs stand into late winter: F_1 Celtic, F_1 Tundra (longest standing).
Savoy type – distinct crinkled emerald green leaves; hardiest of all; may stand into mid-spring: Ice Queen (early), Wivoy (late).

Red cabbage
Red forms of summer and autumn cabbage. Stand for many weeks when mature without deteriorating.
Distinct flavour; used fresh and pickled.
Excellent cooked with apple. Very decorative when growing.
In my experience less prone to pests and diseases than other types of cabbage.
Main cropping season for summer types mid-summer to mid-autumn.
Main cropping season for autumn types mid-autumn to early winter.
Some cvs suitable for lifting and storage before heavy frost.
For standard cultivation see summer and autumn cabbage.
For very early crop of summer cvs can sow in modules in early autumn, over-winter the seedlings under cover, and plant out in early spring as soon as the soil is workable. The system produces exceptionally fine and heavy heads.

Cultivars
Ruby Ball – for summer.
Autoro, Hardoro – for winter.

Ornamental cabbage
Very decorative form with distinctly variegated foliage.
Mainly used for decoration; edible (but only just). For cultivation see companion volume *Salads for Small Gardens*.

Pests and diseases on brassicas
The following are the most common pests found on cabbages and other brassicas. For organic gardeners, growing brassicas under fine nets is highly recommended to keep out the flying pests, such as flea beetle, aphids and whitefly, cabbage root fly, butterflies and moths with destructive caterpillars, and birds. For other control measures see Pests and Diseases p.66.

Flea beetle Nibbles holes in young leaves, often at seedling stage. Spray or dust as soon as noticed.

Mealy aphids Grey-green, waxy looking aphids, in colonies on leaves and stems causing puckering throughout summer but worse in late summer. Squash by hand, spray, or try moving ladybirds on to attacked plants. Can stunt plants seriously. Aphids over-winter in stumps so pull out and burn by early summer.

Cabbage whitefly Clouds of small white insects fly up when plants disturbed throughout summer. Not normally seriously damaging, but can spray when first noticed. Also over-winter in stumps so pull out and burn by early summer.

Caterpillars Eggs laid by various types of cabbage white butterflies and moths, mainly from mid-summer to autumn. Watch out for eggs (mainly on leaf undersides) and young caterpillars. Squash or spray them, or use biological control.

Cabbage root fly Potentially one of most serious pests. Adult flies (which emerge roughly when cow parsley is in flower) lay eggs at base of young brassica plants; hatched grubs tunnel into roots causing plants to collapse. Standard advice is to dig up and burn attacked plants; however, with oriental greens, I have washed off grubs, trimmed back foliage and successfully re-planted. Physical barriers best preventive measures (see Pests and diseases p.72).

Slugs and snails Damage most serious in early stages; keep a constant watch and destroy.

Birds Attacks most serious initially, at seedling stage; later on birds attack mature plants in winter.

Clubroot (Finger and toe) Soil borne disease resulting in grotesque swellings (not unlike dahlia tubers) on roots; plants collapse and die. Lift diseased roots very carefully and burn them; never compost them. Difficult to eradicate because spores can last 20 years in soil. Practising rotation, improving drainage, and liming to raise pH to slightly alkaline level help prevent and control. Heavy mulching may be beneficial.

In infected soils, raise plants in pots – 15cm (6in) pots ideal – and plant out at late stage to give them a head start. Or concentrate on fast growing brassicas, such as Texsel greens and CCA oriental seedlings, which will be ready before the plants become seriously infected.

VSR **intensive systems, *standard heads
PP red cabbage

CALABRESE (Italian broccoli, green sprouting broccoli)
Brassica oleracea Italica Group
Fairly compact brassica growing 60cm (2ft) tall. Forms central, green, cauliflower-like head about 15cm (6in) in diameter and, after that is cut, broccoli-like side shoots. Not very hardy, but very useful brassica for small gardens because normally matures in under four months and can be closely spaced. Delicious, undervalued vegetable.

Site and Soil
See Cabbage, but tolerates poorer soil.

Cultivation
Dislikes transplanting. Where possible sow *in situ* (three seeds per station, thinning to one after germination), or sow in modules and plant out. Space plants 23cm (9in) apart for highest overall yield.
Sow: 1 From early/late spring until mid-summer for succession.
     2 Late summer/early autumn, planting under cover, for example in cold greenhouse for very early crop. Use an early cv. Plants may be killed in severe winter, but worth a gamble.
Calabrese must grow steadily; water well in dry weather.
Can give nitrogenous top dressing or foliar feed in summer after cutting central head to stimulate growth.

Pests and Diseases
See Cabbage.

Harvesting
Main season early summer until frost, depending on cv.
Pick main head just before flower buds open; side shoots then develop.
Pick constantly to encourage more shoots to develop.
If attacked by caterpillars, soak in salted water before cooking to entice them out.
Boil or steam heads until just tender.
Thick shoots can be peeled, then boiled or steamed. Freezes well.

Cultivars
In order of maturity:
F₁ Mercedes, F₁ Green Comet, F₁ Citation, F₁ Shogun.

VSR**

CAPSICUM see Peppers

CARROTS *Daucus carota*
With careful planning and successive sowing of different types you can have garden carrots for at least nine months of the year, making this an excellent vegetable for small gardens. Flavour of homegrown far superior to bought carrots.
Classified according to type, though there is a considerable overlap between groups.

Earlies:
Mature within 10-12 weeks. Short or squarish/round roots.
Mostly used fresh, but some Nantes cvs also suitable for storage. Generally sweet flavoured.
Types within earlies group:
Round/square rooted cvs – suitable for heavy and shallow soils.
Amsterdam cvs – finger-shaped; smooth; excellent raw.
Nantes cvs – somewhat larger.

Maincrop:
Mature in 20-24 weeks. Larger, longer carrots, used fresh but, because of bulk, also suitable for winter storage.
Chantenay cvs – medium sized; reputation for good flavour.
Berlicum cvs – larger, later maturing.
Autumn King cvs – potentially highest yielding, but unsuitable for heavy soils and areas with short growing season.

Site and Soil
Sheltered situation for early carrots; open site for maincrop. Carrots thrive in light, deep, fertile, stone-free, well-drained soil. Roots cannot penetrate and swell in heavy clay or compacted soil.
Dig in plenty of well-rotted compost or manure several months beforehand; growth apt to be sappy and the roots tend to fork in freshly manured ground. Carrots also fork – on encountering a stone – in very stony ground.
Foliage pretty, so can look good in flower beds and other, decorative garden situations.

Cultivation
Early crop:
Especially useful crop, maturing early summer onwards.
Use round, or Amsterdam or Nantes cvs.
Minimum soil temperature for germination 5°C (41°F), but at 10°C (50°F) seeds germinate three times faster.
Worth trying primed seed; often helps to overcome adverse weather conditions during germination. (See p.41.)

Carrots need very fine seedbed.
Never sow in weedy ground, as difficult crop to keep weed free.
See 'carrot fly' below for advice on thinning.

Sowing options
1 Sow under cloches or in cold frames, late winter (in warm areas), early spring (colder areas). Warm soil beforehand if necessary.
   On very light soils broadcast seed, or sow in 7·5-10cm (3-4in) wide bands, spacing seeds 2cm (¾in). No thinning of seedlings should be necessary.
   On heavy soils can sow in bands or drills 15cm (6in) apart; thin to about 5cm (2in) apart.
   Remove cloches or frame lights in mid- or late spring when temperatures rise. Carrots ready in early summer.
2 Sow at same time as above, and cover with perforated or fleecy films. Sow in shallow drills, laying films over the top of the drills.
   Remove perforated films when the carrots have about five leaves (usually after about ten weeks); fleecy film can be left until maturity unless very hot weather. F_1 Nantes cvs are very suitable for this treatment.
3 Sow *round cvs only* in modules indoors in propagator in late winter.
   Can sow up to four seeds per 4-5cm (1½-2in) cell; transplant outside 'as one' after hardening-off, spacing 7·5-10cm (3-4in) apart.
   Can protect with cloches, films and so on.
   (Long rooted cvs unsuitable for multi-sowing in modules as roots twist around each other. They *can* be sown singly in modules, but must be planted out before the tap root starts to develop.)
   Successional sowings with early types.
4 Sow in open from early spring until mid-summer for summer supply of fresh carrots.
   Sow in drills 15cm (6in) apart. Thin in stages to about 4-5cm (1½-2in) apart for medium sized carrots, or wider spacing for larger carrots. Very wide spacing – up to 10cm (4in) apart, has been shown to encourage quick maturity and growth in early carrots.
5 Make final outdoor sowing late summer (colder areas), early autumn (warmer areas), for young carrot crop in late autumn/ early winter. Cover with cloches or fleece early or mid-autumn.
6 Sow under cover (in unheated greenhouse or polytunnel, or outdoors under fleece) in mid-autumn using F_1 Nantes cvs. Success depends on severity of winter, but can result in very early carrots in late spring.
Note: Carrot seed can also be sown mixed with annual flowers (see Space Saving p.102).

Maincrop sowings for fresh use and storage:
Use any maincrop cvs.
Sow mid-spring to mid-summer.
Sow in drills 15cm (6in) apart. Thin as for successional sowings (4) above.

Weed carrots carefully in early stages of plant growth; once established leaves blanket soil so further weeding unnecessary. Mulch between rows to retain soil moisture.

Carrots only require moderate amounts of water: excessive water encourages leaf growth at expense of roots.

Root splitting often occurs when heavy rain follows dry period; can prevent by watering just enough to stop soil drying out completely and keeping soil mulched.

Pests

Carrot fly The most serious pest on carrots. Fly lays eggs at base of plants; when hatched tiny maggots tunnel into roots. Foliage becomes bronzed, seedlings die, larger plants weakened; mined carrot roots don't store well. Several generations of flies each year.

Adult flies are low flying so most successful methods of control are to grow within 60cm (2ft) high barriers, or in boxes raised off the ground, or under fine nets or cloches (see Pests and Diseases pp.72-3).

The following practices minimize damage:

~ Sow early (generally before mid-spring), and late (towards beginning of early summer) to avoid worst attacks.

~ Sow thinly to minimize need for thinning, as smell of thinnings attracts adult flies. Thin in evening or in still conditions. Nip off unwanted seedlings just above ground level. Bury all thinnings in compost heap Water and firm remaining plants after thinning.

~ Where problem is serious aim to lift early carrots by early autumn, maincrop carrots by mid-autumn; this prevents another cycle hatching and lessens following year's attacks.

~ Remove all carrot debris; never leave it on the ground.

~ Grow cvs with some resistance, such as the fodder carrots (which are pale but quite edible). New cvs with resistance are being introduced, but are not so far of high quality.

~ Cutworms can attack young plants. Water heavily when larvae noticed.

Harvesting

In light soils pull roots out carefully as soon as they reach required size. In heavy soils it is advisable to fork out to avoid breaking roots; water soil beforehand if dry.

Storage options:

(Carrots withstand light frost, but damaged by heavy frost.)

1 Leave in soil. Best method for retaining flavour.

Only feasible in light, well-drained soil where few slugs. Impractical where mice and rats likely pests.

Unless getting very early frosts, allow foliage to die back, then cover plants with black polythene film.

Cover film with generous layer – up to 30cm (12in) thick – of straw, bracken or insulating material.

On exposed sites can put low hoops over the top to help to keep insulation in place.

2 Lift and store indoors.

Lift before heavy frost.

Cut off leaves 1cm (½in) above roots. Reject all the diseased and damaged roots.

Lay roots in layers in boxes or tubs, each layer separated by 1cm (½in) of sand, sifted ashes or light soil.

Put in frost-free shed or cellar.

Cover with fine mesh if mice likely to be a problem.

3 Storage in clamps outdoors.

Make clamp in sheltered spot.

Start with 20cm (8in) layer of straw on ground.

Pile carrots on top in a heap, to a maximum height of 60cm (2ft). Cover with 20cm (8in) layer of straw and, in cold areas, a 15cm (6in) layer of soil. This can be taken from around base of heap to improve drainage.

Cultivars

In recent trials the following cvs have proved especially suited to organic growing, as they have exceptional natural vigour and good leafy tops, which suppress weeds.

Earlies: Nairobi, Newmarket – both Nantes types, suitable for use fresh and stored.

Maincrop: Bangor (Berlicum type); Autumn King Vita Longa (Autumn King type).

Otherwise use standard cvs.

Round carrots (improved modern cvs): 'Rondo', 'Early French Frame Lisa', 'Parmex'.

VSR*** PP

CAULIFLOWER, MINI *Brassica oleracea* Botrytis Group

Most types of cauliflower occupy too much ground, for too many months, to justify space in small gardens. Exception is 'mini-cauliflowers' where plants grown close for diminutive heads, excellent for freezing and small portions. (See also green curded 'Romanesco' opposite.)

Site and Soil

Reasonably fertile, slightly acid or slightly alkaline soil; lime if very acid. Avoid freshly manured soil and soils with high levels of nitrogen, which will make growth too leafy. Mini-cauliflowers well suited to 90cm-1.2m (3-4ft) wide beds.

Cultivation

Small curds mature at more or less same time, so advisable to make several successive sowings.

Sowings

1 Late winter, in modules or seedtrays in propagator at 20-25°C (68-77°F) for crop early summer. Plant out after hardening-off.

2 Early spring to mid-summer, in seedbed, *in situ*, or in modules, for crop from early summer to mid-autumn

3 Early autumn, in modules or seedtrays. Over-winter in cold frames, plant out following spring for early summer crop.

Space plants 12-15cm (5-6in) apart each way.

If sowing *in situ* sow two to three seeds per station, thinning to strongest seedlings after germination.

Keep ground well watered and weeded throughout growth.

Pests and Diseases
See Cabbage; normally few problems as in ground for fairly short time.

Harvesting
Small curds ready anything from 12-16 weeks after sowing; mature fastest in late spring/early summer.

Cut heads when 4-7.5cm (1½-3in) in diameter.

Cook or freeze whole.

Curds 'go over' quickly, so don't leave long once useable size.

Cultivars
Idol, Lateman, Montano.

Note: These are early summer cauliflower cvs, the type currently recommended for mini-cauliflowers. Their drawback is rapid deterioration once mature. Present trials may indicate some autumn cvs more suitable, lasting longer when ready for harvesting. Watch gardening magazines and catalogues for developments.

VSR*

Green curded autumn cauliflower 'Romanesco'
May be worth growing in small garden as excellent flavour. (Often listed as calabrese.)

Sow late spring, space 60cm (2ft) apart, harvest early autumn.

CELERIAC (Turnip-rooted celery)
Apium graveolens var. *rapaceum*
Bushy plant, 45cm (18in) high, 30cm (1ft) across, celery-like leaves, swollen base of stem edible; good substitute for celery as hardier, less prone to disease.

Site and Soil
Open site, but tolerates light shade provided plenty of moisture. Fertile soil, rich in organic matter.

Cultivation
Likes long growing season and plenty of moisture all the time.

Sow late winter/early spring in a heated propagator; mid-spring in cold greenhouse or under cloches. Germination of seedlings is often erratic. Be patient!

Sow in modules; or sow in seedtrays, pricking out 6cm (2½in) apart, preferably into boxes/containers 7·5cm (3in) deep, when plants are large enough to handle.

Don't start hardening-off outside until weather warm. Plant end late spring/early summer. Plant 30-38cm (12-15in) apart, base of stem at ground level. Water thoroughly in dry weather; keep plants mulched.

Weekly liquid manure from early summer onwards very beneficial.

Remove lower ageing leaves as season progresses to expose 'bulb'.

Pests
Celery leaf miner (celery fly) Most common pest, tunnelling into leaves causing blisters. Remove diseased leaves and burn. Growing under fine nets prevents attacks. Never plant seedlings with blistered leaves.

Slugs Attack in early stages.

Harvesting
Can be used from early autumn until late spring.

Can normally leave in soil throughout winter, if well-protected with thick layer of straw or bracken tucked between plants; or cover with frost-proofing fleece film.

In very cold areas lift in autumn before severe frost, trim off outer leaves leaving central tuft, and store under cover in boxes of sand.

If ground needed in spring, lift remaining plants and heel in (see p.184). Celeriac bulb can be grated raw in salads, puréed, boiled, used in soups or served with cheese sauce.

Unfortunately rough outer skin harbours dirt; scrubbing it clean is a (worthwhile) chore!

Leaves normally remain green all winter; strong flavour, but can use sparingly in salads or for celery seasoning. Can also dry leaves for use as celery substitute in cooking.

Cultivars
'Balder', 'Monarch', 'Snow White', 'Tellus' – among many good cvs.

VSR*

CELERY *Apium graveolens* var. *dolce*
Distinctly flavoured plant grown mainly for its crunchy stems. Traditional 'trench celery' unsuitable for small gardens as requires considerable space over several months. 'Self-blanching' types and 'leaf celery' more appropriate and better value.

Self-blanching
Long stemmed plants, on average 45cm (18in) high. Not frost hardy.
In standard cvs stems cream or yellowish; can be partially blanched to make whiter and possibly sweeter flavoured.
In 'American Green' cvs stems green, with no blanching necessary; good flavour.
Leaf or cutting celery:
Robust, very hardy plants closely related to wild celery.
Quite bushy and leafy with thin, fine stems.
Height from 30-45cm (12-18in), depending on cv.
Mainly used for soups and flavouring in winter months.

Site and Soil
Open site, very rich soil and plenty of organic matter. Leaf celery less demanding than self-blanching.

Self-blanching
Cultivation
Sow in seedtrays or modules early spring in propagator, or mid-spring under cover.
Sow on the surface, or lightly covered with sand, as seeds need light in order to germinate.
Alternatively, buy plants late spring/early summer.
Do not sow too early; if temperature falls below 10°C (50°F) for more than 12 hours, plants liable to 'bolt' (run to seed).
Don't put outside to start hardening-off until weather is warm.
Plant beginning of early summer in block formation at equidistant spacing to get a blanched effect. Space plants 15cm (6in) to 27cm (11in) apart.
The wider the spacing the heavier the plants and thicker the stems.
Do not plant too deeply.
Take precautions against slugs.
Tuck straw around standard cvs in mid-summer to increasing blanching.
Water generously or plants liable to bolt or become stringy.
Feed weekly with liquid manure from early summer onwards.

Pests and Diseases
Slugs, celery fly See Celeriac.
Celery leaf spot Debilitating disease, leaving small brown spots on leaves and stems. Seed borne and difficult to control organically. Dusting leaves with old soot may prevent attacks.
Use good quality seed; unwise to save your own. Burn any diseased foliage. Can try spraying several times with Bordeaux mixture when diseased leaves first noticed.

Harvesting
On average stems ready for cutting within 14 weeks of sowing.

Will stand until frost though condition deteriorates.
Green cvs have shorter period of peak quality.
Best to cut before outer leaves become pithy.
Can cut individual stems at soil level, or lift whole plant.
In the USA celery is lifted before the first frost and stored in cellars for winter use.

Leaf celery
Cultivation and Harvesting
Sow throughout growing season in seedtrays or modules.
Plant outside 13cm (5in) apart.
Can also multi-sow in modules, up to eight seeds/cells, planting out in 'clumps' 20cm (8in) apart.
Late summer sowing can be planted under cover in autumn for extra quality plants during winter.
Can cut plants frequently, starting about four weeks after planting. Will regrow and remain productive over many months, though eventually runs to seed in spring.
If few plants left to run to seed in second season will self-sow. Young seedlings can be transplanted to wherever required.

Cultivars
self-blanching – Celebrity, Lathom Self-Blanching, Greensleeves (standard x green cross), Hopkins Fenlander (green), F_1 Victoria (good flavour).
Leaf celery – Amsterdam cvs; Parcel – very decorative, recently introduced cv with deeply crinkled, parsley-like leaves.

VSR **Self-blanching, ***Leaf celery
Leaf celery PP

THE CHICORIES Cichorium intybus
This is a large group of plants, closely associated with Italy. They are extremely robust, tolerant of wide range of climate and soil conditions, and rarely seriously troubled by pests and diseases. The main season of use is from late summer to spring. Chicories are characterized by slightly bitter flavours, which may account for their lack of popularity but by shredding the leaves, using seedlings and blanching appropriate types to sweeten them they become very palatable. Red chicories are extremely decorative.

Chicories are mainly used in salads, but can also be cooked. For small gardens the red chicories, 'Sugar Loaf' chicory and 'Witloof' or 'Belgian' chicory give the best returns. All chicories produce very tall, beautiful spikes of sky blue (edible) flowers when they run to seed in the second season. For the more unusual types of chicory, see *Salads for Small Gardens* (p.248).

Red chicory (outside Italy now widely known as 'radicchio')
Ground-hugging plants, typically with variegated or reddish green, loose leaved heads early in season, becoming deeper red and forming tight little hearts with sweeter, crisp inner leaves in cooler weather. Improved modern cvs develop deeper coloured, tighter heads, much earlier.
Most cvs moderately hardy. The narrow-leaved, non-hearting 'Treviso' types exceptionally hardy. Some red chicories can be forced like 'Witloof' chicory to produce white, pink-tipped chicons in winter.
Grows best in fertile, moisture-retentive soil but very adaptable. Useful for intercropping, as tolerates light shade from overhanging plants. Natural season from summer to early winter, but can be extended to following spring by growing under cover in winter.

Cultivation
Traditional method, suitable for older cvs:
Broadcast seed in patches outside, in weed free soil, from late spring to mid-summer. Curiously, plants seem to thin themselves out, some growing larger at expense of weaker ones. If appear overcrowded in late summer thin to 10-13cm (4-5in) apart.
Methods for improved modern cvs:
1 For early summer crop:
   Sow early maturing cvs in seedtrays or modules in mid- and late spring. Transplant outside after hardening-off. Protect with cloches or crop covers in early stages.
2 For main summer and autumn outdoor crop:
   Sow as above from late spring to mid-summer.
3 For winter/early spring crop under cover, sow mid-/late summer, transplanting under cover in late summer/early autumn.
Space plants 20-35cm (8-14in) apart depending on cv.
Keep weed free; otherwise little attention needed.
In late autumn can cover remaining plants outdoors with low polythene film tunnels or straw to extend the season.
During winter outer leaves (especially of plants grown under cover), may develop rots. Remove infected leaves carefully. Plants often recover in warmer spring weather.
Note: 'Treviso' chicory can either be sown broadcast, or raised as single plants sown in summer.

Harvesting
Once hearts form either cut across crown, or cut individual leaves as required. Leave stumps to resprout; they will produce more loose leaves over many weeks.

Forcing
Some of the 'Verona' cvs and 'Treviso' can be lifted in late autumn and forced in the same way as 'Witloof' chicory' (see pp.163-4).

Cultivars
Alouette, Cesare, Medusa – for early and summer crops.
Palla Rossa Bella, Palla Rossa Verona – Verona type.
Treviso – non-hearting, very hardy type, with deep red pointed leaves.
Castelfranco – traditional variegated type.

VSR** PP

'Sugar Loaf' chicory

Green-leaved low-growing plants, forming large, dense, conical heads. Inner leaves creamy and naturally blanched, so sweeter than most chicories (hence its name); flavour still slightly bitter, but very refreshing. Highly productive as can be grown as CCA seedlings and/or for heads, and responds to CCA treatment at every stage. Once established plants appear to have excellent tolerance to drought, possibly because of deep roots.

Reasonably hardy. Headed crop previously grown mainly for late summer and autumn use, but some new cvs suitable for earlier summer crop, while others have increased frost resistance allowing for later crops. Responds well to being grown under cover in winter months, for example in cold greenhouses, treating as semi-mature CCA crop to increase resistance to frost. (See Space Saving p.105.) Can be grown almost all year as seedling crop.

Cultivation
CCA seedling crop (any cv can be used)
1 Make first sowing early spring *in situ* under cover. Sow broadcast in patches, or in narrow drills 7.5-10cm (3-4in) apart, or in wide drills. Start cutting when leaves 5-8cm (2-3½in) high; continue as long as leaves tender. Can then thin out to 20-25cm (8-10in) apart, allowing remaining plants to heart up.
   For continuous cutting keep plants well watered; give occasional liquid feeds to stimulate growth if seems necessary.
2 Continue with outdoor sowings as above, as soon as soil is workable. Can sow at intervals throughout summer, but spring sowings generally prove most useful. Treat as early sowings above. Can protect with crop covers or cloches in the autumn to prolong season of usefulness.
3 Make final sowing early autumn under cover for winter crop.

Headed crop
1 For early summer crop, sow appropriate cvs in seedtrays or modules in spring. Plant about 25cm (10in) apart.
2 Sow in early and mid-summer as above or *in situ*, thinning to 25-30cm (10-12in) apart. Plants can be covered (see red chicory) in late autumn before frost to prolong season. Heads can be pulled up by roots. Keep for several weeks in cold cellar or frost-free shed. Protect with straw.

3 Sow in mid- to late summer as opposite, transplanting under cover in early autumn. Even if there is not time for large heads to develop, plants will resprout over a long period if cut at semi-mature stage.

Cultivars

Various Italian 'cutting chicories': Trieste, Milano – mainly used for CCA seedlings; may form small heads.
F_1 Jupiter – versatile headed cv suitable for any sowings.
Scarpia, Poncho – headed types suitable for summer sowings.
Note: 'Misuglio' is an Italian mixture of various types of chicories, which can be broadcast together to make a colourful patch, which is productive over several months.

VSR ****CCA seedlings, ***headed

'Witloof' or 'Belgian' chicory

The parsnip-like roots are forced in darkness to produce white buds or 'chicons' during winter. Much more easily grown than most people tend to imagine. Used raw in salads or cooked braised, or use as an ingredient in cheese, ham or egg dishes. The newer cvs are a great improvement on the old ones.

Cultivation

Being closely related to dandelion, 'Witloof' chicory is not fussy about soil. Avoid freshly manured ground, which can lead to over-lush growth and fanged roots.
Sow in late spring/early summer
1 Thinly, *in situ*, in drills about 30cm (12in) apart.
2 In modules for transplanting. (Chicory does not otherwise transplant very successfully.)
  Thin or plant about 23cm (9in) apart.
  Little further attention required during summer, other than weeding, and watering in very dry weather. Mulching advisable.

Forcing methods (see diagrams p.164)

Chicory can either be lifted and forced indoors, or forced *in situ*. Indoor methods more convenient; *in situ* method said to produce better flavoured chicons.
Forcing in pots indoors:
~ As long as the soil not heavily frosted, lift roots for forcing any time from autumn to the end of the year.
~ Dig up plants; leave somewhere sheltered, such as a lean-to shed, for a week or so to allow moisture to pass back into the roots from the leaves.
~ Trim off the leaves about 2.5cm (1in) above the root.
~ Trim off wispy side roots; discard any roots that are less than 4cm (1½in)

Forcing Chicories in the Greenhouse

Lift roots in early winter; leave for about a week then trim off the leaves 2.5cm (1in) above root

Pot several roots, pat closely together into a flower pot, cover with a pot of similar dimensions

Chicons ready for harvesting; cut about 2cm (¾in) above soil level, leaving the root to resprout

Store until required for forcing between layers of sand or soil

'Witloof' and 'Treviso' chicories being forced in the dark under a greenhouse bench

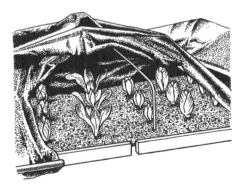

diameter across the top. Trim root tips back to about 20cm (8in) if too long for pots.

~ Store roots until required for forcing. Either lay them flat in boxes, between layers of sand, in a shed, or lay them in a 30cm (12in) deep trench in the garden, covered with soil.

~ Force a few at a time in a 23-30cm (9-12in) flower pot filled with soil or old potting compost to support the roots. (All nourishment comes from the roots, so good quality soil is unnecessary.) Select three to five roots of roughly the same size. Pack them upright, fairly close together in the pot, with the necks about 2.5cm (1in) above the soil.

~ Water lightly. Cover the pot with another upturned pot of the same size. Block the drainage hole with tinfoil or a stone to exclude light.

~ Put the pot indoors at a temperature of 10-18°C (50-64°F).

~ Inspect from time to time. Remove any rotted leaves and water lightly if dry. Firm chicons normally develop within about three weeks.

~ Cut them about 2cm (¾in) above the root. If not eaten immediately wrap them in brown paper to prevent them greening; can keep in the fridge. If the roots are left after the first cut they resprout to produce a smaller second crop of loose, but tender, blanched leaves.

Can also force roots in boxes or any container of sufficient depth: allow at least 20cm (8in) headroom for the chicon.

Forcing in a greenhouse
~ Prepare the roots (p.163).

~ Instead of planting in pots, plant in greenhouse soil, for example in the ground under the staging.

~ Devise a method of excluding light completely, for example – cover the area with black polythene film anchored over wire hoops or erect boxes or boards to black out the area.

Chicons normally take longer to develop than when they are forced in pots indoors. If temperatures rise rapidly in spring may get aphid attacks or develop rots. Use them up quickly!

Forcing *in situ* outdoors
~ In late autumn cut back the leaves as for lifted chicory.

~ Cover the stumps with 15-20cm (6-8in) of sand, light soil, or sieved ashes to make a ridge over them.

~ Can cover the ridge with cloches or low polythene film tunnels to bring on the chicons sooner.

~ Chicons push through from late winter to early spring, depending on the weather. Scrape away the covering to cut them.

Cultivars
Apollo, Videna, F_1 Zoom.

VSR*

CHINESE CABBAGE (Chinese leaves) *Brassica rapa*
Pekinensis Group

Very fast growing, mild flavoured brassica. 'Hearted'/ 'headed' type most common: has characteristic white marbled veining on leaves; crisp-leaved hearts. Squat 'barrel' forms particularly compact; tall cylindrical forms generally later maturing.

'Loose-headed'/'semi-headed' type very much looser; used mainly as CCA crops at semi-mature and seedling stage. The 'fluffy top' loose-headed cvs have beautiful creamy centres, crepe-like leaves; excellent salad vegetables. Chinese cabbage not very hardy but withstands some frost if protected; suitable for CCA cropping under cover in winter.

Site and Soil

Fairly open site, though tolerates light shade in mid-summer, provided plenty of moisture and not cramped. To maintain fast growth requires very fertile, moisture-retentive soil, limed if acid.

Cultivation

Like many oriental greens, Chinese cabbage tends to bolt (run to seed prematurely) if sown early in year (apart from where grown as CCA seedlings). Most types best sown summer for late summer/early autumn crop. Ideal crop to follow peas, early potatoes and broad beans.

Bolting tendency exacerbated by low temperatures in early stages, by dry conditions and by being transplanted.

CCA seedlings

Sow *in situ*, broadcast or in drills. Use loose-headed cvs as many hearted cvs have rough textured leaves at seedling stage. Make first sowings under cover in early spring.

Follow with outdoor sowings as soon as soil workable. Can protect with crop covers or cloches.

Continue sowing outdoors until late summer. Make final sowing under cover early autumn.

Cut seedlings when useable size, leaving to resprout unless plants have started to bolt.

Headed crop

For main crop: sow *in situ* or in modules from early to late summer. Space plants about 30cm (12in) apart.

For early crop: can try sowing late spring/early summer in propagator, using bolt resistant cv. Maintain minimum temperature of 18°C (64°F) for first three weeks after germination. Protect plants with cloches or crop covers after planting.

For late crop: sow end summer, transplanting under cover early autumn. Either grow at standard spacing, or space plants about 13cm (5in) apart, for regular cut of small leaves during winter. Can be very productive.

Mulch after planting. Keep weed free and well watered.
Unlike most brassicas, Chinese cabbage has very shallow roots, therefore needs frequent, moderate watering, especially when the plants are nearing maturity.
Responds to liquid feeds throughout growth if soil not very fertile.

Pests and Diseases
See Cabbage. Subject to all common brassica problems. Growing under fine nets to deter flying pests highly recommended.

Harvesting
Headed types ready 9-10 weeks after sowing; loose-headed types two to three weeks earlier; seedling crops from four to five weeks after sowing.
Cut heads about 2·5cm (1in) above base and leave to resprout.
Plants under cover run to seed in following spring, producing tender flowering shoots. Cut these for use like broccoli
Heads can be lifted before onset of frost and stored for several weeks in cool, dry, frost-free conditions, or in a fridge.
Use Chinese cabbage raw in salads, or cook lightly, for example by steaming or stir-frying. Delicate flavour completely destroyed by boiling, in ways used for European cabbage.

Cultivars
F_1 Kasumi – barrel type with good bolting resistance.
F_1 Tip Top – barrel type with reasonable bolting resistance.
F_1 Jade Pagoda – tall cylindrical type.
F_1 Ruffles (previously Eskimo) – fluffy top loose-headed type; has reasonable bolting resistance.
Santo/Minato Santo – loose-headed type.
Note: Improved cultivars are continually being introduced.

VSR **headed, ***CCA; Fluffy top types PP

CHOY SUM *Brassica rapa* var. *purpurea* & var. *oleifera*
Various Chinese greens are grown for the delicately flavoured young flowering shoots and stems, eaten like broccoli. Most productive types for small gardens are purple-flowered pak choi (var. *purpurea*) and hybrid flowering rape (var. *oleifera*).

Site and Soil
Fertile, moisture-retentive, well-drained soil, as growth must be rapid to produce tender shoots.

Cultivation and Harvesting
Purple-flowered pak choi:
Pretty, branching plant, with purple stems and yellow flowers, growing

about 30cm (12in) high by the time it reaches maturity.
Adapted to cool weather; fairly hardy – survives -5°C (23°F).
Best sown late summer for autumn/early winter crop.
Sow *in situ* or in modules.
Space about 38cm (15in) apart in good soil; can be a little closer in less fertile soil.
For good quality winter crop plant under cover in early autumn.
Plants normally ready in less than two months from sowing.
Keep cutting shoots when 10-15cm (4-6in) long, before buds open. Will produce more shoots over several weeks or months.
Can eat raw in salads or lightly cooked. (See Chinese Cabbage.)

VSR* PP

Hybrid flowering rape

The new cv 'F$_1$ Bouquet' is far more productive than old cvs and the best value. Very attractive; excellent flavour.
Can grow about 45cm (18in) high, with light green, savoyed leaves, chunky succulent stems and heavy clusters of yellow flower buds.
Adapted to cool weather; survives light frost.
Sow as for purple-flowering pak choi for outdoor crop and winter crop under cover.
Space plants 15-20cm (6-8in) apart.
In addition, early summer sowings are sometimes successful.
Cut shoots while tender before buds open, but with a hint of yellow colour showing; first cuts sometimes made when plants no more than 20cm (8in) high. Leave plants to resprout.
In Japan also used as cut flower!

VSR** PP

CHRYSANTHEMUM GREENS (Chop suey greens, Shungiku)
Chrysanthemum coronarium
Decorative form of garden chrysanthemum with pretty creamy yellow flowers, grown for the aromatic, distinctly flavoured and nutritious leaves. Grows to about 15cm (6in) high in the leafy phase; even taller when flowering.
Naturally healthy and relatively hardy plant; generally grows best in cool weather.
Small and fast growing, so is particularly useful for catch cropping and intercropping. Does well in containers.

Site and Soil
Not fussy about soil or site, though grows more lushly in fertile soil with plenty of moisture. Will tolerate light shade in summer, and grows reasonably well in low light levels in winter.

Cultivation

Can grow as CCA seedling crop or as single plants.

Can sow for much of the year, but tendency to run to seed rapidly in hot weather and dry conditions. Spring and mid-summer/autumn sowings probably most productive and useful.

Very fine seed, so sow shallowly.

1 For very early crop sow early spring under cover.
2 Follow with outdoor sowings as soon as soil workable.
3 Sow towards end of summer for autumn crop which can be covered with cloches or crop covers to improve quality.
4 Sow early autumn under cover for good quality winter crop.

For CCA seedling crop sow thinly, either broadcast, or in single drills or wide drills, spaced 13cm (5in) apart.

For single plants sow *in situ*, or in seedtrays or modules. Space plants about 10cm (4in) apart.

Harvesting

First cut of CCA seedlings can normally be made four to five weeks after sowing when 5-10cm (2-4in) high. The younger the leaves the more tender they are. Leave the plants to resprout.

Single plants normally ready six to eight weeks after sowing. Can be cut or pulled whole, or individual leaves can be cut as required. Continue cutting regularly in order to keep plants tender. Remove any flower buds which appear.

Cut back hard if stems start to become woody; plants often regenerate.

Leave a few plants to run to seed at the end of the season; they may self-seed usefully

Leaves wilt rapidly, so use as soon after picking as possible.

Young leaves can be used sparingly in salads, but older leaves tend to be strong flavoured and best cooked lightly for example steamed, stir-fried, or cooked like spinach. May become bitter if over-cooked. Flower petals are also edible.

Cultivars

New cvs, such as 'Maiko' broader leaved and more productive than old; but currently named cvs rarely listed in seed catalogues.

VSR*** PP

CLAYTONIA see Purslane, winter

CORN SALAD (Lamb's lettuce, mâche) *Valerianella locusta*
Low growing, small-leaved, hardy annual.
Meek appearance belies its exceptional robustness. Invaluable ingredient for winter salad.
Requires little space; ideal for intercropping, undercropping.

Rarely troubled by pests or disease.

Two types: the floppier 'large-' or 'broad-leaved' English type, and the darker green, squatter, perkier looking 'green' type. Latter more popular in western Europe and also reputedly hardier, but probably less productive than the English type.

Site and Soil

Undemanding plant to cultivate as it is adaptable to a wide range of conditions. Will grow in full sun or light shade; tolerates fairly dry and fairly moist situations. Growth more lush in fertile, well-cultivated soil, but tolerates poorer soil.

Cultivation

Can grow as single plants or as CCA seedlings. Former seems to be the most productive method.

Sow:

1 Late winter/early spring under cover for late spring/early summer crop.
2 Early/mid-spring outdoors for summer use.
3 Early/mid-summer outdoors for autumn use, though may bolt prematurely in hot weather.
4 Late summer/early autumn outdoors for winter and spring use when most value. These sowings may provide pickings throughout winter until spring. Can protect with cloches/crop covers, even bracken, in early winter to improve quality.
5 Early autumn under cover for productive, good quality winter crop, which will continue growing on warm days when the outdoor plants stop growing.

Sow *in situ* in narrow or broad drills about 10cm (4in) apart, or broadcast.

Can also sow in seedtrays or modules for transplanting.

Space plants 10cm (4in) apart each way.

Broadcasting and wide drills most appropriate where grown as CCA seedling crop.

For good use of space can broadcast or plant between brassicas; or on the onion bed to follow on when onions lifted.

Harvesting

Mature plants ready in 12 weeks; seedlings several weeks earlier.

With single plants either pick individual leaves as required, or cut across head leaving plant to resprout, or pull up the whole plant. (This is done where corn salad is marketed, as it otherwise wilts rapidly after picking.)

Cut CCA seedlings as soon as useable size. They will resprout at least once, maybe several times.

Plants eventually run to seed; young flowers are edible in salads.

Can leave some plants to self-seed. Often prove very useful.

Mild flavour. Excellent for adding to salads, especially to complement sharp-flavoured winter salad plants.

Cultivars
Dutch, Large-Leaved English – standard type.
Jade, Cavallo, Verte de Cambrai, Vit, Vollhart – green types; best reserved for later sowings.

VSR***

COURGETTES see Marrows

CRESS see Mustard

CUCUMBER *Cucumis sativus*
Tender, mainly climbing plants, grown for their fruits.

Main types
Greenhouse/indoor   smooth cucumbers often 45cm (18in) long. Must be grown in greenhouses to survive. Require high temperatures, high humidity and careful cultivation. (For cultivation see specialist books, Further Reading pp.248-9.)
Ridge/outdoor – (The name 'ridge' stems from originally being grown on ridges to improve the drainage.) Much more rugged types, with greater resistance to pests, diseases and cold conditions. Various types within the group:
Traditional cvs – fairly stubby, rough, prickly-skinned cucumbers. Plants sprawl rather than climb.
Japanese cvs – result of modern breeding. Relatively smooth cucumbers up to 30cm (12in) long. Very healthy and robust. Climb up to 1.8m (6ft), depending on cv.
Bush cvs – mainly compact, non climbing US cvs, resembling bush courgettes. Suitable for large containers or where climbing cvs inappropriate. Fruit quality continually being improved.
Gherkins – very small ridge cucumbers suitable for pickling. Sprawling plants.
Round fruited – several old cvs with apple shaped, very juicy fruits. Not as rugged as some cvs.
Following applies only to outdoor ridge cucumbers.

Site and Soil
Sunny sheltered site; tolerate light shade in summer. Reasonably fertile, moisture-retentive, humus-rich soil. Site often prepared by filling 30cm (12in) deep, 45cm (18in) wide hole or trench with rotted manure or compost, and covering with 15cm (6in) soil.
Although normally grown outdoors or in frames, ridge cucumbers can be grown in greenhouses. In cold districts it may be essential to grow them under cover; the Japanese cvs will prove most productive. See also Cultivation in frames p.172.

Cultivation

Sow indoors mid-spring, in propagator or at minimum temperature of 20°C (68°F).

Sow seeds 2-2·5cm (¾-1in) deep on their side; sow two to three seeds per 5-7·5cm (2-3in) pot, thinning to strongest after germination has taken place.

Harden-off well and plant outside late spring, provided no risk of frost. Can protect with cloches or fleecy films at first, especially if weather becomes cold, windy or wet.

Plant climbing cvs 38-45cm (15-18in) apart; sprawling cvs should be planted 75cm (30in) apart.

Stagger sowing dates to prolong season as cucumbers only crop for limited period.

Alternatively sow *in situ* under jam jars or cloches for protection, in late spring or early summer. Nothing gained by sowing in cold soil: wait until soil temperature around 20°C (68°F).

Thin to one seed per station after germination. This method can be very successful as cucumbers do not transplant well.

Protect young seedlings against slugs.

Training

Train Japanese cvs against trellis, up cane tripods, wire or nylon netting; 23cm (9in) square mesh adequate. Tie in if necessary. Allow for 1 to 2m (3½ to 6½ft) growth.

Nip out growing point when top of support reached.

Older cvs climb less vigorously, but cucumbers better quality if grown against support and encouraged to climb even a metre or so. Growing point can be nipped out after six or seven leaves have formed in order to encourage stronger secondary growths which will fruit on side shoots. Tie in if necessary.

Keep weeded, well watered; mulching recommended.

Liquid feeding beneficial mid-summer onwards.

Syringing with water in hot weather helps control red spider mite.

Pollination

Ridge cucumbers insect pollinated, so whether grown outdoors or under cover, male flowers must *not* be removed, as is done with greenhouse cvs, which set fruit without pollination and become bitter and swollen if they are pollinated.

Cultivation in frames

Useful method for growing ridge cucumbers in cold districts, or in poor seasons. If possible train cucumbers off the ground, for example on a horizontal trellis (see diagram p.95). Keep frames well ventilated during the day. In hot weather spray regularly to keep down red spider mite. Top dress with good soil if roots appear on the surface.

Pests and Diseases

Aphids Problem in some seasons.

Slugs Particularly serious in early stages.

Red spider mite Problem in warm dry weather. Foliage becomes rusted. Burn badly infected leaves. Try spraying with derris. Biological control may be successful outdoors in summer months.

Mosaic virus Leaves become mottled and distorted. Burn young infected plants and leaves from older plants. Older plants may recover though yields lowered.

Powdery mildew White patches develop on leaves. No remedy. Grow resistant cvs where available.

Harvesting

Outdoor cucumbers crop mid-summer to early autumn.

Keep picking to encourage growth.

Small cucumbers can be pickled like gherkins.

Cultivars

Masterpiece, Mastermore (good mildew resistance) – short fruited types.

F₁ Burpee Hybrid, F₁ Burpless Tasty Green, Chinese Long Green, F₁ Tokyo Slicer, Yamato – Japanese types.

Crystal Apple (Lemon) – attractive, crisp, well-flavoured round fruit.

Bush Crop, Bush Champion – non-trailing bush cvs.

Conda – gherkin.

VSR*

ENDIVE *Cichorium endivium*

Low growing, loose-leaved plants; useful for year round salads. Natural flavour slightly bitter, but can be blanched to sweeten.

Types

Curled, *frisée* – pretty, fine, indented leaves; fairly flat head.

Broad-leaved, Batavian, *scarole/escarole* – larger plants, somewhat coarser, broader leaves, often with incurved, creamier coloured leaves in centre.

Broad-leaved types generally more disease and cold tolerant, and grow well in low light levels of winter. So most useful as lettuce substitute in late summer to late spring period.

Curled types better suited to summer cropping, but some reasonably hardy and grow well in winter. Ever increasing choice of good cvs, but each suited to sowing at certain periods. Be guided by catalogue and packet information.

Site and Soil

Summer crops need reasonably high fertility (dig in plenty of manure and compost), and good supply of moisture throughout growth. Winter crops need good drainage, but tolerate lower fertility: excess nitrogen can lead to lush growth making them prone to rotting diseases. Open site normally best; summer crops tolerate light shade.

Cultivation
Can grow as single plants, or CCA seedlings. Curled types most suitable for CCA seedlings.

Sow:

1 Early spring (under cover) to plant outside for early summer crop, or *in situ* for early crop CCA seedlings. Need temperature of about 20°C (68°F) to germinate. Plants may bolt (run to seed prematurely) if prolonged cold snap occurs.
2 Mid-/late spring for main summer supply.
3 Early/mid-summer for autumn supply. Can protect with cloches/crop covers to improve quality. May stand well into winter in mild areas. Use hardy cvs for later sowings.
4 Late summer, to plant under cover for winter crop. Use hardy cvs.
5 Beginning of autumn *in situ* under cover for winter CCA seedlings. Use hardy cvs.

For single plants sow *in situ*, or in seedtrays for transplanting, or in modules. Germination sometimes erratic: sowing in seedtrays and modules advisable in hot weather. Keep seedlings cool until germinated.

Space plants 25-35cm (10-15in) apart, depending on cv.

For CCA seedlings sow broadcast, or in narrow or wide drills about 10cm (4in) apart.

Keep winter crop reasonably well watered and mulched to prevent 'tipburn', where leaf margins dry out.

Blanching
Whether blanching considered necessary largely a matter of taste. Many modern cvs have fairly tight heads, so leaves to some extent blanched naturally with only a hint of bitterness. Curled types look very attractive blanched to near whiteness.

Plants can be completely blanched by excluding all light, or partially blanched so outer leaves remain green.

Normally ready within about ten days, but varies. Use quickly once ready or they will deteriorate.

~ Blanch a few plants at a time when fully mature – generally about 12 weeks after sowing.
~ Leaves *must* be dry or plants will rot when covered. Curled types most prone to rotting.
~ Partially blanch tall growing types by tying up heads. Partially blanch flat headed types by covering centre of plant with dinner plate or similar laid on plant. Or use purpose made blanching caps, which may only cover centre, or may be large enough to cover plant completely.
~ Completely blanch plants by covering with a bucket, or large inverted

flower pot with drainage hole blocked to exclude light, or blanching cap. Or replant under cover in darkened area as for 'Witloof' chicory, but without cutting back the leaves.

Harvesting

Cut across head when mature. Plants normally resprout several times, though they are less likely to do so after blanching. Endive responds well to CCA treatment at any stage, though the plants may run to seed rapidly in hot weather.

Protected winter crop can remain productive throughout winter into early spring.

CCA seedlings often ready within five weeks of sowing. Number of cuts depends on sowing time and cv.

Mainly used raw in salads, but can be cooked: often braised.

Cultivars

Curled: Ione – early and summer sowings.
Pancalière – any sowings; fairly hardy.
President, Ruffec, Wallonne – hardiest; summer sowings.
Broad-leaved: Golda, Casco d'oro, Cornet de Bordeaux – all versatile cvs.

VSR**; Curled type PP

FLORENCE FENNEL (Sweet fennel)
Foeniculum vulgare var. *azoricum*

Beautiful feather-leaved annual plant, growing about 45cm (18in) high; grown for swollen 'bulb' at base of stem.

Site and Soil

Must have well-drained, moisture-retentive soil, rich in organic matter. Prefers light sandy soil, but tolerates heavier soil.

Cultivation

Risk of fennel bolting rather than hearting if sown too early in the year or checked by dry or cold conditions. Must be grown fast. Some modern cvs have good bolting resistance.

Sow:
1 Late spring/early summer for outdoor summer crop.
2 Mid-summer/late summer to plant under cover for autumn use.
Fennel dislikes root disturbance.

Preferably sow in modules or *in situ*; otherwise in seedtrays, pricking out when very small, planting at four to five-leaf stage.

Space plants 30cm (12in) apart each way.

Watch for slugs in early stages.

Keep well watered; mulch to retain moisture and keep down weeds. Can earth up bulb when it starts swelling to blanch it, but not essential.

Tolerates light frost; cloche protection in autumn prolongs season.

Harvesting
Cut just above ground level when bulb formed. Leave stem to resprout with tasty smaller shoots. Aniseed-flavoured bulb used raw or braised. Use fern for flavouring. Flavour and appearance similar to closely related, perennial, herb fennel.

Cultivars
Perfection, Sirio, Sweet Florence – standard cvs.
Fino/Zefa Fino, Cantino – good bolting resistance (but not infallible!)

VSR* PP

GARLIC *Allium sativum*
Garlic bulbs form underground. Hardy plant; leaves grow 20-25cm (8-10in) high. Used fresh and also stored for winter. Some types keep longer than others. Many garlic strains available, but naming and descriptions haphazard! Where available, use strains adapted to your climate, and guaranteed disease-free.
Some types require a four to six week period of below freezing temperatures to break dormancy: these *must* be planted in autumn (see below).

Site and Soil
Open, sunny site. Does best on light, well-drained soil; avoid very heavy, poorly drained soil, unless taking special measures (see below). Lime soil if acid. Moderate level of fertility sufficient. Avoid freshly manured soil. Garlic seems to respond to potash; can work fresh bonfire ash into ground before planting. Reasonable levels of moisture needed in growing season.

Cultivation
Plant plump, healthy cloves, ideally about 1cm (½in) diameter, broken off from garlic bulb. Discard puny cloves.
The earlier garlic planted, the better.
On suitable soil plant early to late autumn *in situ*.
Depth of planting can vary; on light soils can plant up to 10cm (4in) deep. Plant less deeply in heavier soil, but cover cloves by at least 2.5cm (1in) soil. Plant flat end downwards.
For highest yields space cloves 18cm (7in) apart.
Where no alternative to growing on very heavy or poorly drained soil:
1 Plant in modules in autumn. Over-winter in cold frames; plant sprouted cloves outside in spring.
2 Plant *in situ* as early in spring as soil workable.
   To improve soil and drainage put layer of coarse sand or potting soil beneath bulbs when planting.

Or work soil into little ridges about 10cm (4in) high, and plant in the ridges, pushing the cloves below the surface.

Once established garlic requires little attention other than the occasional weeding.

Harvesting

Unlike onions, garlic should be lifted when leaves *start* to turn yellow, generally mid- to late summer. Better to lift garlic too soon rather than too late, or bulbs shatter and may start sprouting.

Bulbs may be quite deep; dig up carefully. (Always handle garlic carefully, as bruises lead to rots in store.)

Dry garlic outside for week to ten days, ideally in sunny, breezy conditions. If weather wet hang in greenhouse or conservatory with good through draught. They don't need to be baked excessively.

Store hanging in bunches or plaited, or laid on wooden shelves or in boxes, in dry, frost-free conditions. Ideal temperature 5 10°C (41-50°F). (Moistening the leaves first makes them easier to plait.)

Bulbs keep from six to 12 months depending on cv.

VSR*

Note: For cultivation of garlic chives see companion volume *Salads for Small Gardens*.

HAMBURG PARSLEY *Petroselinum crispum* var. *tuberosum*

Very hardy, dual purpose parsley. Edible roots 17-20cm (6½-8in) long, up to 7·5cm (3in) diameter. Deep green foliage remains green even in severe winters; can be used as a parsley substitute in cooking. Easily grown. Valuable winter vegetable.

Site and Soil

Will grow in open or semi-shade; appreciates moist situation. Tolerates poorer soil than most root crops. Soil preferably manured in the previous autumn.

Cultivation

Requires long growing season to develop large roots.

Sow early/late spring in drills 25cm (10in) apart. Thin to 13cm (5in) apart. Germination slow; can mix with radish seeds to mark rows.

Alternatively 'station sow', sowing radish or small lettuce cv such as 'Tom Thumb' or 'Little Gem' between 'stations'.

Can also sow in modules. Plant out before the tap root starts to develop.

Can also sow mid-summer, to stand winter and give earlier crop in the following year.

Keep weed free; mulch and water in dry summer.

Can leave in soil all winter.

Can cover with bracken, leaves, etc to make lifting easier in frost.
Can be lifted mid-/late autumn and stored in moist sand in shed, but some flavour is unfortunately lost in the process.

Harvesting
Ready late summer until following mid-spring.
Scrub roots before cooking; they discolour if peeled.
Roast under joint, mash with swedes grate in salads, fry as chips.
Excellent, sweet flavour. Roots can be dried for flavouring.
Use foliage for flavouring and garnishing in cooking.

VSR* PP

ICEPLANT *Mesembryanthemum crystallinum*
Fascinating, fleshy-leaved sprawling plant. Leaves covered with bladders that sparkle like dew! Not hardy. Grown in hot climates as spinach substitute, but much better used as a salad plant.

Site and Soil
Not fussy about soil provided well. Sunny site or light shade. Can be grown as undercrop.

Cultivation
Naturally perennial, but grown successfully as a half-hardy annual in cool climates.
Sow indoors in seedtray or modules mid-/late spring.
For early pickings, plant few under cover late spring.
Plant main crop outside mid-/late spring after risk of frost is over. Protect with cloches in early stages.
Space plants about 30cm (12in) apart.
Alternatively sow *in situ* outdoors after risk of frost.
Plants require little attention once they are established. Remove any flowers that appear.
For a late summer follow-on crop under cover take cuttings from established plants in mid-summer. Plant under cover when rooted.
Mature plants survive light frost; cloche in late summer to extend season and maintain quality.

Harvesting
Young leaves and stems, forming tips of the 'branches', are edible. Start by picking the young; pick constantly to encourage more tender growth.
Older leaves and stems become coarse.
Very succulent, so leaves don't wilt like most green vegetables, but keep fresh several days. Refreshing, slightly salty taste.

VSR** PP

KALE, CURLY (Borecole, Scotch kale)
Brassica oleracea Acephala Group

One of hardiest brassicas with deeply crinkled green or blue green leaves. Valuable in cold climates for winter/early spring greens. Both leaves and young shoots edible. Height ranges from 30-90cm (1-3ft) high with similar spread; dwarfer forms very compact, but taller probably more productive. Growing as closely spaced 'mini veg' and CCA seedlings useful techniques for small gardens. Normally healthy and free of pests and diseases.

Ornamental kale

Highly decorative, multi coloured forms grown mainly for ornamental colours in winter. Can be used for garnish, and, sparingly in winter salads. For cultivation see companion volume, *Salads for Small Gardens*.

Site and Soil

Less fussy than most brassicas, though does best in fairly rich, well-cultivated soil. Needs good drainage. Lime soil if acid; preferably manure previous autumn or for previous crop. Fairly resistant to clubroot; may succeed where other brassicas fail.

Cultivation and Harvesting

1 For main winter/spring supply.
   Sow mid-/late spring, thinly in seedbed, or in seedtrays or modules for future transplanting.
   Plant out in permanent position early/mid-summer.
   Space plants 30-75cm (1-2½ft) apart, depending on cv – the closer spacing for dwarf cvs.
   If necessary water in early stages to ensure well established.
   Keep weed free. Remove any lower rotting leaves.
   Dwarf plants can be covered with cloches/crop covers in autumn to make leaves more tender.
   Can give seaweed-based fertilizer following spring to stimulate shoot production.
   Pick leaves for use from about late autumn onwards. Pick a few at a time to encourage fresh growth and prolong the season.
   Side shoots develop early spring, typically from late winter until about mid-spring. Pick when young and tender, about 10-12cm (4-5in) long. More will develop over several weeks. Stop picking when flower buds form or stems become coarse.
2 Mini-veg (cv F_1 Shobor recommended for this technique)
   Sow from early to late spring, *in situ*, in rows 15-20cm (6-8in) apart, or in seedbed, in seedtrays or in modules for transplanting.
   Grow plants at equidistant spacing, 15-20cm (6-8in) apart each way.
   Can normally start picking about 18 weeks after sowing: ie late summer from first sowings.

Pick or cut individual leaves as required for use, leaving the plants to resprout.

They stand in good condition for many months without becoming tough. Will over-winter so picking can continue into following spring. If required can cover with cloches or crop covers in autumn to make leaves more tender.

3 CCA seedling crop

Provided soil workable, sow under cover mid- or late winter.

Sow thinly, *in situ* in single or wide drills about 15-20cm (6-8in) apart. Cut as seedlings when 5-7·5cm (2-3in) high, or thin out a little and cut as greens when 15-20cm (6-8in) high. If sown under cloches/crop covers outside, remove covers in early spring.

Kale has fairly strong flavour. Use tender young curly kale leaves and shoots in salads. Otherwise steam, stir-fry, or cook in minimum amount of water. Serve with butter or 'Glorious Garnish' sauce: 5:1 mix of vegetable oil and light soya sauce, plus crushed garlic. This is delicious and well worth trying! With its deep colour and attractive curly leaves kale makes an excellent winter garnish.

Cultivars

Modern F_1 hybrids probably give best value in small gardens.
Darkibor, Fribor, Showbor – F_1 hybrids.
Dwarf Green Curled – older cv.

VSR *Single plants, CCA seedlings, **Mini-veg; PP

KOHL RABI *Brassica oleracea* Gonglodes Group

Odd looking, under-rated, rather beautiful looking brassica. Plants grow about 30cm (1ft) high. Stem swells into a ball-like, 'mid air' bulb roughly 5-7·5cm (2-3in) diameter. Purple- and green- (often known as white) skinned forms; the former may be the best flavoured, the latter hardier. Kohl rabi very nutritious; bulbs have delicate turnip-like flavour. Young leaves also edible.

Withstands drought, heat and clubroot well. May succeed where other brassicas, such as turnips, fail.

Small kohl rabi grown as 'mini veg' very appealing: particularly useful crop for small garden.

Modern cvs great improvement on older ones.

Site and Soil

Fertile, light sandy soil ideal, but tolerates heavier soil.

Cultivation

Valuable catch crop and for intercropping, as can mature within eight weeks of sowing. (See pp.105-9.)

Make several sowings for continuous supply. Green-skinned cvs are generally faster maturing and used for earliest sowings.

Don't sow at soil temperatures below 10°C (50°F) as there is a high risk of plants bolting prematurely in such circumstances.

Sow:

1 For early summer crop sow mid-winter/early spring, in gentle heat indoors. Sow in modules, and transplant outside, after hardening-off, when no more than 5cm (2in) high. Space plants about 25-30cm (10-12in) apart each way. (Considerably closer spacing can also prove perfectly successful.)

Can protect with cloches or crop covers in early stages.

2 For main summer crop sow in modules or *in situ* outdoors, from early spring until late summer. Plant or thin to spacing above.

Thin early as development is checked if seedlings become overcrowded. Station sowing about 10cm (4in) apart helpful practice.

Purple-skinned cultivars traditionally sown from early summer onwards.

3 If kohl rabi popular in household, make late sowing under cover in late summer/early autumn for early winter crop.

Keep plants weed free. Mulching beneficial to retain soil moisture and encourage fast growth.

Mini-kohl rabi

(Cv F₁ 'Rolano' is recommended for this technique)

Sow *in situ* outside from late spring until late summer, in drills 15cm (6in) apart. Thin plants to 2·5cm (1in) apart.

Best harvested at ping pong size when very tender: normally ready within nine weeks of sowing.

Regular sowings will give supplies from early summer right through until mid-autumn.

Late sowings can be covered with cloches to prolong season.

For a very early crop sow from early spring onwards. Only recommended in warm areas, or under cover.

Pests and Diseases

Slugs In the early stages and *pigeons* early in the year likely problems.

Flea beetle and *cabbage root fly* Occasionally attack. May also be affected by *clubroot*, but normally matures fast enough to avoid serious attack.

Harvesting

With old cvs standard advice was to eat when no larger than tennis ball size, as larger bulbs became 'woody'. Modern cvs remain tender when larger, and stand in good condition longer.

Can be left in the ground in early winter and mild weather. In colder conditions can lift and store in boxes of sand in frost-free shed. Remove outer leaves, but leave central tuft of leaves on bulb. Some flavour lost when stored.

Cook leaves and bulbs separately. Cook bulb unpeeled, as best flavour said to be just below the skin. Steaming recommended. Can be boiled/steamed then stuffed; served with sauces; grated raw in salads.

Cultivars
F₁ Lanro, Rolano, F₁ Rowel – white-skinned.
Delicacy Purple – purple-skinned.

VSR** PP

KOMATSUNA (Mustard spinach)
Brassica rapa Perviridis Group
Diverse group of Japanese greens, created by crossing various brassicas. Generally have large, glossy, bright green leaves. Komatsuna group notable for vigour, versatility, healthiness and tolerance to wide range of temperatures. Some cvs exceptionally hardy. Reputedly very nutritious. Mainly grown for cooked greens, but can be used in salads. Flavour depends on cv; generally in cabbage spectrum with hints of mustard and spinach. Excellent value in small gardens.

Site and Soil
Open site; fertile, moisture-retentive soil. Like all oriental greens needs to grow fast with plenty of moisture throughout growth.

Cultivation
Can grow as single plants, harvested at any stage from small to fully mature, or as CCA seedlings.
Komatsuna responds well to CCA treatment at every stage.
Although most cvs very hardy, growing some plants under cover in winter recommended: plants will be exceptionally tender-leaved, and more productive in mid-winter than outdoor plants.
Sowings for single plants
1 Sow from early to late summer for the main late summer/autumn/winter crop outdoors.
2 Sow late summer/early autumn for plants to be transplanted under cover for top quality winter to spring crop.
 Sow *in situ* outdoors, or in seedtrays or modules for transplanting.
 Either space plants about 10cm (4in) apart for small plants harvested young, or 30-35cm (12-14in) apart for large plants harvested over a long period.
Sowings for CCA seedlings
1 Sow mid-/late winter under cover for early crop
2 Sow early spring, as soon as soil workable, until late summer outside for summer to autumn crop. Early and late sowings can be protected with cloches to improve quality.
3 Sow early autumn under cover for winter/spring crop. Sow thinly *in situ*, broadcast, or in narrow or wide drills about 10cm (4in) apart.

Cut seedlings from about 10cm (4in) high onwards. Several cuts can usually be made.

Pests and Diseases
Theoretically susceptible to all brassica pests and diseases (see Cabbage), but in practice a healthy crop. Growing under fine nets recommended in summer months to protect against flying pests.

Harvesting
Number of days from sowing to harvesting depends on the cv and when sown. Averages are: seedlings 20-35; small plants 35 (summer) to 60 (winter); large plants 55 (summer) to 80 (winter).
Cut whole heads of young plants, or single leaves of larger plants when useable size. Leave plants to resprout; they normally remain productive over many months.
Plants eventually run to seed in late spring.
The young flowering shoots tasty raw or cooked. If eating raw, have trial taste first.
Some cvs very peppery at flowering shoot stage.
Use young leaves, young stems, flowering shoots and shredded older leaves raw as an ingredient in salads. Otherwise cook by any methods suitable for greens or kales.

Cultivars
Komatsuna, Tendergreen, F₁ Green Boy.

VSR ****CCA seedlings, ***Single plants

Note: Excellent winter hardy cvs 'Hiroshimana' and 'Shirona' (technically considered types of loose Chinese cabbage), perform like komatsuna. Seed currently only rarely available. Where obtained grow like komatsuna and use for winter greens.

LAMB'S LETTUCE see Corn Salad

LAND CRESS (American land cress, Upland cress)
Barbarea verna
Hardy, low-growing, fast-maturing, glossy leaved plant.
Flavour almost identical to watercress. Underrated salad crop, available all year round.

Site and Soil
Plenty of organic matter in soil. Succeeds in damp, semi-shaded positions most vegetables dislike. Ideal for small city gardens.
Borders that receive little sun are quite suitable. Can intercrop between taller or widely spaced vegetables.

Cultivation

Sow early spring to early summer for summer use; mid-summer to early autumn for winter/spring use. (Generally considered the most useful crop.)

Can plant late sowings under cover for top quality winter crop.

Sow broadcast, or in drills 23cm (9in) apart; water drills thoroughly beforehand in dry weather. (See Tools and Techniques p.47.)

Can also sow in seedtrays or modules and transplant.

Thin or transplant to 15-20cm (6-8in) apart.

Young seedlings sometimes attacked by flea beetle. Spray with derris or grow under fine nets.

Normally ready within eight weeks of sowing.

May run to seed prematurely in hot weather/dry conditions; keep plants well watered.

Pick leaves as required. Leave plants to resprout, though, in my experience, they are not always very productive.

Will stand outside all winter, but quality much improved by protecting with cloches, or even with light covering of straw or bracken.

Plants run to seed early following spring. Will often conveniently seed themselves if left undisturbed in dampish soil. If dense crop of seedlings result, treat as CCA seedling crop. Can transplant seedlings if required.

Mainly used as salad plant. Can be cooked as a substitute for watercress.

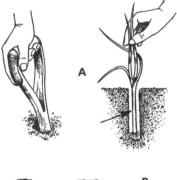

VSR**

LEEKS (*Allium porrum*)

Very hardy winter vegetable in onion family, grown for long white shaft.

Site and Soil

Open site. Succeeds in most fertile, well-cultivated soil preferably prepared and manured previous autumn; or dig in compost or well-rotted manure before planting. Dislikes compacted soil. Good crop to grow where garden troubled by clubroot: may help to reduce clubroot infection.

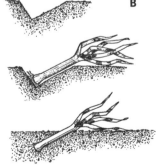

Above (A) Planting leeks in a 15-20cm (6-8in) deep hole
Below (B) 'Heeling in' leeks in a shallow angled trench

Cultivation

Long growing season essential for large leeks, but smaller, faster growing 'mini leeks' a delicacy ideally suited to small gardens. (See p.186.)

Leeks divided roughly into types according to their approximate season of maturity.

'Earlies' – main season autumn; 'mid-season' – main season winter; 'lates' – main season spring. Earlier cvs generally taller, paler, less hardy. Later cvs shorter, broader, darker often blue green leaves, hardier.

Leeks germinate poorly at soil temperatures below 7°C (45°F).

Best sown in seedbed, seedtrays or modules for transplanting, as this enables deep planting which helps to get nice long white shaft. Sow about 2·5cm (1in) deep.

Can sow *in situ* if easier.

Leeks respond well to being multi-sown in modules. Sow three to four seeds per module. Plant 23cm (9in) apart each way.

For continuous supply make several sowings, starting with earliest cvs.

1 Indoors in propagator late winter/early spring. Harden-off well before planting out. Mainly early cvs.

2 Indoors, or outdoors if soil workable, early/mid-spring. Can sow under cloches. Mainly mid season cvs.

3 Indoors or outdoors late spring. Late cvs.

Plant leeks 10-15 weeks after sowing, ideally when about 20cm (8in) tall. Planting can spread from early to late summer.

Key to growing large leeks – good soil, long growing season, large transplants, wide spacing.

For highest yield of average size leeks space plants about 23cm (9in) apart each way; or grow 15cm (6in) apart in rows 30cm (12in) apart. This will allow for intercropping with lettuce, or winter salads such as corn salad or winter purslane.

Closer spacing, that is 10-15cm (4-6in) apart, also gives reasonable sized leeks.

Leeks *can* be planted on the flat, but normally planted in holes to get blanched stem.

Make 15-20cm (6 8in) deep hole with dibber. Drop leek in hole. Water gently with fine spout.

Allow earth to drop into hole naturally in due course, so leek stems becomes blanched.

Note: Traditional practice of trimming leaf tips and root ends before planting probably lowers yields, but leaf tips can be trimmed off if they are dragging on the soil.

Pests and Diseases

Leeks relatively trouble free.

Slugs Enjoy leaves but effect not as devastating as might be expected.

Cutworm Grubs can attack roots of young plants. Watering heavily when grubs young by far the best remedy.

Rust Disease giving leaves rusty colour; seems to be on increase. No remedy at present. Leeks normally still useable though unsightly and yields probably lowered.

Harvesting
Leeks ready from early autumn until late spring. Pull as required, using less hardy, early cvs first.
If the ground is required for cultivation in the spring, uproot leeks and 'heel in' (see diagram p.184). First make a shallow, angled trench in soil; lay the leeks in it. Cover stems with soil so that only leaves protrude.

Mini-leeks (Recommended cvs: King Richard, Lancelot, Lavi)
Cultivation
Sow early spring to mid-summer *in situ* either in shallow wide drills, spacing seeds 6mm-1cm ($\frac{1}{4}$-$\frac{1}{2}$in) apart, or in rows 15cm (6in) apart, spacing seeds 1cm ($\frac{1}{2}$in) apart.
Pencil thin leeks ready for pulling after about 13 weeks when 15-20cm (6-8in) tall.
In my experience can leave standing for many weeks without loss of quality; in mild winters they are still useable and tender the following spring, even after over-wintering. Can be cooked or used as a raw ingredient in salads.

Cultivars
Trials have indicated the following cvs are especially recommended for organic gardeners. In order of maturity:
King Richard, Blue Green Autumn Verina, Blue Green Autumn Cortina, Blue Green Winter Derrick.
Musselburgh – reliable late cv.

VSR** PP

LETTUCE *Lactuca sativa*
Most widely grown salad plant of all, ideally suited to temperate cool climates. Divided into headed and loose-leaf types. Normally green, but very attractive red-and bronze-leaved forms of all types widely available.

Headed types
Note: 'Cabbage head': general term embracing both 'butterhead' and 'crisphead' types.

Butterhead/roundhead
Flattish, gently rounded heads with soft, buttery textured leaves. Mostly well flavoured, but the leaves wilt soon after picking. Generally faster growing than crispheads, but tendency to run to seed once mature, especially in warm weather.

Crispheads

Compact hearts of crisp leaves. Generally slower maturing/slower bolting than butterheads. Includes very crisp 'Iceberg' type – name given to types sold with outer leaves stripped off. (Many find 'Icebergs' poorly flavoured, though reddish cvs seem better flavoured.) Reddish tinted 'Batavian' group considered well flavoured.

Cos/Romaine

Large, tall, upright, somewhat loose-hearted lettuces. Thick, slightly bubbled leaves with sweet 'real' flavour. Slower to mature than the cabbage heads; many cvs are relatively hardy. 'Semi-cos' group: small framed; crisp-hearted: exceptionally sweet cos lettuces typified by the well known cv 'Little Gem'. One of the best cvs to choose for small vegetable gardens.

Loose-leaved types

'Salad Bowl' type

Plants form loose tuft of leaves and occasionally, small, loose heart. Much slower bolting than headed lettuces; ideal for CCA harvesting over many weeks or months. Very productive where space limited. Generally vigorous and healthy. Very versatile in use. Soft, mild flavoured leaves wilt rapidly once they are picked. 'Salad Bowl' cvs have given name to group. Characterized by indented leaves, in some cvs rounded indentations like oak-leaves. Very deeply curled 'Lollo' types highly decorative and could be grown in flowerbeds.

'Cutting lettuces'

Group of traditional continental cvs used for CCA seedling crops. Give very quick returns throughout growing season. Smooth and crisp-leaved cvs are available.

Stem lettuce/Celtuce

Oriental type grown for its thick stem. For cultivation see companion volume *Salads for Small Gardens* and *Oriental Vegetables* (see p.248).

Site and Soil

Light, well-drained, fertile soil. Dig in plenty of well-rotted organic matter beforehand to make soil moisture retentive. Avoid very dry soils. Rotate around garden to prevent build up of the soil pest, root aphid. Open site normally preferable, but summer lettuce tolerates light shade. Small cvs like 'Little Gem' and 'Tom Thumb', and CCA seedlings, useful for intercropping.

Cultivation

With successive sowing, choice of appropriate cv and use of protected cropping, can pick lettuce almost all year round, though for headed crop in mid-winter heated greenhouse normally necessary. (See p.188 for principal sowings.)

Headed lettuce can be sown *in situ* or in a seedbed, in seedtrays, or in modules for transplanting.

In situ sowing advisable for mid-summer sowings, as lettuce transplants badly in dry conditions. (Alternatively raise in modules and transplant.) Sow seed 1-2cm (½-¾in) deep.

Start thinning when about 5cm (2in) high. In cool conditions thinnings can be transplanted to give a succession, normally maturing about ten days later.

High temperature dormancy

Lettuce germinates well at low temperatures, but germination is erratic if the soil temperatures are above 25°C (77°F) within a few hours of sowing. Potentially a problem from around late spring onwards. Can be overcome by:

~ Sowing between 2 and 4pm, so critical period occurs in the evening or at night.
~ Watering the soil before sowing to reduce the soil temperature.
~ Keeping seed in a fridge for a week or two before sowing; this effectively breaks the dormancy.
~ Sowing in seedtrays or modules, and then putting them in a cool place to germinate.

Transplant at four- to five-leaf stage, so the lowest leaves are just above soil level.

Equidistant spacing strongly recommended as lettuces blanket soil well when mature. Spacing varies with the cv. On average:

~ Small cvs 15-20cm (6-8in) apart each way.
~ Standard butterheads 27cm (11in) apart each way.
~ Crispheads 33-38cm (13-15in) apart each way.

Large cos and 'Salad Bowl' 35cm (14in) apart each way.

(If growing in rows adjust the spacing accordingly, see Tools and Techniques p.43.)

Mulching after planting very beneficial.

Lettuce requires little attention once established, other than keeping it weed free.

Must be grown fast with plenty of water. In dry weather weekly watering at rate of 22 litre/m² (4gal/yd²), recommended. Critical period for watering a week or ten days before maturing.

Extra feeding not normally necessary in fertile soil; apply seaweed-based fertilizer during growth if plants seem to be below par.

Principal sowings

For continuous supply sowing 'little and often' recommended; helps to overcome the problem of lettuce bolting prematurely.

1 Spring sowing in unheated greenhouses, frames or cloches for late spring/early summer crop.

~ Sow from late winter in warmer areas, or from early spring where the weather is colder. Can make first sowings in gentle heat in propagator.

~ Thin out or transplant outside in early/mid-spring. Can protect with crop covers initially; remove them after three or four weeks, or earlier in very hot weather.

~ Use cos types; butterheads recommended for early sowings; 'Salad Bowl' types.

2 Main outdoor summer sowings for early summer to mid-autumn crop.

~ Sow in succession as soon as the soil is workable in spring until about mid-summer. Make mid-summer sowings *in situ* or sow in modules to transplant later on.

~ Lettuce grows at different rates throughout the season: for continuous supply make 'next' sowing when the seedlings from previous sowing appear through the soil.

~ In late autumn can cover with cloches to prolong the season. Use any types *except* butterheads recommended only for early sowings. Choose mildew resistant cvs for late sowings.

3 Autumn sowing of hardy outdoor lettuce, maturing late spring/early summer following year.

~ Sow *in situ* late summer or early autumn, thinning to no more than 7.5cm (3in) apart. (Thin to final spacing in spring.)

~ Although hardy, covering with cloches or crop covers will improve both the quality as well as giving earlier maturity. Use cos and hardy butterheads cvs.

4 Autumn and winter sowings in unheated greenhouses, maturing between late autumn and late winter or early spring

~ Sow from late summer to mid-autumn, choosing the optimum time specified for each cv.

~ Can sow earlier sowings in seedbeds outside or in seedtrays or modules for transplanting into greenhouses or frames.

~ Sow later sowings *in situ* in greenhouses or frames, or in seedtrays or modules for transplanting. Use only butterhead or crisphead cvs recommended for winter greenhouse production.

Cut-and-come-again seedlings
Highly productive method of lettuce growing in limited space. Cut small leaves when 5-10cm (2-4in) high.

Normally ready three or four weeks after sowing; usually resprout to give a second, occasionally even a third cutting. Use 'cutting' lettuces or 'Salad Bowl' types.

Can sow throughout growing season, but mid-summer sowings may bolt rapidly or quickly become coarse. Under most conditions the following prove most productive sowings:

1 Very early spring under cover.
2 Spring outdoors.
3 Late summer/early autumn outdoors.

4 Early/mid-autumn under cover. (This sowing often productive during winter until the following spring.)

Sow in narrow or wide drills about 10cm (4in) apart. Aim to space seeds about 1cm (½in) apart.

'Leaf lettuce' system

Very productive method of growing lettuce leaves (ie unhearted lettuce) developed at the Wellesbourne research station for catering industry. Devised to give succession of crisp cos lettuce leaves – without having to cut up head.

This formula has been developed in the UK to a keep family of four supplied with lettuce from a small area from late spring to autumn, sowing roughly a square metre (yard) each time (see Seasonal Guide to Main Garden Jobs p.240).

~ Make a succession of small sowings. Each is cut twice – as with CCA seedlings above, cutting when leaves 8-13cm (3½-5in)high.

~ Sow in fertile, weed free ground; keep well watered.

~ Sow in rows about 13cm (5in) apart; aim to space plants about 2·5cm (1in) apart.

To compensate for varying growth rates throughout the season:

~ Sow weekly from mid- to late spring. Make the first cut 50 days or so later; second cut after another 50 days, ie from mid- to late summer.

~ Sow weekly in late summer to maintain continuity. Make first cuts about 24 days later in early autumn; second further 31 days later in mid-autumn.

~ Unless you are experimentally inclined, only use tested cos cvs such as 'Lobjoits', 'Valmaine', 'Paris White Cos'. Others may become bitter under this system.

Pests and Diseases

Slugs, snails, cutworm, leatherjackets Attack below and above ground in early stages. Take standard control measures.

Birds Can be damaging. Protect with fine nets or black cotton.

Leaf aphids Take standard control methods as soon as noticed.

Root aphids White, soil inhabiting aphids; colonize roots and cause sudden wilting. No remedy. Practise rotation. Use cvs with some resistance such as 'Avondefiance', 'Musette', 'Sabine'.

Various rotting diseases Most common in early spring and autumn. Grow plants well; thin seedlings early; avoid overcrowding. Use cvs with good disease resistance.

Harvesting

Headed types – normally pulled up when required. Heads maturing in early spring can be cut across stump, which may resprout to give secondary (very useful, but less than perfect looking) head in about five weeks time. Later in season secondary leaves tend to be bitter.

With 'Salad Bowl' types cut across head or pick individual leaves as they are required.

Lettuce normally used raw in salads, but can be cooked and used in soup. Good way of utilizing bolted plants.

Cultivars

Enormous choice!

Butterhead – Debbie, Marvel of Four Seasons, Tom Thumb, Hilde (early sowing), Novita, Columbus, Cynthia (winter under cover), Valdor (hardy ing).

Crisphead – Windermere, Lakeland, Webb's Wonderful, Kelly's (winter under cover), Rouge Grenobloise, Regina Ghiacci/Queen of the Ice (Batavian type); Saladin, Lakeland (Iceberg type); Tiger, Sioux (reddish icebergs).

Cos – Winter Density, Lobjoits Green Cos, Valmaine, Corsair.

Semi-cos – Little Gem, Jewel, Bubbles

Salad Bowl – Catalogna, red and green 'Salad Bowl', red and green Lollo, Valeria (red 'Lollo'), Lumina

VSR ***CCA, leaf lettuce, Salad Bowl types

**summer lettuce, protected winter lettuce

*over-wintered outdoor lettuce

PP Salad Bowl types

MARROWS (Vegetable marrow/ summer squash) & COURGETTES *Cucurbita pepo*

Tender, often climbing, annuals. Marrows and courgettes same vegetable. Courgettes simply immature fruits picked young – but only some marrow cvs suitable for use as courgettes.

Many types of marrow: mature fruits can be long, round, flat, fluted (custard marrow or 'Patty Pan'), club shaped.

Colour can be green, yellow, white, grey or striped.

Mainly used fresh, although some marrows can be stored for short periods of time.

Flowers and shoot tips edible.

Modern hybrid bush courgettes very productive and compact – about 45cm (18in) high, 60-90cm (2-3ft) spread. Suitable for small gardens.

Trailing types commonly trail 1.5-1.8m (5-6ft). Economical of space when trained upwards on supports. (See Space Saving p.100.)

Site and Soil

See Cucumbers.

Cultivation

Sowing: see Cucumbers.

No advantage in starting prematurely as extremely susceptible to cold weather; however very fast growing once established.

Can make second sowing of courgettes in early summer for follow on-crop, as cropping season short.

Plant when two good leaves, with third developing.

Plant bush types about 90cm (3ft) apart; climbing types 45cm (18in) apart if climbing; 1.2m (4ft) apart if trailing.

To save space can plant trailing types under sweet corn. Alternatively train in neat circle by pinning leading shoot down with twigs or wire pin, leaving enough space for stem to expand. Plants often produce useful secondary roots on stem.

Make sure climbing types have sufficiently strong supports; may need to be tied in to supports, especially in early stages. Less vigorous types like round-fruited 'Little Gem' and 'Table Dainty' can be trained up strings. Keep mulched and well watered; don't water in full sun or plant may get leaf scorch.

Can liquid feed from mid-summer if growth appears to be slowing.

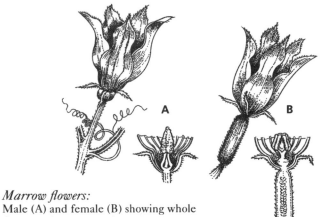

Marrow flowers:
Male (A) and female (B) showing whole flower and a cross section

Pollination

Marrows have separate male and female flowers; pollination by insects normally necessary to get fruit.

Female flowers distinguished by small, embryonic fruit behind petals (see diagram above).

In very cold seasons and early in year fruits may fail to set, and are worth hand pollinating.

Select fully open male flower, strip off petals, push it into centre of female flower. Either leave it there or use to pollinate another flower.

Natural tendency for male flowers to be produced early in year – and for female flowers to be produced later. Frustrating! No remedy other than waiting or using parthenocarpic cv.

Parthenocarpic cvs
Newly introduced cvs (such as F_1 Moreno) in which fruits set without pollination. Worth trying where setting problems encountered, though current cvs may be less robust than standard cvs.

Pests and Diseases
See Cucumber.
Cucumber mosaic virus Common problem; some recently introduced cvs have good resistance (see below).
Mildew My own observation that custard marrow 'Patty Pan' has better resistance than most cvs.

Harvesting
Courgettes can be ready within seven or eight weeks of sowing.
Pick long types from very small up to 10-15cm (4-6in) long; patty pan types best flavour when no larger than 6-7·5cm ($2\frac{1}{2}$-3in) diameter.
Must keep picking regularly to prevent courgettes developing into marrows and to encourage further cropping.
Plants will be destroyed by first frost.
Many methods of cooking; normally peeling unnecessary.
Pick marrows when size required.
For winter storage leave few on plant until end of season so skins can harden. Cut before frost.
Hang in nets in cool airy place at temperature of 7-10°C (45-50°F).
Normally keep for about two months.

Cultivars
F_1 hybrids highly recommended for small gardens.
F_1 Defender, F_1 Supremo, F_1 Tiger Cross – bush courgettes with mosaic virus tolerance.
F_1 Ambassador, F_1 Early Gem – bush types, suitable for courgettes and marrows.
F_1 Gold Rush – bush courgette, yellow-fruited.
Rondo de Nice, Tender and True – bush types, round fruit.
Custard White, F_1 Sunburst – large bushes, 'Patty Pan' type fruits.
Little Gem, Table Dainty – small round fruits.
Vegetable Spaghetti, Long Green Trailing – trailing marrows.

VSR** PP

MIBUNA GREENS *Brassica rapa* var. *nipposinica*
Attractive, fast growing Japanese brassica, closely related to mizuna greens. Healthy, narrow, strap-like leaves, 30-45cm (12-18in) long, forming dense clumps 25-30cm (10-12in) or more across. Moderately hardy plant, surviving about -6°C (21°F) in the open. Tolerates wide range of temperatures but is most useful as late summer to winter greens.

Inclined to bolt prematurely from spring sowing.

Very pleasant, mild mustard flavour. Can be used raw in salads or cooked. Grow as single plants or as CCA seedlings; not quite as productive as mizuna. For cultivation see Mizuna Greens. 'Green Spray' only cv currently available.

VSR** PP

MIZUNA GREENS (Kyona, Potherb mustard)
Brassica rapa var. *nipposinica*

Beautiful Japanese brassica with glossy, serrated, dark green leaves with narrow white stalks. Mature plants form clumps up to about 27cm (11in) high, often over 30cm (12in) across. Very adaptable, vigorous, easily grown plant; tolerates high and low temperatures. If kept cropped will survive about -10°C (14°F) in the open.

Pleasant, mild mustard flavour. Used as mibuna.

Site and Soil

Does best in fertile soil, but tolerates wide range of soils and conditions. Mid-summer crop requires plenty of moisture or may bolt prematurely. Normally open situation, but tolerates light shade mid-summer. Very decorative; can grow in flower beds in patches or as edging.

Cultivation

Very versatile plant. Grow as single plants or as CCA seedlings.

Excellent for undercropping and intercropping both as single plants kept compact by constant cutting or as CCA seedlings.

For sowing methods and times see Komatsuna.

In addition late spring to early summer sowings may succeed, as mizuna has more resistance to bolting prematurely from spring sowings than many oriental greens. Still some risk of bolting in very dry conditions.

Space plants 10cm (4in) apart for small plants, 20-23cm (8-9in) apart for medium plants, 30cm (12in) apart for large plants. Thinnings can be transplanted or used in salads.

Excessive rainfall or snow can cause winter crop to rot.

Protect outdoor crops with cloches or low polytunnels if these conditions are likely to occur.

Pests and diseases

Theoretically, the plants are subject to common brassica pests (see Cabbage), but in practice *flea beetle* on young plants most serious problem. Take standard measures, or grow under fine nets to protect from all flying pests.

Harvesting

May be able to cut CCA seedlings within about three weeks of sowing, especially if growing conditions have been good; larger plants within six to eight weeks. Pick single leaves or cut across whole plant about 5cm (2in) above ground level; leave to resprout. Can be cut frequently – sometimes up to five times before running to seed. May even resprout again if flowering heads cut back.

Cultivars
Mizuna – deeply serrated leaves.
F_1 Tokyo Beau, F_1 Tokyo Belle – broader leaved, hardier hybrids.

VSR ***Single plants, ****CCA seedlings; PP

MUSTARD Sinapsis alba, SALAD RAPE Brassica napus var. napus, GARDEN CRESS Lepidium sativum
Seedlings used in salads and sandwiches all year round. Can grow indoors or in the garden.

Cultivation indoors
Sow in shallow boxes, seedtrays, or other shallow containers on thin layer of well-sifted soil, soilless compost, bulb fibre or sifted leaf mould, or on dishes on damp flannel or moist blotting paper.
If soil or equivalent base used, seedlings should give a second crop.
Water sowing medium gently before sowing.
Sow seeds fairly thickly and evenly on surface; press in gently with board; do not cover with soil.
Cover container or put in dark to encourage rapid growth.
After a week move into light for two or three days to become green.
Cut for eating when 4-5cm (1½-2in) high.
Mustard normally germinates faster than cress, so if wanted together, sow three days after cress, in same or separate container. New cvs of cress much faster growing; can be sown at same time. Milder flavoured salad rape seed can be substituted for mustard. In practice germination rates of different cvs of mustard, cress and rape variable. Worth doing small trials to test; then sow slowest germinating first.
Flavour also varies; some cress cvs more pungent than others.
At day temperature of 15-18°C (59-64°F) older cvs cress ready for cutting ten days after sowing; mustard and rape after seven days.
Sow for succession at weekly or ten-day intervals all year round.

Cultivation outdoors
Light soil; open site spring and autumn; shaded site in summer.
Spring and autumn sowings best value; summer sowings run to seed fast.
Broadcast seed in small patches, or intersow, for example between newly planted brassicas.
In cool weather and moist soil four or five cuts can be made in succession. Rape is mildest in flavour, slowest to run to seed; can be left to grow

20-25cm (8-10in) high for use as greens. Provides pickings over many months. (In my view mature cress and mustard become too peppery.)

Useful sowing: early/mid-autumn under cover, for example in unheated greenhouse or frame. (Can sow after tomatoes cleared.) Make one or two cuts in early winter. Growth normally ceases in mid-winter, but re-starts very early in spring. Continue cutting until plants run to seed in spring. Very early sowings under cover also recommended.

Cultivars
Cress – Armado (fast growing, hot flavour); Broad-leaved – large-leaved; Greek – distinctive type, well flavoured.
Super Salad – (fast growing, large leaves, mild flavour).
Mustard – Tilney.
Rape – Broad-leaved Essex.

VSR****

MUSTARDS, ORIENTAL *Brassica juncea*
Large group of rugged oriental vegetables gradually being introduced to the west. Varying degrees of hardiness; mostly at their best during the winter. Leaves somewhat coarse, but gutsy flavour. Stems often thickened and exceptionally well flavoured. Worth growing for 'something different' in winter. Best used steamed or stir-fried.
Note: Of those currently available in west, following probably most suitable for small gardens. Consult *Oriental Vegetables* (see Further Reading p.248) for more information and other types. Be prepared for considerable confusion over names in seed catalogues!

Site and Soil
Not as fussy as many brassicas, but do best in fertile, moisture-retentive, well-drained soil, on open site.

Cultivation
Fast growing like most oriental greens; generally mature within two to three months of sowing.
Tendency to bolt from spring and early summer sowings.
Main sowing: mid- to late summer for autumn to spring crops.
Can transplant some under cover in early autumn for more productive, top quality, winter crop.
Outdoor plants can be covered with cloches/row covers in winter to improve quality, but not essential.
Mustards run to seed in spring after planting and become very hot flavoured.
Generally healthy plants free of pests and diseases. Slugs and flea beetle in early stages most likely problems. Take standard control measures.
Best sown in seedtrays or modules and transplanted. Can be sown *in situ*.

Large leaved mustard 'Amsoi' (also called Indian mustard)

Large-leaved, thick-stemmed plant. Easily grows 30cm (12in) high and has an equal spread; plant grows considerably larger when kept under cover. Moderately hardy. Traditional oriental pickling mustard with excellent flavour.

Sow as opposite. Space plants about 38cm (15in) apart; or grow more closely for smaller plants.

Cut whole plant or individual leaves as required. Will resprout over many weeks, especially where grown under cover.

Large leaved purple mustards – 'Red Giant', 'Osaka Purple', 'Miike Giant'

Handsome large-leaved mustards. Crepe-like leaves with varying degrees of purple tints. Grow about 27cm (11in) high with similar spread. Reasonably hardy. Very decorative.

Sow as opposite, spacing plants about 30cm (12in) apart.

Harvest as 'Amsoi' above; re-growth not quite as vigorous.

Can also sow from spring (first sowing under cover) to summer as CCA seedling crop. Seedlings make colourful, spicy addition to salads. Sow frequently as will run to seed fairly fast. Make late sowing early autumn under cover for winter seedlings.

Common or leaf mustards (Gai choy)

Medium sized leaves, often with serrated edges. Can grow up to about 30cm (12in) high, depending on cv. Reasonably hardy. Quite strong flavour. Strong tendency to bolt from spring sowings.

Sow and harvest as for 'Amsoi'. Space plants about 23cm (9in) apart.

Can also grow plants more closely, spacing plants about 10-15cm (4-6in) apart, for harvesting at younger stage when the leaves reach about 15-20cm (6-8in) high.

Green-in-the-snow (Serifong/Xue-li-hong) mustard

Very vigorous, extremely hardy, plants with strong flavoured, serrated leaves. Plants generally 25cm (10in) high and similar spread.

Sow as common mustard. Can grow at various spacings, from about 10-25cm (4-10in), for harvesting at different stages.

VSR **Purple-leaved; PP

ONIONS *Allium cepa*

Large family of strongly-flavoured, biennial and perennial plants. With careful choice of cvs, possible to have homegrown onions from the garden almost all year round.

'Bulb' onions – main source of culinary onion. Bulbs can be used both fresh or stored. Only certain cvs suitable for storage. Some types grown very closely to obtain miniature onions for pickling.

'Salad' or 'spring' onions – grown for young green leaves and small, rudimentary bulbs. Used mainly for salads/seasoning. These are selected cvs of bulb onions.

Site and Soil

Open site; fertile, thoroughly-dug, well-prepared soil. Good drainage essential. Onions (especially spring onions) sensitive to acidity, so lime if soil acid. Ideally manure soil several months before sowing or planting; growth too lush if freshly manured. In spite of permanent 'onion patch' tradition, advisable to rotate over minimum four year cycle if possible to prevent build up of eelworm (nematodes) and soil borne diseases.

Cultivation
Bulb onions

Long growing season essential; bulb formation initiated when certain day length reached, and onions never 'catch up' if sown late. Must grow correct cvs for your climatic zone, or will fail to develop bulbs.
Sow:
1 Early spring for (a) main summer supply of fresh onions (ready mid-summer onwards) and (b) storage onions (lifted in late summer/early autumn). These will keep until mid-spring.
2 Late summer/autumn for over-wintering onions maturing early to mid-summer following year. Use Japanese over-wintering types or special, autumn planting sets. These onions only suitable for short term storage.
Note: Grow shallots (see p.222) to bridge gap between last stored onions and first fresh onions.

Seeds or sets?

Onions raised either from seed or from tiny bulbs known as sets. Each has pros and cons.
Advantages of seed: available for all cultivars; less prone to bolting; generally more flexible sowing times; cheaper. Advantages of sets: easier to grow; less prone to disease; usually avoid onion fly attacks; may give reasonable crop in poor soil; onion has 'head start' so ready earlier, better chance of maturing where growing season short. Disadvantages: only available for some cvs; more prone to bolting; sowing date critical for heat treated sets (see opposite); more expensive.

Main summer supply of fresh onions and storage onions
Growing from seed
1 For early start, especially in cold areas, sow indoors late winter in seed-trays or modules, at temperature of 10-16°C (50-61°F).
Once germinated don't expose to temperatures above about 13°C (55°F) before planting out.
Prick out at 'crook neck' stage, when seedlings about 1cm (½in) clear

of soil but still bent over; space about 5cm (2in) apart.

Where modules used can multi-sow up to six seeds per module, planting out as one (see p.61).

Harden-off well before planting out mid-/late spring at two-leaf stage. Space as for direct sown onions below.

Note: Onions can be started much earlier, in early winter, but inadvisable unless you have good greenhouse conditions.

2   Sow *in situ* outdoors as soon as the soil is workable in spring.

Never sow in cold or wet soil. If necessary warm with cloches/films beforehand, or sow under cloches.

Rake seedbed to very fine tilth. Sowing in 'stale seedbed' (see Pests and Diseases p.67), good practice to deter bean seed fly, which may attack onion seedlings.

Sow thinly in rows about 30cm (12in) apart. Thin in stages. Use thinnings as spring onions. Eventual size of onions determined by spacing. For maximum yield of average size onions: 4cm (1½in) apart. For large onions: 7·5-10cm (3-4in) apart.

Can also get reasonable yields with onions grown at equidistant spacing 15cm (6in) apart each way.

Space multi-sown modules 25-30cm (10-12in) apart each way.

Growing from sets

Only plant firm, medium sized sets. Large sets most prone to bolting. (Beware cheap offers of large sets!) Some sets 'heat treated' to destroy flower embryo and prevent premature bolting. Must not be planted too early: follow instructions when purchased.

Plant untreated sets as soon as soil workable in late winter to mid-spring. Plant heat treated sets late spring or when recommended.

Push gently into soil so tips at or just below surface level; otherwise birds pull them out.

Space 15cm (6in) apart each way for average size bulbs; 18cm (7in) apart each way for large bulbs.

Can protect with black cotton where birds a problem. (See Pests and Diseases p.76.) If birds uproot, carefully dig up and replant. Pushing sets back into soil damages developing roots.

Water onions in early stages until crop established. Normally no need to water in later stages of growth. Overwatering damaging.

Keep weed free, especially in the six to eight weeks after seedlings have appeared.

Where onion fly serious can grow under fine nets.

Over-wintered onions for early crop following summer

1   Using hardy Japanese cvs:

Sowing date critical. Onions must be 15-20cm (6-8in) high by mid-autumn to survive winter conditions. If too far advanced risk of bolting in spring and also more vulnerable to severe weather.

Recommended sowing times in UK:
- – North England and Scotland, early August.
- – South West and South Wales, end August.
- – Rest of England, second and third week August.

Sow *in situ* as for spring-sown onions. Water drills well if weather dry.
Sow in rows 30cm (12in) apart. Space seed 2·5cm (1in) apart to allow for losses during the winter. Thin to 5cm (2in) apart in spring.

Can apply foliar feed in spring to boost growth.

Note: In some areas local hardy cultivars recommended for late summer/autumn sowings.

2 Using autumn sets

Introduced in 1980's. Have proved excellent method of raising earliest onions, with good record of surviving cold winters.

Plant early to late autumn, 20-27cm (8-11in) apart each way.

Ready for use about mid-summer.

Can lift and store for a few months.

Pests and Diseases

Onion fly Small maggots attack seedlings which turn yellow and die. Sow in stale seedbed (see p.67); grow under fine nets.

Mildews, rots Attacks worse in poor seasons. No organic remedies. Harvest onions carefully to minimize the chances of rots developing in storage.

Harvesting and storage

Fresh use: lift onions when they reach a useable size.

Storage onions: wait until foliage starts to die down and tops bend over naturally. Although a traditional and much-illustrated practice, don't bend tops over artificially: can lead to storage rots.

Ease bulbs gently from ground. If weather good spread on upturned wooden boxes outdoors to dry for ten days or so. Ready when skins are paper dry.

If weather turns wet, finish drying indoors or in greenhouses. Handle gently; storage rots start with tiny cuts and bruises. Store in well-ventilated, frost-free shed or cellar, ideally at 0°C (32°F). Suspend bulbs in bunches or plaits; or knot individually in nylon stockings; or spread on trays.

To prolong storage life of onions cut off any fresh roots which develop in late winter.

Cultivars

Dual purpose cvs for use fresh use and storage – F_1 Caribo, Rijnsburger Robusta, F_1 Hygro, Sturon, Mammoth Red (red), Southport Red (red). Japanese type for early use fresh – F_1 Express Yellow, Imai Yellow, Senshyu Semi-Globe Yellow, F_1 Buffalo, F_1 Keepwell.

Sets for autumn planting–Unwin's First Early, Radar.

VSR **bulb onions from sets, *bulb onions from seed

Spring Onions
Cultivation

Prepare seedbed as for maincrop onions.

For summer/autumn supply sow in succession, every two or three weeks, from early spring to early summer.

For over-wintered crop for use following spring, sow in mid- and late summer. In cold areas use very hardy cultivars, or sow under cover.

Sow thinly in 7·5-10cm (3-4in) wide drills, or narrow drills as close as 10cm (4in) apart.

Space seeds 2-3cm (¾-1¼in) apart, to give useful sized spring onion.

Pull as soon as they reach a useable size. No further thinning is necessary. Water in dry conditions.

Cultivars

White Lisbon – standard cv; White Lisbon Winter Hardy – hardiest cv.

VSR**

Pickling Onions
Cultivation

Can be grown on fairly poor, dry soil, though do best in fertile soil.

Sow spring, *in situ*.

To get small, thumb sized onions of pickling size aim for about 30 plants per 30cm^2 (1ft^2).

Sow in rows 30cm (12in) apart, thinning to 6mm (¼in) apart; or sow in wide drills, allowing about 1cm (½in) between plants. Generally no need to thin; competition keeps the bulbs small.

Normally sown about 1cm (½in) deep, but in Holland commercial pickling onions sown 4-5cm (1½-2in) deep to keep them white.

Allow foliage to die down, and harvest as for bulb onions.

Don't leave too long in soil or may resprout.

If not pickled immediately can store until required for pickling.

Cultivars

Paris Silver Skin, Barletta, Brunswick (reddish brown), North Holland Flat Yellow Plastro, Purplette (purple).

Perennial onions

The following perennial onions can be very useful, especially in winter. For cultivation see companion volume *Salads for Small Gardens*.

Welsh onion (Ciboule) *Allium fistulosum* – forms clumps of thick, hollow leaves; very hardy. Use for green onion all year.

Oriental bunching onion *Allium fistulosum* – thick hollow leaves, and sometimes thick, leek-like stems. Naturally perennial but grown as annual or biennial. Some cvs very hardy. Can use green leaves all year round; in some types stems can be earthed up like leeks.

Everlasting onion *Allium perutile* – finer leaved type that does not set seed, so has to be raised by dividing clumps.

Egyptian or tree onion *Allium cepa* Proliferum Group – fairly frail plant; produces tiny aerial bulbs which can be harvested mid-winter.

ORIENTAL SALADINI *Brassica* spp.

Mixture of oriental greens. Originally devised in 1991 in conjunction with Suffolk Herbs seed company, to give a 'taster' of recently introduced oriental greens. Primarily used for CCA seedlings both under cover and in open, but has proved very versatile. With successive sowings can provide greens for salads and cooking for much of the year. Original UK mixture included pak choi, loose-headed Chinese cabbage, purple mustard, mibuna, mizuna and komatsuna. Looks pretty growing on account of variation of leaf colours and textures.

Cultivation
Sow as for CCA seedlings. (See Space Saving p.103.)
Requires reasonably fertile soil, with plenty of moisture if several cuts being made over long period.
Make successive sowings, broadcast, or in narrow or 7.5-10cm (3-4in) wide drills. Sow in weed free soil.
Sow thinly aiming for seeds about 1cm (½in) apart.
Sow:
1 Late winter/early spring under cover.
2 Mid-/late spring outdoors.
3 Late summer/early autumn outdoors.
4 Autumn under cover.
In addition mid-summer sowings may be successful in cool districts, but there is otherwise a risk of seedlings bolting rapidly, and growth being coarser, in hot weather.
Keep well watered. If growth seems to be flagging can feed with seaweed-based fertilizer.
Although subject to the common brassica pests (see Cabbage), most likely pests are flea beetle in the early stages and slugs. Take appropriate measures. Growing under fine nets beneficial to protect against flying pests.

Harvesting
Several alternatives:
For salad seedlings
Cut seedlings when about 5-10cm (2-4in) high, about 1cm (½in) above soil level, normally within three to four weeks of sowing. Leave to resprout. Depending on the season, they will resprout two or three times. Use raw in salads. Lovely bright colour and refreshing flavour.

For larger 'stir-fry' leaves
Either thin the seedlings to 2·5cm (1in) apart from outset, or thin after a

couple of cuts have been made so remaining plants grow larger. Cut when about 15cm (6in) high for cooking as greens.

For larger plants
From late summer sowings can prick out individual seedlings. (Seedlings of various types can be distinguished fairly early by differing leaf form and by their colour.)
Plant 20-30cm (8-10in) apart, outdoors or under cover. Allow them to develop into full sized plants. (For further cultivation see under individual plants.) They may remain productive over winter and into following spring.

Mature and flowering shoots
In some cases oriental seedlings more or less thin themselves out, with some plants developing at the expense of others. Longer leafy shoots develop. Cut for use raw (if tender) or for cooking.
Eventually the shoots run to seed. Cut them in bud stage. (See Choy Sum.) Use raw or lightly steamed. Most will prove very sweet flavoured.

Windowsill/window box saladini
Oriental saladini can be grown in a seedtray on a windowsill, or in any shallow container. Use good potting compost.
If started indoors move to good, even light as soon as germinated.
Normally only one cut can be made.

VSR**** PP

PAK CHOI (Celery mustard) *Brassica rapa* Chinensis Group

Large group smooth-leaved, very attractive, fast growing oriental greens. Leaves typically have broad white (sometimes green) midribs, widening at base to give mature plant characteristic rounded butt. Closely related to Chinese cabbage.
Many types. Height ranges from small stocky cvs 8-10cm (3-4in) high, to tall types up to 45cm (18in) high. Most cvs only moderately hardy, but very useful under cover in winter month.
Leaves, stems and flowering shoots all excellent raw and cooked. Mild flavour, often refreshingly juicy; crisp texture.
Rosette pak choi – distinct, hardy, type. See p.204.

Site and Soil,
See Chinese Cabbage.

Cultivation
For general cultivation, pests/diseases see Chinese Cabbage.
Very versatile: can use at any stage from small seedlings to flowering shoots. Responds well to CCA treatment as seedlings, semi-mature and mature plants. CCA seedlings one of most productive crops.

Like Chinese cabbage, tendency to bolt from early sowings, unless grown as CCA crop. Some cvs have reasonable bolting resistance.

CCA seedlings (see Chinese Cabbage p.166)

For spring and early summer sowings use bolt-resistant cultivars where available, though can usually get at least one cut from standard cultivars before plants run to seed.

Mature and semi-mature plants (see Chinese Cabbage, Headed crop p.166)

Make last sowing about six weeks before first frost expected.

Sow *in situ*, or in seedtrays or modules to transplant.

Spacing depends on cultivar and stage being harvested.

Small plants and squat types: 13-15cm (5-6in) apart.

Medium sized plants: 18-23cm (7-9in) apart.

Large plants: up to 45cm (18in) apart.

Use thinnings in salads, or, in cool conditions, transplant elsewhere.

Harvesting

CCA seedlings

Cut at any stage from 4-13cm (1½-5in) high. Depending on season, first cut may be made within three weeks of sowing. Two or three further successive cuts often possible.

Mature and semi-mature plants.

Either cut individual leaves as needed, or cut across head about 2·5cm (1in) above ground level leaving it to resprout, or pull up entire plant. Often ready within six weeks of sowing. With CCA treatment semi-mature and mature heads may remain productive over several weeks or months. Especially useful for plants under cover in autumn/ early winter, as cut back plants have more resistance to frost. Plants eventually run to seed. Young and mature flowering shoots mild flavoured; use before buds open.

All parts can be used raw in salads when young, or cooked lightly when mature, for example by steaming or stir-frying.

Cultivars

Chingensai – medium sized, green stem, slow bolting.

F_1 Joi Choi – large sized, white stem, reasonably hardy.

Mei Qing Choi – medium sized, green stem, good heat and cold tolerance.

Tai-Sai – elegant tall, 'spoon-leaved' type; delicate flavour.

Watch out for new cvs being introduced as pak choi continues to become more popular.

VSR ***Single plants, ****CCA seedlings

Rosette Pak Choi (Tatsoi) *Brassica rapa* var. *rosularis*

Distinct, striking type with rounded, dark green, crepe-like leaves. Leaves upright in hot weather, but later form flat, very symmetrical rosette. Leaves small in older cvs; larger in newer cvs. Excellent flavour; more pronounced than most pak choi cvs.

Grows best in cool weather. Hardier than other types of pak choi. In well-drained soil may survive -10°C (14°F), but may not survive in prolonged wet winter weather unless protected.

Grow either as CCA seedlings or as single plants.

Strong tendency to bolt from early sowings; most productive sowings mid- to late summer for autumn/winter crop.

Sow as pak choi opposite. Can transplant under cover in autumn for top quality plants.

Space 15cm (6in) apart for small plants; 30-40cm (12-16in) apart for the larger plants.

Slightly slower growing and less productive than standard pak choi.

Either cut individual leaves as required, or cut across plants leaving them to resprout. (For further information see *Oriental Vegetables* p.248.)

VSR** PP

PARSNIP *Pastinaca sativa*
Very hardy vegetable, grown for well-flavoured root. Roots vary from fairly stocky to about 20cm (8in) long.

Site and Soil
Open site. Grow best on deep, light, stone-free, well-drained soil. High level of fertility unnecessary. Soil preferably manured for previous crop. Lime if acid. On shallow and heavy soils grow shorter-rooted cvs.

Cultivation
Long growing season necessary to develop good-sized roots.

Use fresh seed, as viability falls off rapidly.

Normally sown *in situ*, but can sow in modules and transplant, provided planted out before tap root starts to develop.

Theoretically can sow from late winter until late spring. However, germination slow, and in practice very high failure rate with early sowings. In cold areas, or cold heavy soils, better to delay sowing until early, mid- or late spring.

If necessary warm the soil before sowing by covering it with cloches/films, or sow under cloches.

Prepare seedbed with fine tilth.

As germination slow, advisable to 'station sow' (see Tools and Techniques p.44), sowing radish between stations to mark rows. (Can use small lettuces if stations at least 18cm (7in) apart.)

Grow small types in rows 20cm (8in) apart. Thin to 5-10cm (2-4in) apart.

Grow large types in rows 30cm (12in) apart. Thin to 13-20cm (5-8in) apart.

Alternatively can grow at equidistant spacing (see p.43).

After final thinning hoe carefully to avoid damaging crowns, and mulch between rows.

Extra watering not normally necessary, unless soil drying out completely.

In this case recommended to water every two or three weeks, giving roughly 11 litre/m^2 (2 gal/yd^2) each time.

Pests and Diseases
Canker Crowns crack, then invaded by fungi. Most likely to occur where there is drought, over-rich soil or crown damage. Small roots less vulnerable. Where canker common, use resistant cultivars, or sow slightly later, ie mid-/late spring.
Celery fly Blisters leaves. Pick off and destroy diseased leaves.

Harvesting
Roots available early autumn to following mid-spring.
Best left in soil all winter though can be stored in boxes of sand in shed. Frost improves flavour. Foliage dies down, so mark position of rows. Can be covered with straw or bracken to assist lifting in frost. Lift and heel in when growth restarts in spring (see p.184).
Eat boiled, mashed, fried, roasted under joint, baked with brown sugar.

Cultivars
The following cvs all have good canker resistance:
Avonresister (short-rooted), Bayonet, Cobham Improved Marrow, Gladiator, White Gem, White Spear.

VSR*

PEAS *Pisum sativum*
Fairly hardy annuals in the legume family. Can grow anything from less than 45cm (18in) to over 1.8m (6ft) high; tendrils cling naturally to supports. Fairly space consuming, but worth growing for quality of home grown peas compared to shop peas. Divided into 'shelling' and 'mangetout' types.

'Shelling' peas
Grown for peas within pods, normally eaten fresh as young green peas. Mature peas can be dried for winter use. (Some old cvs and 'marrowfat' types are the best for drying.)
'Petit pois' type are tiny, exceptionally sweet peas.
Shelling pea seed 'round' or 'wrinkled'. Round cvs hardier but less sweet. Wrinkle-seeded cvs sweet flavoured but generally less hardy.
Semi-leafless cvs: types in which most of leaves converted into tendrils, making plants almost self-supporting. Developed for mechanical harvesting but good for small gardens as little staking is required. Compact, generally disease-free (fewer leaves mean better ventilation).

Mangetout (sugar peas/snow peas)
Whole pod is edible. Very well flavoured. Probably best value in small

gardens as heaviest yielding. In classic type pods very long, flat, often curved, and bumpy due to embryonic peas within pod. Other cvs have smaller pods. In newer 'Sugar Snap' type pods rounded, smooth, peas almost 'welded' to pod walls. Crunchy texture; excellent sweet flavour.

Maturity groups

Peas classified according to time taken to mature. 'Earlies': 11 to 12 weeks; 'second earlies': 12 to 13 weeks; 'maincrop': 13 to 14 weeks. Earlier types dwarfer in habit so require less staking, but lower yielding; later cvs taller, higher overall yields, staking more difficult. With a few exceptions can sow most types any time.

Site and Soil

Open site; light shade tolerated in summer. Good drainage essential. Soil must be fertile, deeply worked, preferably manured previous autumn. High levels of nitrogen unnecessary, as nodules on pea roots start fixing nitrogen about five weeks after sowing, meeting plant's needs for nitrogen. Rotation advisable to avoid soil borne diseases.

Cultivation

Sow in weed free soil; peas awkward to weed when growing.

Main sowings:

1 For early summer crop

Use dwarf early cvs.

Sow early spring outdoors, from late winter in mild areas, early or mid-spring in colder areas. Don't sow until soil temperature at least 7°C (45°F). (See also Getting an early start p.208.)

For early sowings can warm soil by covering with cloches/clear film for a week or so beforehand.

Can cover with cloches/films after sowing.

2 For main summer crop

Continue sowing until early summer. The earlier peas are in the soil the better; growth much less vigorous in hot weather. Use mildew resistant cvs for later sowings. For a succession of peas throughout summer you can:

– sow every two to three weeks from mid-spring to early summer using any cv.

– sow three cvs, one from each group, on the same dates in mid- to late spring.

3 For autumn crop

Sow an early/dwarf cv in mid-summer. Something of a gamble as growth will be poor in hot summers; but will make welcome late crop when it succeeds.

4 For late spring crop following year

In mild areas sow hardy over-wintering types in a sheltered place outdoors from mid- to late autumn. Can protect with cloches, but give ventilation on warm days.

Where space is available can also sow late/mid-winter in unheated greenhouses, polytunnels or frames. Use dwarf cvs of ordinary or mangetout types.

Set mouse traps for all these sowings!

During winter pull a little soil around stems to give them extra support and for protection.

Getting an early start

Peas sown outdoors *in situ* early in year very vulnerable in early stages: often fail to germinate. Following methods help get early crop established. Fairly labour intensive: probably only worth doing with relatively small quantities.

~ Germinate seed indoors on moist paper towelling. (See Testing Seed Viability p.60). Sow individual seeds carefully outdoors when tiny radicle seen emerging from seed.

~ Sow indoors, preferably in modules; transplant the young plants after hardening-off.

~ Fill a semi-circular piece of guttering with light soil or potting compost; sow pea seeds in it. Keep in cool greenhouse or sheltered place outdoors. When the seedlings well established, gently push the soil/compost out of the gutter into a shallow trench, of similar dimensions, made in the ground.

Sowing and spacing

Sow 2.5-4cm (1-1½in) deep. Not necessary to rake seedbed to fine tilth as seeds relatively large.

For main sowings space dwarf and semi-leafless cvs about 5cm (2in) apart, taller cvs about 7·5cm (3in) apart.

For autumn/early spring sowings sow as close as 2·5cm (1in) apart to compensate for higher seed losses.

Spacing for longer cropping period

Research has shown that peas sown/planted as much as 12cm (4½in) apart each way crop over much longer period due to less competition. For this system grow peas in bands of three rows, each row 12cm (4½in) apart. Thin to correct spacing after germination. Allow 45cm (18in) between bands.

Many sowing patterns can be used. Choice influenced by support system. Typical systems:

~ Single rows with supports behind.

~ Double rows 23cm (9in) apart with supports down centre.

~ 15-23cm (6-9in) wide, flat bottomed drills with supports behind. Space seeds evenly across drill or sow in parallel rows.

~ Evenly spaced patches or circles, up to 90cm-1.2m (3-4ft) diameter,

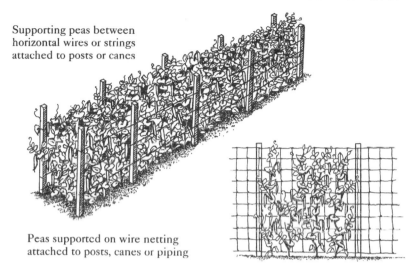

Supporting peas between horizontal wires or strings attached to posts or canes

Peas supported on wire netting attached to posts, canes or piping

with main support system around the periphery. In this case make holes with small dibber; drop peas in hole, making sure they touch the bottom and are not suspended in air.

Traditionally space between adjacent broad drills/pairs of rows roughly that of height of peas. In practice peas often grown closer with no ill effect, though access more awkward.

Protect from birds after sowing with black cotton or wire pea guards.

Mulch heavily as soon as seedlings established to keep down weeds.

Only water in early stages if conditions exceptionally dry; overwatering can result in leafy growth at expense of pods.

If weather dry once peas starting to flower water to increase yields. Water weekly at rate of 22 litre/m^2 (4gal/yd^2).

Supporting peas (see diagrams above)

Support peas as soon as the first tendrils appear – usually when the plants 7.5-10cm (3-4in) high. Plants never really recover fully once they flop on the ground.

Dwarf and semi-leafless cvs, and peas grown in patches *can* be grown without supports, but benefit from a few twigs/brushwood pushed among them to keep stems and lower leaves off the ground.

Supports must be strong as mature crop becomes weighty. Can use:

~ Criss-crossed brushwood or pea sticks where available. The more branched they are the better. They should be at least 1.5m (5ft) high for tall cvs.

~ Between parallel wires or strings attached to wire or posts (see diagram).

~ Wire netting, or nylon or string net, of 5-10cm (2-4in) mesh. Height of 1.2-1.5m (4-5ft) normally sufficient. Attach firmly to upright posts or

piping to keep taut. Can anchor wire netting with bamboo canes pushed in and out of wire and into ground (see diagram p.209).
~ Patented pea support systems, such as netting on tent-shaped frame placed over pea rows after sowing.

Pests and Diseases
Mice Can devastate early and winter sowings, burrowing down for seeds. Set mousetraps.

Birds Most serious in early stages but may attack throughout growth. Protect with nets if necessary.

Pea moth Attacks in summer; maggots found in peas. Spray with derris when flowering, or grow under fine nets to deter adult fly.

Pea weevil Nibbles leaf margins in spring, retarding seedlings. Spray with derris when noticed.

Pea thrips/thunderflies Most serious in a hot summer. Pods become silvered and distorted. Spray with derris.

Various mildews, wilts and rotting diseases Attack at different stages depending on the weather. Practise rotation, burn unhealthy and diseased leaves; use disease resistant cvs if the problems are being encountered regularly.

Harvesting
Shelling peas Pick while pods bright green. Cook shelled, or to conserve flavour, cook pods whole and shell afterwards.

Dried peas Leave pods on plants till they turn brown towards end of season. Pull up plants. Finish drying hung by roots in airy place, for example well-ventilated greenhouse. When pods split open shell peas and store in airtight jars.

Mangetout (flat types) Pick when outline of peas just visible through skin and pods snap cleanly in half. In their prime for fairly short season. Some types need strings removed from pods. Good sliced raw in salads as well as cooked lightly, for example steamed or stir-fried. If left to mature can eventually shell peas like ordinary peas.

'Snap pea' type Pick while green, plump and easily snapped in half. Use like flat mangetouts. Later can treat as shelled peas.

At end of season cut off plants at soil level and dig in roots to return nitrogen to soil from root nodules.

Cultivars
Earlies:
Feltham First (round seeded), Hurst Beagle – shelling peas.

Second earlies:
Daybreak, Early Onward, Kelvedon Wonder, Minnow (petit pois) – shelling peas.

Dwarf Sweet Green, Edula, Honeypod ('Sugar Snap'), Reizensucker – mangetouts.

Maincrop:
Cavalier (mildew resistant), Dark Skinned Perfection, Hurst Greenshaft, Markana (semi-leafless), Top Pod (mildew resistant), Tristar – shelling peas.
Oregon Sugar Pod, Sugar Snap (snap pea) – mangetouts.

VSR *Earlies, **Maincrop; Semi-leafless PP

PEPPER, SWEET (Capsicum) *Capsicum annuum*
Grossum group
PEPPER, CHILLI *Capsicum annuum*
Longum group
Bushy tender plants, on average 30-45cm (12-18in) tall. Sweet peppers can be used immature or mature. Commonest cultivars in Europe are green when immature, turning red, yellow, orange or purple on maturity. There is tremendous variation in shape: upright, pendulous, square, round, rectangular, tomato (bonnet-shaped), long. In addition there are thick- and thin-walled types (former used for stuffing). Much hotter chilli peppers also very diverse. Plants smaller leaved, pretty. Cultivate like sweet peppers.

Site and Soil
Except in warmest areas, grow peppers under cover for best results. As a rough guide, where tomatoes succeed, peppers will also succeed, though slightly higher temperatures preferred for them to thrive.
Where grown outside choose sheltered, sunny situation.
Need a reasonably fertile but not over-rich soil. Avoid using fresh manure; work in well-rotted compost beforehand. Need high light intensity to flourish.

Cultivation
Can plant in ground, outdoors or under cover, or grow in 20-25cm (8-10in) pots or growing-bags. Dwarf cvs can be grown successfully in pots on windowsills.
Sow indoors early spring in seedtrays or modules. Germination best at about 21°C (70°F).
Sow eight to ten weeks before last frost if planting outside; two weeks earlier if growing under cover.
Lower temperature gradually after germination.
If sown in seedtrays prick out at about the three-leaf stage into 5-8cm (2-3in) pots.
Can pot on again into 10-13cm (4-5in) pots to obtain very strong plants.
Plant in permanent position – indoors, outdoors, or in a container – when the plants reach about 10cm (4in) high and the first flowers are showing.
Space standard cvs 38-45cm (15-18in) apart; dwarf cvs should be spaced 30cm (12in) apart.

Harden-off well before planting outside. Delay planting until all risk of frost is past.

Protect with cloches or crop covers at least in early stages.

Aim to obtain strong bushy plants. Where growth not very vigorous, nip out first, small 'crown' fruit (which develops centrally) to encourage plant to bush out.

If branches weak and spindly when plant 30-38cm (12-15in) high, nip out tips of branches.

Peppers don't normally require supports, but can prop up branches with twigs if branches flopping, or stake if necessary.

If plants growing and fruiting well, supplementary feeding unnecessary. Otherwise feed every ten days or so with seaweed-based fertilizer once fruits start to form.

Water sufficiently to prevent soil and roots drying out, but don't over-water. Keep plants mulched.

Where grown under cover keep well ventilated.

Indoor plants require high humidity. In warm weather damp down (sprinkle with water) or spray/syringe plants frequently; helps fruit to set and discourages greenhouse pests.

Pests and Diseases

Outdoors poor weather the most significant problem!

Aphids, red spider mite, whitefly May be problems under cover. Use biological controls. A good measure to deter whitefly is to interplant with French marigolds.

Harvesting

Start picking green peppers when smooth, glossy, and useable size. Picking early fruits encourages further cropping.

Flavour changes and gets sweeter as fruits mature and colour. In cool areas and poor summers peppers may never mature fully, especially when grown outdoors.

Often continue growing well into autumn.

If frost is likely protect plants at night with cloches (if feasible) or with fleecy film.

Towards end of season uproot remaining plants before frosted. Hang by roots in frost-free shed or greenhouse. Sweet peppers continue to colour and may keep firm for several months. Chilli peppers will dry naturally and keep for two or three years, although flavour will deteriorate.

Cultivars

Early maturing F_1 hybrid cvs highly recommended for cold climates.

Ace, Bell Boy, Queen Star, Redskin (dwarf) – hybrid sweet peppers.

F_1 Apache (dwarf), Hungarian Wax (outstanding flavour) – chilli peppers.

VSR*; Chilli peppers PP

POTATOES *Solanum tuberosum*

Tender annuals grown for the tubers. Enormous choice of cv. Waxy types generally best for salads; floury types for baking, boiling.

Types

'Earlies': mature fastest, on average within 110 days of planting, not very high yielding, normally used fresh.

'Second earlies' and 'maincrop': slower maturing, on average within 120 and 140 days respectively, higher yielding, can be used fresh or stored for the winter.

In most small gardens only 'earlies' worth growing, as quickest returns, require less space, escape most 'maincrop' diseases, ready when prices high, taste delicious when homegrown. (For cultivation 'maincrop' potatoes see Further Reading *The Vegetable Garden Displayed.*)

Site and Soil

Open site; avoid frost pocket. Potatoes tolerate acid conditions, grow on wide range of soils. Deep, fertile, well-drained, medium loams ideal. Manure previous autumn. Often planted in new gardens to improve and 'clean' soil; wireworms which enter them removed when potatoes lifted. Rotate early potatoes over minimum three-year cycle.

Cultivation ('Earlies')

Buy certified seed potatoes mid-winter (mild areas)/late winter. 3kg (6½lb) sufficient for roughly 10m (33ft).

Large tubers generally better for early crops than small/medium sized tubers. (Not always the case with maincrop potatoes.)

Chitting (see diagram right)
This is the process for starting potatoes indoors to shorten growing season. Results in heavier yields, at least three to four weeks earlier. Place tubers 'rose end' (end with most 'eyes') upwards in seedtrays, shallow boxes, or containers such as empty egg trays.

Put in frost-free shed or cool room, in the light but away from direct sunlight. Leave for the shoots to develop.

For extra sturdy growth and early root development line tray with

Chitting seed potatoes in an egg tray

thick layer of newspaper. Spray potatoes lightly with seaweed-based fertilizer every ten days or so once sprouting starts. (Method developed by champion potato grower Charlie Maisey.)

Theoretically potatoes should be planted when sprouts about 2·5cm (1in) long. In practice *can* be planted successfully when very much longer – provided you manage to plant without snapping them off.
Reject unsprouted and diseased tubers.
Plant early/mid-spring. Early planting gives highest yields.
Soil must be moist, but do not plant if wet, sticky or very cold, or if heavy frost forecast.
Make 10-15cm (4-6in) deep drill, or make individual holes with trowel.
Plant tubers 5cm (2in) below soil surface, rose end upwards. Cover them with soil.
Earlies can be 25-30cm (10-12in) apart; rows 38-45cm (15-18in) apart.
After planting, covering with 15cm (6in) compost, straw, or manure beneficial. Gives them extra protection against frost, and helps to conserve soil moisture. Or cover with perforated polythene film or fleecy film to give earlier, heavier crops. Remove film three to four weeks after potatoes have emerged.
Protect young growth from frost with cloches, bracken, or by covering with newspaper at night if frost forecast or seems likely.
Keep weeds down.
Yield of 'earlies' increased by heavy watering. In dry weather water growing plants every 10-14 days at rate of 16-22 litre/sq m (3-4gal/sq yd).

Earthing up
Tubers near surface get pushed upwards as plants grow, becoming green and poisonous. Covering with earth prevents greening. (See also Growing under black film below.)
When plants roughly 15-23cm (6-9in) high, pull soil up around stems, covering lower leaves and leaving only tops exposed.
Earthing up suppresses weeds and may also increase yields.

Growing under black film
Method of growing which saves earthing up. (More suitable for 'earlies' than 'maincrop' as watering throughout summer would be laborious, and temperatures would rise too high.)
After planting cover potatoes with black polythene film. Anchor edges in the soil on either side of potatoes.
When tips of plants start pushing up film from below cut slits or crosses in the film and ease young growths through.
Water carefully through the slits when necessary.
Tubers form very near surface, and are easily lifted by pulling back film.

Pests and Diseases
Potato eelworm Causes 'potato sickness' in old gardens and allotments. Plants are stunted; yields lowered. If suspected, lift roots and plunge into bucket of water. Tiny round brown eelworm cysts will rise to surface if present. Remedy: give up potatoes for seven years or be content with

lower yields, or try new cultivars (see Cultivars) which are resistant to some strains of eelworm. (Maincrop potatoes are prone to many diseases, such as potato blight, which are largely avoided by 'earlies'.)

Harvesting
Open flowers on plants indicate tubers reaching edible size, generally early/mid-summer. Dig as required. Do not leave any tiny tubers in soil as they may carry over disease.

Potatoes in barrels or tubs
Choose cvs with compact growth (see Cultivars).
Use wooden or plastic barrels about 75cm (30in) deep and 60cm (24in) diameter. Prepare good soil or potting compost mixed with plenty of garden compost or well-rotted manure. Put 10cm (4in) layer in barrel. Place four sprouted tubers on top, cover with 10cm (4in) soil compost. Firm down and water. When stems about 15cm (6in) high, add another 10cm (4in) layer. Repeat until plants about 5cm (2in) below rim of barrel. Add final layer of soil or compost. Keep well watered. Apply weekly foliar feed of seaweed-based fertilizer. Harvest when plants flower. Plunge hands into barrel to check if tubers are reasonable size.
(Heavy duty black polythene rubbish sacks can also be used. Make a few drainage holes in the bottom. Roll down the sides when planting, and roll them up gradually as the potatoes develop and sack is filled.)

For late 'new' potatoes
A gamble worth trying for late 'new' potatoes. May give you new potatoes in early winter
Keep back a few of original seed potatoes. Keep somewhere light but as cool as possible, ideally 3-4°C (37-39°F).
Late spring/early summer rub off sprouts that have developed.
Plant mid-summer. Space 15-23cm (6-9in) apart, in rows 60cm (2ft) apart. Can cover with cloches early/mid-autumn.
Unless planted under cover should usually lift by mid-/late autumn as otherwise likelihood of becoming diseased.
If still looking healthy leave in longer, protecting from frost.

Cultivars ('Earlies')
The performance and flavour of potato cvs varies considerably with soil and climatic conditions. Worth trying several cvs, then settling for those that perform best under your conditions.
Accent, *Dunluce, Epicure, *Foremost, Maris Bard, Pentland Javelin (resistant some types eelworm), Premiere Rocket - good earlies under organic conditions.
* = compact cvs suitable for tubs

VSR ('Earlies')*

PURSLANE, SUMMER *Portulaca oleracea*

Tender, low-growing plants with succulent, rounded or oval leaves and fleshy stems. Thrive in warm weather; miserable in poor weather. Green and yellow forms. Green: thinner leaved, probably hardier and more prolific. Yellow: thicker leaved, more succulent, more decorative. Leaves and young stems mainly used raw in salads. Very attractive appearance in salads, deserves to be much more widely grown in areas with suitable climate. Mild flavour with cooling, refreshing quality.

Site and Soil
Light, well-drained soil. Open site in full sun, but sheltered from wind.

Cultivation
Grow either as single plants spaced 15cm (6in) apart, or as CCA seedlings, sown broadcast, or in narrow or wide drills.

Seeds tiny and seedlings damp off easily, so there is no advantage in sowing prematurely.

Sow:

1 *In situ* under cover early/mid-spring as CCA seedlings for very useful early crop.

2 In gentle heat in propagator in seedtrays mid-spring/early summer. Prick out (can prick out into modules) when the seedlings are large enough to handle.

   Harden-off well and plant outside after all risk of frost has past. Can protect with cloches/films in the early stages. Alternatively can plant under cover.

3 For follow on crop outdoors, sow in seedtrays in late spring or in early summer.

4 *In situ* outdoors late spring/early to mid-summer, as CCA seedlings, as long as no risk of frost.

5 *In situ* under cover late summer for useful autumn crop.

Harvesting
In favourable conditions CCA seedlings ready within four or five weeks of sowing; single plants within eight weeks.

Start cutting CCA seedlings when about 5cm (2in) high.

Pick young leaves, shoot tips, stems of single plants as soon as useable size. Pick regularly to encourage further growth, as plants rapidly become coarse. Remove any seedheads that appear as not only are they knobbly and unpleasant to eat, but they inhibit the production of more tender shoots.

When plants start to run to seed towards the end of the cropping period cut stems right back to within about 4cm (1½in) of ground. They will often regenerate.

VSR ***indoor seedlings, **single plants

PURSLANE, WINTER (Claytonia, Miner's Lettuce, Spring Beauty) *Montia perfoliata, Claytonia pefoliata*

Pretty, dainty little plant. Rarely grows more than 20cm (8in) spread, and up to 20cm (8in) high when flowering.

Early triangular leaves on short stalks superseded by larger, semi-circular leaves 'wrapped' around flowering stalks. Leaves, stems and flowers all edible. Mild flavour, succulent texture; use in salads. Can be available all year round, but most useful autumn, spring and early summer. Grows astonishingly fast early in the year. A salad children love.

Site and Soil

Not fussy, but does best on light sandy soil. Tolerates light shade. Be warned: it seeds itself and can become invasive.

Cultivation

Sow:

1   Early to late spring for summer use.
2   Mid- to late summer for autumn harvest. (Plant later sowings under cover.)
3   Late summer/early autumn. Plant under cover for spring crop.

Either sow *in situ* thinning to required spacing, or in seedtrays or modules. Sow shallowly, as seeds are tiny.

Space plants 10-13cm (4-5in) apart each way.

Can also be broadcast in patches for seedling cut-and-come-again crop. Start cutting as soon as leaves large enough to handle.

Reasonably hardy, surviving most winters outdoors if soil well drained, but looks poorly and 'blue' in cold water.

For valuable spring crop have some plants under cover: they will be more luxuriant and ready well ahead of outdoor plants.

Once winter purslane is established, seedlings appear all over the garden in autumn and spring. Transplant them carefully to where you want them, or dig them in as *gratis* green manure.

VSR**** PP

RADISH *Raphanus sativus*

Range of annual and biennial plants of varying hardiness, grown mainly for their roots. Roots have characteristic sharp flavour. Young leaves and seed pods of some cvs edible.

Types

Standard: Small roots; skin colour white, red, pink, yellow, purplish, red and white; round or cylindrical in shape. Can be grown for much of year outside and under cover. Must be used fresh.

Oriental: Large radishes. 'Mooli'/'Daikon' types typically very large, long, white-skinned, white-fleshed roots, often weighing 500g (1lb). Plants much larger than standard radishes. Mainly grown for mid- to late summer use. Used raw or cooked like turnips. 'Beauty Heart' type characterized by pink or green internal flesh and sweet flavour. Fairly large round or long roots. Very decorative.

Winter: Moderately large radishes; round and long forms; skin colour pink or black/violet. Traditional cvs known as 'Chinese' or 'Spanish'. Hardy and will keep well for winter, outdoors or lifted. Use raw in salads or cooked like turnips.

For cultivation of radish seed pods and leaf radish see companion volume *Salads for Small Gardens*. Radish seedlings can be grown like mustard and cress. They have a wonderful spicy flavour and are very productive. For cultivation see Mustard p.195; for suitable cvs see below.

Site and Soil

Well-drained, rich, moist soil, plenty of humus but not freshly manured. Open site for spring and autumn sowings; slight shade for summer sowings of ordinary radish or they run to shed. Light soil, good drainage, plenty of moisture is the secret of success with radishes.

Cultivation

Standard radish

Fast maturing, ready 20 to 30 days after sowing.

Useful for intercropping, marking rows of slow-germinating seeds.

Failures usually caused by sowing in dry position, failing to thin early, or poor tilth on seedbed. Seedlings must never become lanky.

Sow:

1 Outdoors late winter (provided soil warm and well drained) until early autumn; sow short rows at two-week intervals for succession. Early to late summer sowings best in semi-shade, ideally between other crops. Always sow thinly, drills 10-15cm (4-6in) apart; *thin early* to 2-2·5cm ($\frac{3}{4}$-1in) apart. Can also broadcast thinly. Dust with derris if seedlings nibbled by flea beetle.

   Water if weather dry.

   Pull radishes as soon as ready as most run to seed rapidly when mature.

2 Autumn and spring under cover – early and mid-autumn, late winter to mid-spring in frames, cloches or greenhouse.

   If sown very thinly, thinning unnecessary. Give plenty of ventilation; keep well watered.

3 Mid-winter under cover – sow mid-autumn to late winter, using only small-leaved, slower maturing cvs developed for this season. Thin to 5cm (2in) apart. Don't overwater. Leaves turning very dark green indicates watering necessary.

Oriental radish

For most cvs delay sowing until early/mid-summer as tendency to bolt prematurely from earlier sowings. Some cvs have good bolting resistance.

Sow *in situ* 1-2cm (½-¾in) deep. Can sow in sunken drills 4cm (1½in)deep, pulling soil around stems as they grow to give extra support. Radishes very fast growing.

Spacing depends on cv. Average spacing 10cm (4in) apart in rows 23-25cm (9-10in) apart.

Can also sow in modules and transplant, provided planted before tap root starts to develop.

Sow 'Beauty Heart' cvs mid- to late summer. Can sow or transplant under cover for early winter crop.

Most oriental cvs mature in seven to eight weeks; normally stand for several weeks once mature without deteriorating.

Because of being in the soil for a relatively long time it is subject to same pests as brassicas (see Cabbage). Can grow outdoor summer crop under fine nets to protect from cabbage root fly and other flying insect pests. (For further information see *Oriental Vegetables*, p.248.)

Winter radish

Sow *in situ* in open, in moist soil, mid-/late summer.

Drills 30cm (1ft) apart; thin to about 20cm (8in) apart.

Either leave in soil all winter (can be protected with bracken or straw), or lift in late autumn and store in sand in dry shed.

Roots can grow over 50cm (20in) long without becoming coarse.

May keep in good condition until mid-spring. (Leave a plant to run to seed for seed pods. These big radishes generally produce large, very succulent seed pods.)

Excellent raw sliced or grated in salads, cooked in stews or curries, or pickled.

Radish tops edible (just). Cook like spinach.

Cultivars

Standard radish:

Crystal Ball, French Breakfast, Long White Icycle, Pink Beauty, Sparkler.

Pontvil, Red Princ/Prinz Rotin – good bolting resistance.

Helro, Robino, Saxa - suitable mid-winter sowing under cover.

Oriental:

F_1 April Cross, F_1 Minowase Summer Cross – slow bolting.

F_1 Mantanghung – red flesh 'Beauty Heart'; Misato Green Flesh – green flesh.

Winter radish:

F_1 Cherokee, Black Spanish Round, Violet de Gournay.

Specialities:

Munchen Bier – seed pods; Bisai, Jaba – leaf radish and CCA seedlings; Early 40 Day – CCA seedlings.

VSR ***ordinary radish, **winter radish

SALAD ROCKET *Eruca sativa*

Dwarf growing, spicy-leaved salad plant; highly productive, especially as cool weather cut-and-come-again seedling crop. Reasonably hardy.

Site and Soil
Tolerant of moist soils. Slightly shaded site preferable in summer.

Cultivation
With successive sowings in open and under cover can be available all year round.
Make first sowings in cold greenhouse or frame mid-/late winter.
Sow outdoors early spring until early autumn. (Summer sowings in hot weather may bolt very rapidly.)
Sow in early/mid-autumn under cover for winter and spring supplies (see Cress p.195).
Good for intercropping and undercropping, for example among brassicas.
For single plants sow *in situ*, thinning to 15cm (6in) apart, or sow in seed boxes or modules planting out when young. For seedlings broadcast in patches, or sow in wide drills or in bands between other vegetables.
Flea beetle may attack seedlings. Spray with derris or grow under fine nets.
Keep well watered, especially in summer.
Can also be grown in seedtrays or dishes indoors (see Cress p.195).
Start cutting the seedlings when about 5cm (2in) high. As many as five cuts can sometimes be made. Pick leaves from single plants as they are required. Flowers edible. Use as an ingredient in salads.

VSR****

SALSIFY (Oyster plant) *Tragopogon porrifolius*

Hardy biennial growing 90cm (3ft) high, eventually producing beautiful purple flowers. Not demanding of space, but requires fairly long growing season. Cultivated primarily for thinnish roots used in winter, but also for flower buds and chards (blanched young shoots) which develop in spring. (For cultivation of chards and further information on flower buds see companion volume *Salads for Small Gardens*.)

Site and Soil
Open site; moderately fertile, light, stone-free sandy soil best. Avoid freshly manured soil.

Cultivation
Use fresh seed as viability deteriorates fairly fast.
Sow *in situ* outdoors in good seedbed in spring.
'Station sowing' advisable as germination slow (see p.44).
Succeeds at various spacing: rows 30cm (12in) apart, thinning to 10-15cm (4-6in) apart satisfactory.

Little attention required. Rarely troubled by pests or disease.
Water in dry weather; mulch after watering.
Roots can be left in soil in winter, covered with bracken or straw for extra protection; or lift and store in sand in shed.
For flower buds leave in soil for second season. Plants self-seed easily.

Harvesting
Roots ready mid-autumn to following mid-/late spring. Very delicate flavour. Scrub roots, cook unpeeled, squeeze skin off afterwards.
Can be boiled; baked; fried; served in sauces; parboiled and finished in pan with margarine or butter and brown sugar.
Pick flower buds when plump, just before opening, with 7·5-10cm (3-4in) of stalk, which is edible. Boil lightly, cool, dress with vinaigrette.

Cultivars
Mammoth, Sandwich Island.

VSR* PP when flowering

SCORZONERA *Scorzonera hispanica*
Hardy perennial; long, black-skinned, white-fleshed roots. Yellow flowers in second season.

For Site and Soil, Cultivation, Use, VSR see Salsify
Being perennial, roots can be left in the soil for second season to grow larger. Lift one or two roots in autumn. If only finger thickness leave rest in ground until following autumn; they will thicken without toughening.
Can also sow in late summer for use following autumn.

Cultivar
Lange Jan (Long John) – improved modern cv.

VSR* PP when flowering

SENPOSAI HYBRIDS *Brassica hybrids*
Several recently developed cabbage/komatsuna crosses, characterized by natural vigour, healthiness and good tolerance of heat and cold. Will grow into large loose cabbage-like plant, but flavour best picked young for cooked greens, or used raw in salads. Flavour essentially cabbage with hint of spinach. Good value in small gardens. Seeds can also be sprouted, and grown as seedling sprouts (see p.195).

Soil, Site and Cultivation
See Komatsuna. Can be sown throughout growing season.
For maximum returns sow in wide drills and cut when 5-10cm (2-4in) high for use as CCA seedlings.

After one or possibly two cuts thin to 5-7.5cm (2-3in) apart, and cut for use as young greens when 15-20cm (6-8in) high.

Depending on time of year, CCA stage may be reached four to five weeks after sowing, young greens stage six to eight weeks after sowing. For very early crop make last sowing early autumn outdoors; late/mid-autumn under cover.

Excellent lightly steamed or stir-fried.

Cultivars
Senposai No. 2 – currently recommended.
Look out for new introductions in future.

VSR***

SHALLOTS *Allium esculentum*
Reasonably hardy, low growing plant in onion family. Grown for distinctly flavoured bulbs, known as sets. 'Yellow' types larger, best keepers; 'red' types smaller, considered best flavoured. Useful for small gardens as easily grown, excellent keepers, often lasting until first onions ready following year. Tropical in origin, so grow better than onions at high temperatures. Sometimes planted close for very early green leaves, used like spring onions.

Site and Soil
Open site; deeply-worked, well-drained, light soils best. Rotate as for onions. Do not plant on freshly-manured soil: dig and manure for previous crop or previous autumn.

Cultivation
Traditionally raised by planting sets. Drawback to sets: plants have tendency to bolt prematurely; some stocks have become virused and low yielding. (Beware of cheap offers!) However, improved stocks have now been recently introduced. Also seed now available for some cvs is very disease-free, has good bolting resistance, but cultivation more laborious than growing from sets.

Growing from sets
Ideal size for planting about 2cm (¾in) diameter. Larger sets more likely to bolt prematurely.

Remove dry loose outer scales. 0.5kg (1lb) will normally be sufficient for 4.5m (15ft) row.

Generally plant as early as possible: early/mid-winter in mild areas, otherwise late winter/early spring. However, some cvs, for example 'Sante', only suitable for late spring planting. (Follow supplier's directions as to the most appropriate planting time.)

Plant in firm soil for highest yields, 18cm (7in) apart each way. Often planted 15cm (6in) apart in rows 23cm (9in) apart.

Plant in firm soil.

Push set into soil to half its depth, or plant in shallow drill, so only tips protruding. Firm soil around set after planting.

Protect against birds with strong black cotton (see Pests p.76).

If bulbs uprooted by birds, replant carefully (see Growing from Sets p.199).

Keep weed free; can mulch between rows, but take care not to cover developing sets. No further attention necessary.

Each set develops into a cluster of eight to ten sets.

Growing from seed

Sow indoors early spring as for bulb onions, or sow *in situ* outdoors as soon as soil is workable.

Currently recommended method is to space seedlings about 5cm (2in) apart each way. Each develops into a single shallot rather than a cluster. However, they can be spaced further apart, and shallots then likely to develop into clumps.

Green shallot shoots

Plant small sets or seedlings 2·5cm (1in) apart each way in spring, under cover for early crop or outdoors as soon as soil workable. Cut when 7·5-10cm (3-4in) high. Use as green onion substitute.

Harvesting and Storage

Shallots normally ready mid-summer onwards. Lift clumps whole; no need to split them up.

Harvest and store as for bulb onions (see p.200).

Provided sets look healthy, keep small ones to plant following season.

Use in cooking, raw, or for pickling.

Cultivars

Atlantic, Creation (from seed); Sante, Topper – newer yellow cvs.

Pikant, Delicato – newer red cvs.

VSR**

SPINACH GROUP

Several different plants popularly termed spinach. Naming confusing!

True (ordinary) spinach *Spinacia oleracea* – fast growing, moderately hardy, cool weather annual, generally 15-20cm (6-8in) high. Runs to seed rapidly in hot weather. Probably most nutritious and delicately flavoured of group.

Leaf beet *Beta vulgaris* subsp. *cicla* – includes Swiss chard (seakale beet, silver chard), and perpetual spinach (spinach beet). Vigorous, productive biennials, responding well to CCA treatment at every stage. Both are hardier and more heat tolerant than spinach. The leaves coarser and probably less subtly flavoured. Chard cvs grow to about 45cm (18in) high, with thick white or red mid-ribs and stems, cooked as separate vegetables. Perpetual spinach thinner stemmed, not normally as tall growing; when grown as CCA seedlings probably most productive type for small gardens.

New Zealand spinach *Tetragonia expansa* – tender, sprawling perennial, grown as annual in cool climates. Small triangular leaves. Has good drought resistance. Milder flavoured than ordinary spinach.

Spinach beet
Site and Soil
Well-manured ground, limed if acid; moisture-retentive soil best, but withstands dry conditions fairly well. Tolerates light shade. Don't grow near cucumbers as spinach blight caused by cucumber mosaic virus.

Cultivation and Harvesting
Grow as single plants or as CCA seedlings.
For single plants sow in drills about 38cm (15in) apart. Thin in stages to 25-30cm (10-12in) apart.
For seedling crop grow in rows 10cm (4in) apart, or in wide drills or bands, or broadcast.
Thin to about 5cm (2in) apart. Start cutting when the leaves are 5-10cm (2-4in) high.
Several cuts possible if kept well watered.
Sow:
1 Main sowing mid- to late spring outdoors. Will crop during summer and autumn, and frequently through winter into late spring/early summer following year.
2 Mid- to late summer outdoors. Usually less productive crop, but may crop through winter and well into following summer.
3 Make the final late sowing for CCA seedlings under cover late summer/early autumn for good quality winter crop.
Protect young seedlings from birds.
Keep weed free. Water in dry weather; mulching beneficial.
Pick/cut leaves as soon as useful size, leaving plants to resprout.
Pick off any flowering shoots/seedheads to prolong cropping.
Cloche or protect with bracken during the winter as this will improve leaf quality.

Swiss chard (Seakale beet)
Site and Soil
Succeeds on any soil, but best on heavy well-manured soil. Deep roots enable plants to tolerate drought.

Cultivation and Harvesting

Ideal vegetable for beginners: rarely attacked by pests or disease and withstands neglect and maltreatment well.

White-stemmed type most productive. Older cvs of red-stemmed type less productive, more prone to bolting. (See Cultivars below.)

Sow:

1 Spring *in situ* outdoors. For spacing see Spinach Beet.

Alternatively sow in seedtrays or modules and transplant.

These plants crop through summer and autumn, frequently through winter until late spring/early summer the following year, when they run to seed.

Cut leaves individually, leaving plant to resprout.

2 Mid- to late summer as above.

Use as successional crop from autumn until mid-summer the following year. Can transplant some under cover in late summer/early autumn, for a highly productive, very useful early/late spring crop.

Although hardy, plants grown outdoors in winter may develop rots and deteriorate in quality. Covering them with cloches/fleece/low polytunnels beneficial.

Cut back flowering shoots to encourage further cropping.

Cultivars

Fordhook Giant, Lucullus – green-leaved, white-stemmed.

Ruby Chard – reddish-leaved, red-stemmed. Highly decorative old cv but prone to bolting prematurely.

Feurio – new red-stemmed cv; good bolting resistance if not sown until late spring.

New Zealand spinach

Site and Soil

Open site. It does best in well-drained, reasonably fertile soil, but tolerates poorer soil than spinach and leaf beet. It does not require high levels of nitrogen. It is very useful as a ground-cover plant in fairly dry, sunny corners. Can look attractive in flower beds or as path edging.

Cultivation and Harvesting

Germination can sometimes be difficult. Soak the seeds in water overnight before sowing.

Start seeds under cover mid- to late spring. Harden-off before planting outside after all risk of frost is over. Space plants 45-75cm (18-30in) apart each way.

Alternatively sow *in situ*, after all risk of frost past.

It is easiest to 'station sow' in groups, thinning to one seed after germination has taken place.

Keep picking tips and young leaves to encourage further growth.

May self-sow itself and re-appear following year.

Ordinary spinach
In the past spinach was divided into more heat tolerant 'round seeded' types used mainly for spring sown summer crop, and 'prickly seeded' types used for late summer sowing for autumn crop. Modern cvs more adaptable and in practice dual purpose.

Site and Soil
Open site for main sowings. Needs fertile, moisture-retentive soil. Avoid poor, dry soils.

Cultivation and Harvesting
Normally sown *in situ*, but can be sown in seedtrays or modules and then transplanted.
Spinach tends to run to seed in warm weather; can make summer sowings in light shade, for example between beans, peas or sweet corn.
For a continuous crops can make successive sowings at three to four week intervals throughout growing season, but spring and late summer sowings generally most successful.

Sow:
1 Early spring *in situ* outdoors as soon as soil workable. Can cover with cloches/films in early stages.
2 Continue sowing until early summer.
  These crops should provide cuttings until autumn.
3 For autumn/winter crop sow outdoors late summer/ early autumn. Cover with cloches in bad weather. May continue cropping throughout winter into following spring.
4 Make final sowing for CCA seedlings under cover in late summer/early autumn.
Can grow as single plants or as CCA seedlings. Depending on season, plants respond well to CCA treatment. Must have adequate moisture.
For single plants sow in drills 27-30cm (11-12in) apart, thinning them to 15cm (6in) apart.
For CCA seedlings sow thinly in broad drills or in rows 10cm (4in) apart. Leave unthinned, or thin to 5cm (2in) apart if they are not growing very vigorously.

Cultivars
Jovita, Medania, Norvak, Sigmaleaf, Symphony - reliable dual purpose cvs.

VSR ***Spinach beet, **New Zealand spinach, *ordinary spinach; Swiss chard PP

For ORACHE (mountain spinach) see companion volume
Salads for Small Gardens

SWEDE *Brassica napus* Napobrassica Group

Relatively hardy brassica grown for its turnip-like root. Roots normally yellow fleshed, sweeter and milder flavoured than turnips. Purple-skinned (known as 'purple-top') cvs considered best flavoured. Roots generally round, but sometimes misshapen or long: variations probably due to seed quality. Swedes often succeed where turnips fail, but slower maturing.

Site and Soil
See Turnips.

Cultivation
For seedbed and thinning, see Turnips.
Sow thinly or station sow 10cm (4in) apart late spring (in cold regions), early summer (in warmer regions).
Rows 38-45cm (15 18in) apart, thin early to 23-30cm (9-12in) apart.
Can be sown mid-/late summer for spring greens (see Turnips).
Roots ready 20-26 weeks after sowing.
Can be left in ground in most areas in winter, but probably best to lift and store in early winter or may become coarse.
Store outside in clamps as for carrots (see p.156), covered with straw. very cold areas protect with final 10cm (4in) layer of soil.
Forcing: roots can be lifted mid-winter, trimmed, packed into boxes with soil, put in darkness and forced like 'Witloof' chicory (see p.163). Resulting young semi-blanched growths very tasty. Eat raw or cooked when about 10-13cm (4-5in) long.
Young leafy growths develop from roots in soil over winter. Ready mid-/late spring. Eat as greens.

Pests and Diseases
See Turnips. Where mildew a problem grow cv 'Marian'.

Cultivars
Marian (good resistance to clubroot and mildew), Acme, Lizzy.

VSR*

SWISS and RUBY CHARD see Spinach

SWEET CORN *Zea mays*

Half-hardy, sweet form of maize; cobs borne on plants growing up to about 1.8m (6ft) tall. Traditional types lose sweetness very rapidly after picking. More recently introduced 'supersweet' types have enhanced sweetness, retained much longer after picking; however plants less robust, more susceptible to low temperatures. (See also Key facts p.228.) In UK success with sweet corn a gamble in cold districts, but improved hardier cvs continually being introduced. Fastest maturing, early hybrid cvs most suitable for small gardens; later cvs considered better quality. Popcorn is easily grown type of sweet corn (see opposite).

Site and Soil
Open site, sheltered from strong winds. Moderately fertile, well-drained, moisture-retentive soil. Sweet corn performs poorly in dry conditions. Excellent plant for intercropping as well as undercropping (see Space Saving p.109).

Cultivation
Key facts:
~ Requires long, frost-free growing season. (Fastest maturing UK cvs ready about 120 days after sowing; others take several weeks longer.)
~ Seed fails to germinate at soil temperatures below 10°C (50°F) – temperature not normally reached until late spring in south of England. Never sow in wet soil.
~ Does not transplant well unless raised in modules.
~ Male tassels and female cobs borne on same plant. Must be wind pollinated to form full cobs. To assist pollination best to grow in groups or blocks rather than rows.
~ If supersweet cvs pollinated by ordinary cvs sweet quality is lost. If growing latter advisable *not* to grow ordinary cvs in same garden.

Sow:
1 Sow in modules, indoors, in gentle heat, mid-spring. Can pre-soak seed, and sow when just sprouted. (See Testing Seed Viability p.60.) Only sow one seed per module, as tap roots easily damaged if become intertwined. Harden-off carefully and plant outside after all risk of frost. Can be protected with cloches/crop covers in early stages.
2 Sow *in situ* outside, once soil temperature over 10°C (50°F) in late spring. Can sow seeds individually under jam jars or cloches. Once germinated remove any covers during day to harden-off gradually.
Alternatively sow *in situ*, and cover with either:
~ Clear polythene film. Cut slits and pull seedlings through when seen beneath film
~ Crop covers. Remove once plants reach about five-leaf stage.
3 *In situ* in open, early summer. 'Station sow', thinning to one per station after germination.
Space short cvs about 30cm (1ft) apart each way; tall cvs 38-45cm (15-18in) apart each way. Spacing can be increased if more space required for undercropping.
Protect seedlings from slugs and birds.
When 30-45cm (12-18in) high support stems by earthing up to about 15cm (6in) depth. In exposed areas support with canes.
Keep weed free. Mulching in summer beneficial.

Harvesting
Ready mid-summer (in warm regions), late summer into autumn (in colder regions). Usually one or two cobs per plant.
Pick when *just* ripe. Cob quality deteriorates if left on plant once ready.
Test when tassels on cobs well withered, dark brown, by tearing back sheath and pressing seed with finger nail.
If 'watery' unripe; if 'milky' ripe; if 'doughy' over-ripe.
Cook immediately picked, boiling for 10 minutes at most.

Cultivation popcorn
Grow as sweet corn.
Harvest cobs at end of season when becoming hard. Not damaged by light frost.
Pull off husks and dry for several weeks in dry, airy place.
From time to time strip off corn and do trial 'popping'; must be dried to correct moisture level to pop successfully
To 'pop' put oil in bottom of heavy pan, cover with kernels, replace lid, turn up heat. Should pop in minute or two if ready. If not, dry a little longer, then re-test.
Once right moisture level reached strip kernels from cobs and store in airtight jars.

Cultivars
In approximate order of maturity.
Pilot, Earlibelle, Sunrise – early maturing, standard, F_1 hybrids:
Candle, Sweet Nugget, Conquest, Sweet 77 – early maturing, 'super-sweet' F_1 hybrids.
F_1 Peppy – for popcorn.

VSR* PP

TEXSEL GREENS (Ethiopian or Abyssinian mustard/cabbage)
Brassica carinata
Recently developed brassica, with medium sized, glossy leaves. Grows up to about 30cm (12in) high when mature. Reasonably hardy, fast growing, very nutritious, with pleasant spinach/cabbage/hint of garlic flavour. Eaten raw when young and as cooked greens later. Very valuable in clubroot infected gardens, as reaches useful size before becoming infected.

Site and Soil
Open position, but tolerates light shade in mid-summer. Grows best in fertile, well-drained, moisture-retentive soil. Useful for intercropping and catch cropping.

Cultivation
Essentially a cool weather crop, so it may bolt prematurely in hot, dry

conditions. Spring and late summer sowings are probably the best value in small gardens.

Best sown *in situ*.

Can grow as CCA seedlings, or as 'greens' harvested as small plants 20-30cm (8-10in) high. Also suitable for seedling sprouts. (See Mustard, Cress p.195.)

Sow

1 Late winter/early spring under cover, for first spring crop.

2 Outdoors in succession every three weeks' or so, as soon as soil workable in spring until early autumn. This will give continuous supply from early summer to autumn. Mid-summer sowings may not prove worthwhile in warm, dry areas.

3 Under cover in early/mid-autumn for good quality autumn/winter/ spring supply.

For CCA seedlings sow broadcast or in wide drills.

For small plants various spacings have proved satisfactory:

~ For highest yield of small plants either sow in rows 15cm (6in) apart, thinning to 5cm (2in) apart; or in rows 30cm (12in) apart, thinning to 2.5cm (1in) apart.

~ Can also space plants 8-10cm (3-4in) apart each way for small plants; 15cm (6in) apart each way for medium sized plants; 25-30cm (10-12in) apart for large plants.

Protect winter crop with cloches/crop covers to improve the quality of the vegetables.

Pests and Diseases

Normally very healthy, though may be affected by common brassica pests. (See Cabbage.)

Flea beetle Attacks plants in early stages. Take standard control measures. Grow under fine nets if necessary.

Harvesting

CCA seedlings: ready three to four weeks after sowing, depending on season. Spring and late summer sowings generally fastest growing. Cut about 1cm ($\frac{1}{2}$in) above ground. Usually resprout, though may develop bitterness with second cut.

Young plants: ready on average seven weeks after sowing. Either pull whole plant when 20-30cm (8-12in) high, or pick off individual leaves as required, leaving to resprout. Will run to seed after few weeks, but small leaves on seeding stems quite palatable.

In soils that are infected by clubroot successive sowings can be made if plants are pulled up by their roots when harvested, and a three-week gap left before re-sowing.

VSR***

TOMATO *Lycopersicon esculentum*

Tender, naturally sprawling plant grown for fruits. Fruits most commonly red, but also yellow, orange, pink, white. Tomatoes classified both by fruit shape and growth habit.

Main fruit types

Standard – smooth, round, red or yellow tomatoes. Variable flavour.

Beefsteak – very large, smooth, fleshy, mostly well flavoured.

Marmande – large, irregular shape, often ribbed, fleshy, well flavoured.

Oxheart – conical, fleshy, well flavoured.

Plum – rectangular, solid, traditional Italian canning type; mostly late maturing, variable flavour.

Cherry – small, round fruits usually less than 2·5cm (1in) diameter; often (not invariably) sweet or distinctly flavoured.

Growth habit groups

'Indeterminate' – main shoot naturally grows several metres high in warm climate. Side shoots can develop into long branches. When cultivated usually grown as cordons tied to supports; in greenhouses twisted up overhead strings. Side shoots and growing point nipped out to restrict growth. In 'semi-determinate' sub group main shoot naturally stops growing when about 1m (3ft) high. Most 'Marmande' cultivars in this sub group.

'Bush' or 'determinate' – side branches develop instead of main shoot. Plant remains bushy and sprawls on ground over 60-90cm (2-3ft). Requires no side shooting or stopping. Often early maturing. Useful for culture outdoors as no supports required. Good where space limited; can be grown under cloches/low tunnels, or even in hanging baskets.

'Dwarf' – very small, compact types, often no more than 20cm (8in) high. Ideal for container growing or edging beds.

Except for cultivars bred for heated greenhouses, all types can be grown indoors or outside.

Climate limitations

Tomatoes grow poorly at temperatures below 10°C (50°F); most cvs need at least eight frost-free weeks after planting to mature properly.

Also need high light intensity to do well.

So difficult crop in cold areas, and/or where light levels poor.

In UK growing tomatoes under cover gives guarantee of better crop, but in a good summers/warm areas can grow very satisfactory crops outside.

New gardeners should be guided by practice in their area.

Growing system options (Harvesting dates should be treated only as a rough guide; there is considerable variation from one area to another.)

1 Heated greenhouses. For very early summer crops.

2 Unheated greenhouses. Crops ready mid-summer onwards.

   Greenhouse crops can be grown in the soil or in containers.

3 Outdoors in frames, under cloches, or protected with crop covers in the early stages. Ready late summer. Use bush cvs.
4 Outside without protection. Grow in the ground or in containers. Ready late summer/early autumn.

For cultivation in greenhouses see specialist books in Further Reading p.248. Broadly speaking, the systems used outdoors can be adopted for unheated greenhouses, but special attention needs to be paid to the risk of soil sickness and disease. Growing in easily moved polytunnels overcomes soil sickness problem. While some tomato cvs bred specifically for cultivation indoors, in practise most 'indoor' cvs can be grown successfully outdoors and *vice versa*.

Site and Soil
Sunny site, sheltered from wind. In cold areas grow against wall or fence. (Avoid hedges, as ground too dry.) Requires fertile, well-drained soil, limed if acid. Can prepare ground by digging 30cm (12in) deep trench, 30-45cm (12-18in) wide. Work in well-rotted manure, compost and/or wilted comfrey before planting.
Otherwise just grow in reasonably fertile ground. Advisable to rotate over four- or five-year period if possible to avoid build up of soil diseases. Tomatoes in potato family, so rotate accordingly; but in areas affected by blight don't grow *alongside* maincrop potatoes, to avoid cross infection.

Cultivation
1 Indeterminate types (grown as cordons)
Sow indoors early to mid-spring, roughly six to eight weeks before last frost expected.
Sow 2cm (¾in) deep in seedtrays or modules. Ideal germination temperature 20°C (68°F); sow in propagator if necessary. Seedlings can, in fact, withstand much lower temperatures once they are successfully established.
Pot seedlings on into 5-8cm (2-3in) pots of good potting compost at the three-leaf stage.
Keep in good light so plants remain sturdy and don't become elongated and 'drawn'. Gradually acclimatize to lower temperatures.
Harden-off well before planting outside. Delay planting if soil temperature below 10°C (50°F), or further frost expected. Generally plant late spring (under cover), early summer (outdoors).
If plants are being purchased ready to plant out, choose short sturdy plants, grown in individual pots rather than boxes.
Plant when 18-20cm (7-8in) high, with first flowers showing.
Plant 38-45cm (15-18in) apart, either in single rows or in double rows of staggered plants. Plant firmly with the lowest leaves just above soil level. Planting through polythene film mulches helps to keep weeds down and conserve moisture. Use black mulch, or black/white mulch with white

surface upwards. This reflects light up and assists fruit ripening.

Otherwise mulch with organic mulch such as straw or compost once plants established.

Where possible protect with cloches in early stages. When cloches out-grown can protect with polythene film side panels.

Erect supports as soon as possible. Either use strong individual canes or posts at least 1.5m (5ft) high; or erect 1.2-1.5m (4-5ft) high posts at either end of rows, with two or three parallel wires between posts.

As plants grow tie the main stem to canes or wires, allowing for the stems to thicken.

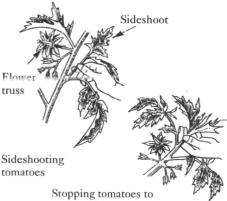

Sideshoot

Flower truss

Sideshooting tomatoes

Stopping tomatoes to encourage fruiting

Remove side shoots (see diagram left, top) and any basal growths, as they develop.

In mid- to late summer 'stop' the plants, to give time for remaining fruits to mature and ripen. In cold areas this will normally be when three trusses have set; in warmer areas after four or five trusses have set. Remove growing point a couple of leaves above topmost flower truss. (See diagram left, below.) Remove and burn diseased and withered leaves.

2 Bush and dwarf types

Sow, raise, harden-off plants as for cordons.

With outdoor *bush* cvs, planting when first flower truss just visible gives best combination of earliness and high yield.

Planting when first flower truss fully open gives earlier fruit, but lower yields overall.

Plant dwarf types 25-30cm (10-12in) apart; plant bush types 45-60 (18-36in) apart.

Can plant through polythene film mulches as for cordon types; helps to keep fruit clean. Can also mulch with straw for same reason, but may attract slugs.

Where feasible, plant under cloches or protect with row covers. (See below for growing bush types under crop covers.)

Let plants grow naturally. No sideshooting or stopping necessary.

Bush cvs under perforated or fleecy films:

System developed by researchers for getting early crop outdoors in cool areas, using bush cvs. Fruits ripen about two weeks ahead of other out-door tomatoes.

Raise plants indoors in normal way; plant out as soon as risk of frost is over. Can plant through mulching films as above.

When planted either cover with perforated or fleecy films laid directly over plants, or lay films over low hoops. Anchor the edges of the films. (See Protection pp.85-6.)

(Note: Unperforated films unsuitable, as temperature and humidity too high, resulting in disease and poor growth.)

Leave film in place until flowers start to press against it. Must then slit it open to allow insects to pollinate; do so gradually to acclimatize plants to colder conditions.

Initially make intermittent cuts in the film roughly 90cm (3ft) long down the centre of the row. Around a week later cut remaining gaps so film flops open.

Don't remove it now, but leave in place on either side of plants as a low windbreak.

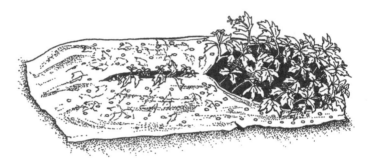

Bush tomatoes grown under perforated or fleecy film.

The tomatoes are weaned in stages: first intermittent slits are cut down the centre. A week later the gaps are cut to expose the plants completely

Watering

Other than in exceptionally dry conditions outdoor tomatoes rarely need extra watering until they start to flower.

If dry weather at this stage give them a heavy watering weekly of about 11 litre/sq m (2gal/yd^2).

Growth will suffer if soil dries out completely, but it's my firm belief overwatering (and overfeeding) lead to poorer flavoured tomatoes.

Feeding

Outdoor tomatoes require far less supplementary feeding than indoor crop, especially if ground well prepared beforehand. If growth poor when second truss is setting feed weekly with organic tomato feed or diluted liquid comfrey.

3 Growing in containers

Tomatoes can be grown successfully in growing-bags or other containers in good potting compost.

For good results the larger the container the better: 20cm (8in) pot minimum satisfactory size.

Raise plants in normal way. Transplant into pots, leaving at least 75cm (30in) headroom, to allow for a top dressing with fresh compost in later stages. With growing-bags, plant through small holes cut in surface film, to minimize evaporation.

If feasible, sink pots into soil or ashes to conserve moisture.

Water carefully so soil neither dries out nor becomes waterlogged

Once first truss starts to set feed weekly with organic tomato feed, seaweed-based fertilizer, or liquid comfrey.

If roots get pushed up to the surface, top dress with either good potting soil or compost.

Pests and diseases

Relatively few problems arise with outdoor tomatoes· poor weather is worst enemy.

Tomato/potato blight Potential problem in wet humid summers, usually appearing mid-summer. Edges of leaves become browned, fruits develop blackened patches. No effective remedy once plants attacked. Can try spraying with Bordeaux mixture when infected leaves first noticed in mid- to late summer.

Harvesting

Pick fruits as they ripen.

Fruit quality ruined by even light frost. If chances of ripening by end of season in open seem slender, cut cordon plants free of supports in late summer, leaving roots in ground.

Mulch ground with straw or plastic films and bend plants down. Cover with cloches or fleecy film.

Cover bush cvs in same way.

Alternatively pull plants up by roots and hang in greenhouse or indoors; green fruits gradually ripen.

Immature fruits ripen slowly in dark cupboards, wrapped or covered in paper – though much of flavour lost. Unripened green fruits can be cooked or used for a delicious tomato chutney.

Cultivars

Enormous choice today. The following perform well outdoors.

Tall growing cvs with good flavour:

Ailsa Craig, Harbinger, F_1 Shirley, Tigerella (striped) – standard types.

F_1 Big Boy – Beefsteak type.

Marmande, Supermarmande – Marmande type.

F_1 Cherry Belle, Gardener's Delight, F_1 Sungold (yellow), Supersweet

100 – cherry type.
Britain's Breakfast – plum-shaped; recommended for freezing.
Outdoor bush types (flavour not normally as good as tall types):
Red Alert, F₁ Sleaford Abundance.
Dwarf bush types:
Phyra (small fruit), F₁ Pixie, Tiny Tim, F₁ Tumbler (small fruit).

VSR**

TURNIP *Brassica napus* **Rapifera Group**
Fast growing brassicas, grown mainly for the roots. Roots can be flat or round, with white or yellow flesh. Can be available for most of year. Fast maturing early types used fresh; slower maturing, hardier types used fresh or stored for winter. Recently introduced small, white Japanese cvs exceptionally sweet and fast growing. (See p.237.) Leafy turnip tops eaten as greens, mainly in spring.
Site and Soil
Open site. Light, humus-rich soils best. Requires higher fertility than for swedes.
Ground preferably manured for previous crop; limed if acid. Avoid dry situations. Moisture throughout growth essential, or turnips become woody. Early types in particular useful for intercropping/catch cropping.

Cultivation
Sow *in situ.*
For turnip roots:
Make successional sowings outdoors, as soon as soil workable in late winter/early spring, until late summer.
Sow in well-prepared, firm seedbed, raked to fine tilth.
Can protect early sowings with cloches/crop covers.
Most useful sowings:
1 Early to mid-spring outdoors (or late winter in mild areas) for early/mid-summer crop. Use early types.
  Sow in rows 23cm (9in) apart. Thin in stages to 10-15cm (4-6in) apart: the wider the spacing the faster the roots develop.
2 Mid- to late summer for fresh or winter storage crop. Use early cvs for fresh crop; winter storage cvs for use fresh or storage.
  Sow storage types in rows 30cm (12in) apart; thin to 25-30cm (10-12in) apart.
Turnips so fast growing *essential* to start thinning early, so adjacent seedlings don't touch. Otherwise they become overcrowded and good roots never develop. Thinnings can be eaten as greens.
For turnip tops:
Sow late summer/early autumn. In mild areas or under cover can extend sowing to mid-autumn. Use hardy types.
Sow thinly broadcast, or in single or broad drills.

Thinning normally unnecessary.
A small patch can give excellent returns.

Pests and Diseases
Subject to same pests as all brassicas (See Pests and diseases on brassicas p.151), but being fast growing often relatively trouble free.
Flea beetle Most likely problem on seedlings. Use standard remedies, or grow under nets, at least in early stages.
Clubroot Yellow fleshed cvs reputedly less susceptible to clubroot.
Powdery mildew Sometimes a problem in dry weather; no remedy.

Harvesting
Spring/summer turnips: some cvs ready within six weeks of sowing. Sweetest and most tender if pulled young when no more than 2·5-4cm (1-1½in) diameter.
Winter turnips: ready within 10 to 12 weeks after sowing. Pull when roots reach a useable size.
In most areas can leave in soil in winter, provided soil well drained.
Where winters severe or soil heavy either protect with good covering of bracken or straw, or lift before end of year and store indoors in boxes, or outdoors in clamps as for swedes.
Turnip tops: best used when 10-15cm (4-6in) high in early spring, when vegetables most scarce. Cut frequently 2·5cm (1in) or so above ground level leaving to resprout. Often resprout over many weeks before running to seed. Can dig in remaining plants as green manure.

Note: The white Japanese cvs very fast maturing; some cvs ready within 35 days of sowing. However *some* cvs (for example 'F₁ Tokyo Cross') bolt prematurely from early spring sowings. Delay sowing until early summer. Others have good bolting resistance.

Cultivars
Snowball, Purple Top Milan – early types.
F₁ Tokyo Cross, F₁ Tokyo Top (good bolting resistance) – white Japanese early types.
Golden Ball (Orange Jelly), Manchester Market, Green Top Stone – suitable for use fresh and storage.

VSR***

CHAPTER TEN

Perennial Vegetables

A few perennial vegetables are covered here briefly. Globe artichokes and asparagus are undoubtedly luxuries in a small garden but, if space is short, are decorative enough to be grown in a flower bed. A small patch of sorrel is excellent value. Perennial cauliflower and Good King Henry are worthwhile, old-fashioned stand-bys. Rhubarb, although eaten as a fruit, well deserves its traditional, permanent corner in even the smallest plot.

For more detailed information on perennial vegetables see companion volume *Salads for Small Gardens* and *The Vegetable Garden Displayed*.

ARTICHOKE, GLOBE *Cynara scolymus*
Handsome plant with beautiful silver leaves; 60cm (2ft) high and 90cm (3ft) spread. Immature flower buds eaten as delicacy. Likes sunny well-drained site, fertile soil. Plant in the spring in rows or groups 75-90cm (2½-3ft) apart each way. Mulch every spring, water in dry weather, apply liquid feed in the summer. Protect in the winter with bracken. Season mid-summer to early-autumn; cut buds before scales start to open. Replace plants after three seasons by taking offsets in early spring.

ASPARAGUS, *Asparagus officinalis*
Lasts many years so grow in permanent bed. Soil must be well drained and completely free of perennial weeds. Work in plenty of organic matter beforehand. Either buy one-year-old crowns and plant 30-45cm (12-18in) apart in spring, or raise plants by sowing seed in spring in small pots or modules and transplanting into permanent position in autumn. Plant crowns about 10cm (4in) below surface. Do not cut spears for eating until plants are in third season, then cease cutting annually in early summer. Keep weed free by hand weeding or mulching. Foliar feed in summer beneficial but plants not very greedy. Cut down foliage to ground level when it turns yellow in autumn. Mulch with well-rotted manure or compost in autumn. Some modern cvs are very productive. May be able to start cutting in second season.

GOOD KING HENRY (Mercury, or Poor Man's Asparagus)
Chenopodium bonus-henricus
Flourishes in good soil, tolerates poor soil and light shade. Sow outdoors late spring/early summer, or start indoors and transplant. Thin to 38cm (15in) apart. Leaves eaten like spinach in summer; young shoots and flower buds in early spring. Cut back foliage in autumn, cover plants with straw to 'force' shoots. Old plants can be divided to increase stock. Can remain productive for many years.

PERENNIAL CAULIFLOWER/BROCCOLI
Brassica oleracea Botrytis Group
Perennial form of cauliflower, but best replaced every two to three years as vigour declines. In spring produces smallish central cauliflower head, and masses of broccoli-like side shoots with small heads. Very useful in 'vegetable gap'. Cv 'Nine Star Perennial' almost invariably used. Sow spring, preferably in small modules. Plant out after hardening-off. Or 'station sow' in spring thinning to strongest seedling after germination. Grow in fertile, well drained soil. Space plants about 90cm (3ft) apart. May need staking in windy situation. Protect from birds, especially in winter/spring. Cut main head first and side shoots once about 4cm (1½in) diameter. Young stems and small leaves also edible. When plant starts to run to seed and coarsen cut back all remaining shoots. Keep mulched and well watered.

RHUBARB *Rheum x cultorum*
Large, deep rooting plants often up to 90cm (3ft) high and 1.2-1.5cm (4-5ft) diameter. Grown for pink stems, stewed for fruit. Grows in wide range of fertile, well-drained soil; tolerates acid soil. Best to plant bought sets (pieces of root with buds) of disease-free stock. Plant while plants dormant, during winter. Plant with buds about 2·5cm (1in) below ground level, 75 90cm (2½ 3ft) apart. Don't pull any rhubarb in first season; pull lightly second season. Afterwards pull as long as stems firm. Give heavy dressings of manure every autumn/spring to maintain fertility. Cut back seed heads that appear. Can raise from seed, but quality of plants variable. For very early crop lift well-established plants in early winter, when dormant but after exposed to frost. Plant in tubs in darkness indoors. Or cover *in situ* with upturned ashcans or rhubarb blanching pots in late winter/early spring.

SORREL *Rumex acetosa*
Low growing, hardy perennial plant, delicious, sharp, lemon flavour. Sow *in situ* or transplant, spring or autumn. Either treat as annual and thin to 10cm (4in) apart using whole plant, or grow as perennial, thin to 38cm (15in) apart, pick individual leaves. If cloched in autumn can be used almost all year round. Tolerates light shade and poor dry soil, but lusher in fertile, moist conditions. Cut off seedheads as they appear. Renew plants every three years or so. Use in salads, cook with spinach and chard, or make sorrel soup.

Much smaller-leaved 'Buckler-leaved' sorrel *R. scutatus* very strongly flavoured; excellent ground-cover plant.

Seasonal Guide to Main Garden Jobs

General Note

The term 'under cover' includes cloches, frames, low and walk-in polythene tunnels and unheated greenhouses. Timings are based on 'average' UK conditions. In cold districts, make spring sowings and plantings slightly later and autumn sowings earlier. The reverse applies in milder districts.

Only a few perennial and minor vegetables are included in this guide.

CCA = cut-and-come-again seedlings.

MID-WINTER

Sow under cover (mild areas only): broad beans, lettuce, peas, radish. CCA: cress, komatsuna, oriental saladini, salad rape, salad rocket, senposai, 'Sugar Loaf' chicory, Texsel greens.

Plant: Mid-autumn-sown lettuce (under cover), garlic (on light soils).

Jobs: diggings and manuring when soil not frozen.

Sort through stored crops; remove any rotting vegetables.

Hoe through crops under cover.

Blanche endive and force 'Witloof' chicory.

Force rhubarb indoors.

Place seed order.

LATE-WINTER

Sow in heat: celeriac, celery, leeks, onions.

Sow under cover: beetroot, broad beans, Brussels sprouts, summer and autumn cabbage, carrots, chrysanthemum greens, leeks, lettuce, main crop and spring onions, radish, peas (warm areas only). CCA: as mid-winter plus curly endive, cutting lettuce, komatsuna, mizuna greens, oriental saladini, cress, pak choi.

Sow outdoors in favourable conditions: broad beans, kohl rabi, onions, parsnip, peas, radish, spinach.

Plant: spring cabbage, garlic, onion sets, Jerusalem and globe artichokes, shallots.

Jobs: digging and manuring light soils unless ground frozen. Start preparing seedbeds.

Start chitting seed potatoes.

Force 'Witloof' chicory and rhubarb.

Lift parsnips and heel if sprouting.

Thin over-wintered onions.

EARLY SPRING

Sow in heat: aubergine, celery, celeriac, peppers, tomatoes.

Sow under cover: dwarf beans (warm areas), beetroot, Brussels sprouts, carrots, cauliflower (mini), celery, celeriac, endive, leeks, lettuce, winter purslane, CCA seedlings (see late winter) plus summer purslane.

Sow in open: broad beans, summer, autumn and winter cabbage, calabrese, corn salad, chrysanthemum greens, endive (curled), kale, land cress, lettuce, spring and main crop onions, parsley, parsnip, peas, radish, shallots, spinach beet, spinach, peas, turnips. CCA: komatsuna, lettuce, oriental saladini, pak choi, salad rocket, senposai, spinach, Texsel greens.

Plant: Jerusalem artichokes, garlic, lettuce, autumn-sown onion seedlings, onion sets, early potatoes, shallots.

Prick out: tomatoes, and other seedlings germinated in heat.

Jobs: continue preparing ground for sowing.

Hoe through over-wintered crops in open and under cloches.

Feed over-wintered spring cabbage, kale, onions with seaweed-based fertilizer if looking 'jaded'.

Lift, divide and replant chives and Welsh onions.

Lift and heel in remaining leeks, parsnips and celeriac.

Prepare ground for tomatoes.

MID-SPRING

Sow in heat: courgettes, cucumbers, iceplant, summer purslane, New Zealand spinach, tomatoes.

Sow under cover: dwarf beans, celeriac, celery; and slightly later: runner beans, chicory (early red), cucumber, marrows, summer and winter purslane, sweet corn, tomatoes.

Sow in open: asparagus pea, beetroot, broad beans, Brussels sprouts, sprouting broccoli, autumn and winter cabbage, calabrese, carrots, cauliflower (mini), 'Witloof' chicory, chrysanthemum greens, corn salad, endive, Hamburg parsley, kohl rabi, land cress, leeks, lettuce, main crop, spring and pickling onions, parsley, parsnip, peas, radish, salad rape, salad rocket, salsify, scorzonera, spinach beet, summer spinach, Texsel greens, turnip, CCA seedlings as early spring.

Prick out: aubergine, celery, celeriac, peppers, tomatoes.

Plant: Brussels sprouts (sown under cloches), spring cabbage, lettuce, onion sets, potatoes.

Jobs: keep hoeing and weeding, especially among seedlings.

Remove old brassica stumps.

Earth up early potatoes.

Support peas.

Prepare ground for tomatoes if not already done.

Watch out for flea beetle attacks in brassica seedlings.

Harden-off seedlings started under glass.

Feed over-wintered vegetables (see early spring).

Start mulching if soil is warm.

LATE SPRING

Sow under cover: chicory (early red), cucumber, iceplant, marrows and sweet corn.

Sow in open: broad, French and runner beans, beetroot, sprouting broccoli, summer, autumn and winter cabbage, calabrese, carrots, cauliflower (mini), all chicories, corn salad, endive, fennel, iceplant, kale, kohl rabi, land cress, lettuce, spring and pickling onions, Hamburg parsley, peas, summer and winter purslane, radish, salad rocket, salsify, scorzonera, spinach beet, summer and New Zealand spinach, swede, Swiss chard, turnip. CCA: komatsuna, oriental saladini, pak choi, senposai, Texsel greens.

Sow in open when nearing early summer: cucumbers, marrows, sweet corn.

Prick out or pot up: aubergines, celery, celeriac, cucumbers, marrows, peppers, tomatoes.

Thin out: beet, carrots, lettuce, parsnip, radish, spinach, turnip.

Plant (when ready): Brussels sprouts, French and runner beans (raised under cover), summer, autumn and winter cabbage, celery, celeriac, leeks, lettuce.

Plant out under cloches initially: aubergines, cucumbers, courgettes, peppers, sweet corn, tomatoes.

Jobs: harden-off seedlings under cloches/crop covers.

Protect seedbed against birds.

Watch out for blackfly, carrot fly, cabbage root fly, flea beetle, onion fly and take protective measures.

Keep hoeing and weeding: start mulching.

Earth up early potatoes; protect with soil if frost threatens. Support peas.

Start sideshooting tomatoes.

Mulch all established vegetables.

EARLY SUMMER

Sow in open: French and runner beans, beetroot, calabrese, carrots, cauliflower (mini), all chicories, Chinese cabbage, chrysanthemum greens, corn salad, courgettes, cucumber, endive, iceplant, kohl rabi, komatsuna, land cress (light shade), lettuce, mibuna and mizuna greens, pak choi, peas, summer purslane, summer and oriental radish, salad rocket, spinach beet, summer and New Zealand spinach, swede, sweet corn, turnip .

Thin: Direct sown vegetables such as beans, beetroot, carrots and lettuce.

Plant: Brussels sprouts, sprouting broccoli, autumn, summer and winter cabbages, celery, celeriac, fennel, iceplant, kale, leeks, marrows, peppers, summer purslane, tomatoes, sweet corn.

Jobs: pinch out broad bean tops.

Hoeing, weeding, mulching.

Stake and earth up brassicas, when planted out.

Side shoot, stake and tie tomatoes.

Watch out for pests as in late spring.

MID-SUMMER

Sow in seed boxes or modules to transplant under cover, mainly for winter: red and 'Sugar Loaf' chicory, corn salad, endive, fennel, land cress, lettuce, oriental mustard, salad rocket, Swiss chard, winter purslane.

Sow in open: dwarf French beans (to cloche later), beetroot, spring cabbage (in cold areas only), cabbage for spring greens (toward the onset of late summer), carrots, chicory, (red and 'Sugar Loaf'), Chinese broccoli, Chinese cabbage, choy sum, endive (curled and broad), kohl rabi, komatsuna, land cress (in light shade), winter lettuce, mibuna and mizuna greens, spring onion, pak choi, oriental mustards, peas (dwarf), radish (summer, oriental and winter), senposai, spinach, spinach beet, Swiss chard, turnips (for storage), winter purslane. CCA: oriental saladini, salad rape, salad rocket, spinach.

Thin: beetroot, carrots, lettuce, oriental greens, swedes.

Plant: sprouting broccoli, Brussels sprouts, summer, autumn and winter cabbage, calabrese, kale, leeks, oriental greens.

Jobs: keep weeding, hoeing, mulching.

Tie, stake, side shoot and 'stop' cordon tomatoes.

Tie climbing cucumbers, feed, water if dry, top dress roots with compost if necessary.

Watch out for cabbage caterpillars.

Water and feed celeriac, celery, cucumbers, leeks, marrows; water French and runner beans where necessary.

Earth up and stake Brussels sprouts and other greens in exposed sites.

Pinch out cucumber and climbing bean tops when they reach the top of their supports.

Start harvesting shallots.

LATE SUMMER

Sow in seed boxes or modules, to transplant under cover: as mid-summer plus calabrese (toward the onset of early autumn), Chinese cabbage, Chinese broccoli, choy sum, fennel, komatsuna, mibuna and mizuna greens, pak choi, senposai.

Sow *in situ* indoors: summer purslane.

Sow in open: spring cabbage (beginning of late summer), Chinese broccoli, Chinese cabbage, Chinese leaf mustard, chrysanthemum greens, corn salad, land cress, winter lettuce, spring onions, Japanese and traditional over-wintering onions, summer, oriental and winter radish, spinach beet, Swiss chard, winter spinach, Texsel greens, turnips (to eat small and for tops).

Sow to cover later: beetroot, carrots, endive, winter lettuce, winter purslane, Texsel greens.

Thin: beetroot, carrot, Chinese greens, spinach, turnips, etc.

Plant outside: leeks.

Start planting under cover: crops sown mid- to late summer for winter cropping under cover.

Jobs: 'stop' cordon tomatoes, feed if necessary, spray with Bordeaux mixture against blight in wet conditions.

Earth up and stake winter greens; watch out for caterpillars.

Water and feed as in mid-summer.

Harvest garlic, shallots and onions.

EARLY AUTUMN

Sow under cover: calabrese, radish; CCA: chrysanthemum greens, corn salad, cress, endive, 'Sugar Loaf' chicory, komatsuna, lettuce, mibuna and mizuna greens, mustard, oriental saladini, salad rape, salad rocket, senposai, spinach, Texsel greens, winter purslane.

Sow outside: spring cabbage, corn salad, endive, kohl rabi, land cress, winter lettuce, and last sowings of ordinary radish, winter spinach, turnips for tops.

Thin: outdoor winter radish, spinach, Swiss chard, turnips for storing.

Plant: spring cabbage, garlic, autumn onion sets, winter lettuce, and under cover: crops sown mid- to late summer for transplanting under cover.

Jobs: ensure greens earthed up, staked; watch out for caterpillars. Finish harvesting onions.

Cut down tomatoes to ripen off indoors or under cloches.

Bring in storage marrows before frost.

Continue feeding celeriac and leeks.

Cover late sowings of dwarf beans, carrots, endive, lettuce, oriental greens, radish, salad crops, with cloches or low polythene tunnels.

MID-AUTUMN

Sow under cover: winter lettuce, CCA: cress, salad rape, salad rocket, Texsel greens.

Sow outside: broad beans, hardy peas.

Plant: spring cabbage, garlic, autumn onion sets, winter lettuce, and under cover plant: endive, remaining salad and oriental greens from late summer sowing.

Thin: carrots, corn salad, winter lettuce, autumn onion sets, swedes.

Jobs: lift and store carrots, beetroot (cold areas).

Start blanching endive.

Cut down Jerusalem artichokes.

Earth up leeks.

Lift chicory for indoor forcing; cut back and earth up chicory for outdoor forcing.

Lift storage cabbage before heavy frost.

Clear away pea sticks, bean poles.

Start digging and manuring on heavy soil.

Mulch celeriac and parsnips with straw.

Protect red chicories, other salad plants and oriental greens with cloches, low tunnels or straw to improve quality.

LATE AUTUMN AND EARLY WINTER

Sow: broad beans, hardy peas.

Plant: garlic.

Jobs: digging and manuring on heavy soil.

Force 'Witloof' chicory; blanch endive.

Protect celeriac from frost with bracken.

Occasionally hoe through crops under cloches and around over-wintering crops.

Check stored vegetables; remove any rotting ones.

Mark positions of over-wintering root crops in case of snow.

Remove yellowing leaves from brassicas.

Thin or transplant protected over-wintered lettuce 5cm (2in) apart in late auutmn.

Lift and store late-sown beetroot, carrots, turnips, swedes.

SEASON AND MONTH CONVERSION CHART

JANUARY	*MID-WINTER*	JULY	*MID-SUMMER*
FEBRUARY	*LATE WINTER*	AUGUST	*LATE SUMMER*
MARCH	*EARLY SPRING*	SEPTEMBER	*EARLY AUTUMN*
APRIL	*MID-SPRING*	OCTOBER	*MID-AUTUMN*
MAY	*LATE SPRING*	NOVEMBER	*LATE AUTUMN*
JUNE	*EARLY SUMMER*	DECEMBER	*EARLY WINTER*

Note: North and south applies to the northern hemisphere and opposite applies to the southern hemisphere.

Economy Tips

With a little ingenuity gardening can often be made cheaper. My thanks go to the readers of *Garden News* for many of the ideas below, which were first published in *Garden News*, and also to the editor for permission to reproduce them.

Sowing/propagation

For containers use:
2 litre (½gal) plastic cans. Cut in half vertically to make two containers (one with handle), or horizontally to make one container and one funnel.
Plastic can be painted for attractive plant holders.
For other improvized containers see Sowing Indoors, p.53.

For compost use:
Sifted soil from deciduous woods.

For crocks use:
Polystyrene broken into lumps.
Foam rubber in pieces or sheets.

For labels use:
Ice cream wooden spoons; plastic pots, washing-up liquid containers cut into narrow strips; write with a chinagraph pencil.
Flat stones from beach placed on ground as row markers; write with Indian ink, or paint.
Write on plastic labels in pencil; erase with rubber or by scrubbing.
Can re-use many times.

For sowing larger seeds or pricking out use:
Large nails or metal skewers.
Metal shoe horn for getting seedlings out of boxes.

To save compost when sowing few seeds only:
Crock container normally, half-fill with potting compost, finish off with seed compost. Sow seeds very thinly. They germinate in seed compost, and grow on into potting compost. Pricking out will be necessary.

Re-cycled modules:
Make holes in upper surface of used tea bags. Saw seeds in them.

Sifting soil for seed compost use:
Kitchen sieve, or replace bottom of baking tin with perforated zinc.

Seed sowing if you cannot stoop:
Drop seeds down plastic or metal tubing. Best for peas, beans, pelleted seed.

To heat frame or cold greenhouse:
Use a night light or small lamp under inverted flower pot.

If no greenhouse heating:
Heat a cupboard indoors using a 40 watt bulb. Bring seeds and seedlings inside at night in early spring, when night temperatures drop sharply and place them in the heated cupboard.

Tools

Paint tool handles bright colours so that they are not mislaid in long grass.
Paint 10, 20, 30cm (4, 8, 12in) markings, etc, on rake handle for measuring.
Use colander for spreading fertilizers evenly.
Stuff old hot-water bottle with foam rubber to make kneeling pad.
Burn bristles off old broom; the remaining flat head on the handle makes a useful tool for breaking clods and levelling a seedbed.
Make a sprayer from washing-up liquid container by sealing original small opening with hot poker, and piercing holes around the seal with sharp or heated pin. Make holder for small tools, or for seeds such as beans, onion sets (to use while sowing) by cutting top corner (opposite handle) out of 2 litre (½gal) plastic can. Make a spade cleaner from an old spoon. Cut off the top half of the spoon 'bowl' with a hacksaw, flatten the remainder with a hammer. Very handy for cleaning sticky mud from the spade.

Compost containers

Make small quantities of garden compost in plastic rubbish sacks with holes pierced in bottom and every 25cm (10in) around sides; alternatively use plastic laundry baskets. Use compost activators as containers are too small to generate much heat.

Wind/frost/bird protection

Protect plants from wind with plastic sheeting pegged to canes with clothes pegs. Use old umbrellas to protect plants from frost. Cut off handles; anchor in soil with handle shaft. Use nets in which oranges, nuts, etc, sowed over seedlings to protect from birds; support them with twigs or wire.

Miscellaneous

Ripen tomatoes by standing on aluminiun foil in sunlight; reflection hastens ripening. *Taking cuttings when space is short.* Wrap cuttings in sphagnum moss, tied securely with wool or raffia; or put cuttings into small pots in potting compost. Drop pot or moss bundle into plastic bag, put teaspoon of water in bag, secure at top, and hang in warm light place indoors.
Watering when on holiday: make wicks about 45–60cm (18–24in) long (or longer if necessary) either from glass fibre lagging or by twisting double wool together until the strand is about 1cm (½in) thick. Fill buckets with water, dangle wicks in buckets and trail other end into pots with require watering.
Dry off and harden old chrysanthemums, herbaceous plants and sunflower stalks to make stakes. They may last several years.
Cut old nylon stockings or tights (cut in spiral starting from top) to make durable and non-chafing plant ties.
Hang onions, garlic, shallots, in old nylon stockings to store for winter.
Can even store 'Dutch Winter White' cabbages this way.
Cut plastic gloves into circular strips to use as elastic bands.
Seal pieces of polythene together (to make cloches) by pressing under damp cloth with cool iron. Protect ironing board with old cloth.

Further Reading

Many of the books below are no longer in print, but can still be obtained through public libraries.

Other books by Joy Larkcom
All Muck and Magic, Channel 4 Television, 1987.
Grow Your Greens, Eat Your Greens, Channel Four Television, 1993.
Oriental Vegetables, John Murray, 1991.
Salads for Small Gardens, Reed Consumer Books, 1995 (completely revised edition of *Salads the Year Round,* Hamlyn Paperbacks, 1980).
Sainsbury's Home Base Guide to Vegetable Gardening, Sainsbury, 1983.
The Salad Garden, Frances Lincoln/Winward, 1984.
The Vegetable Garden Displayed, Royal Horticultural Society, completely revised edition 1992.

General books on vegetable growing
The Complete Know and Grow Vegetables, edited by J. K. A. Bleasdale, P. J. Salter and others, Oxford University Press, revised edition 1991.
The Vegetable Garden, Vilmorin-Andrieux, John Murray 1885, reprinted 1977.

For vegetable growing in greenhouses
The Complete Manual of Organic Gardening, edited by Basil Caplan, Headline Book Publishing, 1992.
Tomato Growing, Louis N. Flawn, Foyles Handbooks, 3rd edition, 1975.
The Organic Greenhouse, Sue Stickland, Henry Doubleday Research Association, Search Press, 1993.
The Organic Greenhouse and Conservatory, Roy Lacey, David & Charles, 1992.
The Collingridge Handbook of Greenhouse Gardening, A. C. Macself and Arthur Turner, Collingridge Books, 1982.
The Encyclopedia of Gardening, Royal Horticultural Society & Dorling Kindersley, 1992.

Comfrey, compost, green manuring
Comfrey, Past Present and Future, Lawrence D. Hills, Faber & Faber, 1976.
The Complete Manual of Organic Gardening (see above).
Worms Eat My Garbage: How to set up and maintain a worm composting system, Mary Appelhof, Flower Press, 1982.
See also Henry Doubleday Research Assocation 'Step by Step' series:
Composting
Making Worm Compost
Gardening with Green Manure

Specialist subjects

Collins Guide to Pests, Diseases and Disorders of Garden Plants, Stefan Buczacki and Keith Harris, Collins 1982.
Container Gardening, Kenneth Beckett, David Carr and David Stevens Frances Lincoln 1982.
Forest Gardening, Robert A. de J. Hart, Green Books, 1991.
How to Grow More Vegetables. . . . by John Jeavons, Ten-Speed Press, 1982 (on intensive deep-bed systems).
Rare Vegetables, John Organ, Faber & Faber, 1960.
See also *The Complete Manual of Organic Gardening* (p.248), for raised beds, organic pest and disease control.

Further advice can currently be obtained from the following organizations. Send SAE for up-to-date list of publications, services, and suppliers of biological agents, soil testing services etc.

If sending specimens by post:
~ Put pests in matchboxes in polythene bags.
~ Wrap leaves and samples liable to rot in wood, wool or damp newspaper. Then put into sealed polythene bags.

Henry Doubleday Research Association (HDRA), National Centre for Organic Gardening, Ryton-on-Dunsmore, Coventry CV8 3LG.
Publish leaflets on all aspects of organic cultivation; operate seed library of heirloom varieties; demonstration garden.

Horticulture Research International, Wellesbourne, Warwick, CV35 9EF.
Research organization for commercial growers. Publish guides, leaflets and posters for gardeners and has an open day.

Royal Horticultural Society, 80 Vincent Square, London SW1P 2PE.
Wide range of publications; advisory service for members; demonstration gardens.

Most gardening magazines answer readers' queries. For up-to-date magazine addresses look in a public library. Send SAE with any queries.

249

ACKNOWLEDGEMENTS

Please take as read my thanks to all those whose help I acknowledged in the original edition in 1976 and the reprint in 1986. More recently, thank you again to the UK mail order seed companies for seed samples and technical advice. Especial thanks to those companies who still maintain trial grounds, which are an invaluable source of information: Elsoms Seeds, E. W. King, Suttons Seeds, Unwins Seeds and Thompson & Morgan Ltd. Thank you to friends at the Henry Doubleday Research Association, the National Institute of Agricultural Botany, Horticulture Research International at Wellesbourne and the Royal Horticultural Society for helping with advice and queries on many occasions. Thank you to the expert vegetable growers in Channel Four's *Grow Your Greens, Eat Your Greens* television series from whom I picked up so many useful tips. In updating this edition thank you to Colin Randel at Suttons Seeds for sharing his work on 'mini-veg', Bill Symondson, whose section on organic pest control in *The Complete Manual of Organic Gardening* I freely used, Terry Marshall, for advice on his ideas on comfrey and 'growing-bag panniers', Keith Boreham for use of his method of supporting runner beans, and Malcolm Burrows and Richard Lovick for technical help on constructing frames and support systems. Thanks to Elizabeth Douglass for all her painstaking work on the illustrations, to John Matthesson for ever willing emergency help on the computer, to my husband Don for, yet again, keeping the garden and house in order while work on the book was underway, and to Robert Snuggs, Anna Mumford, Selina Higgins and Mark Winwood for their enthusiastic support at Reed Books.

INDEX

References in *italic* refer to illustrations. Main references to vegetables are given in **bold**.

Abyssinian mustard 229-30
acidity, soil 15-17, 66
aeration, soil 13
aerobic compost heaps, 29-31, *30*
aerosols, pesticides 69
alkalinity, soil 15-17
Allium cepa **197-200**
A. esculentum 222-3
A. fistulosum 201
A. perutile 202
A. porrum 184-6
A. sativum **176-7**
American land cress 183-4
amsoi 197
anchusa 102
angelica 103
animal manure 25
annual vegetables 130-236
aphids 63, 67, 70, 71, 72, 73, 92
Apium graveolens var rapaceum **157-8**
A. g. var. *dolce* 158-60
artichokes
globe 101, **237**
Jerusalem 99, 103, 132
artificial fertilizers 23
dosage 23
pollution 23-4

ash 27
asparagus 100, **237**
Asparagus officinalis **237**
asparagus pea 102, **132**
aubergine **133-4**

Bacillus thuringiensis 70, 71
Barbarea verna 183-4
bare root planting 54
bark, shredded 48, 49
base dressings, fertilizers 26
basil 102
bean seed fly 67
beans 42, 51, 67, 98, 99
broad 41, 66, 68, 108, 109, **134-5**
dwarf 101, 108, 109, 135-7
field 33
French 41, 99, 100, 101, 108, 109, **135-7**
kidney 135-7
mung 140-1
runner 99, 100, 108, 109, **137-40**, *139*
sprouts **140-1**
beds
built-up raised 40
intensive deep 40
narrow 38-9
raised 39-40
beetroot 42, 47, 65, 67, 102, **141-3**
Bellis perennis 102
beneficial insects 76
Beta vulgaris **141-3**
B.v. subsp. *cicla* 223

bindweed 78
biological control 71-2
bird manures 25
birds 44, 65, 75, *76*, 250
Black Jack 27, *28*
blackfly 63, 66, 68, 70
blood, fish and bonemeal 27
boneflour 27
bonemeal 27
bonfire ash 27
borage 102
borax 24
Bordeaux Mixture 69
borders, vegetables in 100-3
borecole 179-80
boron 11, 24
bottom heat 57-8
Brassica carinata **229-30**
B. juncea **196-7**
B. napus var. *napus* 32, **195-6**
B. n. Napobrassica Group **227**
B. n. Rapifera Group **235-7**
B. oleracea
Acephala Group **179-80**
B. o. Botrytis Group **156**-7, **238**
B. o. Capitata Group **146-52**
B. o. Gemmifera Group **145-6**
B. o. Gonglodes Group **180-1**
B. o. Italica Group **144-5**, **152**
B. o. var. *alboglabra* **143-4**

B. rapa Chinensis Group **203-5**
B. r. Pekinensis Group **166**
B. r. Perviridis Group **182-3**
B. r. var. *nipposinica* **193**-5
B. r. var. *oleifera* **167-8**
B. r. var. *purpurea* **167-8**
B. r. var. *rosularis* **204-5**
brassicas
intercropping 108, 109
see also individual types eg cabbage; cauliflower
broad beans 41, 66, 68, 108, 109, **134-5**
broadcasting seed 45-6
broccoli 66
Chinese **143-4**
green sprouting 152
Italian 152
perennial **238**
sprouting **144-5**
brushing, hardening off 62
Brussels sprouts 42, 66, **145-6**
buckwheat 33
builder's rubble 22
built-up beds 40
bunching onions 201
butterfly caterpillars 70, 71, 73, 92

cabbages 66, 67, **146-8**
autumn **149**
ornamental 101,